Doubleheaders
A Major League History

ALSO BY CHARLIE BEVIS
AND FROM MCFARLAND

*The New England League: A Baseball
History, 1885–1949* (2008)

*Sunday Baseball: The Major Leagues'
Struggle to Play Baseball on the Lord's Day,
1876–1934* (2003)

*Mickey Cochrane: The Life of
a Baseball Hall of Fame Catcher* (1998)

Doubleheaders
A Major League History

CHARLIE BEVIS

McFarland & Company, Inc., Publishers
Jefferson, North Carolina, and London

LIBRARY OF CONGRESS CATALOGUING-IN-PUBLICATION DATA

Bevis, Charlie, 1954–
    Doubleheaders : a major league history / Charlie Bevis.
      p.   cm.
    Includes bibliographical references and index.

    ISBN 978-0-7864-4214-0
    softcover : 50# alkaline paper ∞

    1. Baseball—United States—History. I. Title.
GV863.A1B48   2011
796.3570973—dc22   2010045768

British Library cataloguing data are available

© 2011 Charlie Bevis. All rights reserved

No part of this book may be reproduced or transmitted in any form or by any means, electronic or mechanical, including photocopying or recording, or by any information storage and retrieval system, without permission in writing from the publisher.

Front cover: *from top left* St. Louis Cardinals owner Sam Breadon; Pittsburgh Pirates owner Barney Dreyfuss; a Decoration Day crowd watches the second of two games at Washington Park, Brooklyn, 1887 (all from National Baseball Hall of Fame Library, Cooperstown, New York)

Manufactured in the United States of America

McFarland & Company, Inc., Publishers
  Box 611, Jefferson, North Carolina 28640
    www.mcfarlandpub.com

Table of Contents

Preface		1
1	The First Doubleheader	5
2	Holiday Two-Game Sets	16
3	Emergence of the Doubleheader	26
4	Lure of the Doubleheader	39
5	Early Holiday Doubleheaders	54
6	First Sunday Doubleheaders	64
7	Tinkering with Doubleheaders	74
8	Expansion of the Holiday Doubleheader	90
9	Maturity of Doubleheaders	101
10	Scheduled Sunday Doubleheaders	118
11	Swing-Shift and Other Wartime Doubleheaders	139
12	Twi-Night and Day-Night Doubleheaders	153
13	Decline of the Doubleheader	174
14	"Let's Play Two"	186
15	Extinction of the Scheduled Doubleheader	193
Appendix A: Doubleheader Milestones		205
Appendix B: Doubleheader Records		209
Appendix C: Doubleheaders by Year		212
Chapter Notes		217
Bibliography		225
Index		229

Preface

THIS HISTORY OF THE DOUBLEHEADER examines the trends in conducting "two games for the price of one" in major-league baseball from its inception in 1882 through the 2008 season. However, this book concerns more than just the who, what, and when of baseball doubleheaders; it is also a social and cultural history that explores the why of the development and decline of doubleheaders in terms of elements such as transportation, nature of ballpark spectators, other forms of entertainment, Sunday laws, communication (radio and television), living patterns (urban, suburban, and rural), and labor relations. The Great Depression and World War II also had a significant influence on the use of doubleheaders.

Doubleheaders are what I call a "horizontal" issue, one that cuts across several eras, such as home runs, as distinguished from a "vertical" issue that resides within a distinct period, such as the 1912–1918 Boston Red Sox. Vertical issues can be easier to research and analyze because there is a natural body of information to examine during that specified time. Some horizontal issues lend themselves to research and trend analysis because they exist prominently within different eras, notably the aforementioned issue of home runs. Doubleheaders, however, exist far below the surface of every baseball era. For the most part, the doubleheader is akin to the wallpaper in a room: it exists but is barely recognized as a distinct element from the wall of the room, which itself is hardly ever remarked upon by observers of the dwelling.

My experience researching a similar subsurface horizontal issue for my book *Sunday Baseball: The Major Leagues' Struggle to Play Baseball on the Lord's Day*, published in 2003, helped to limit frustration in my research efforts on the doubleheader. Like the Sunday baseball issue, there was very little secondary research available on doubleheaders, so the research focus was to mine newspapers and baseball publications for bits and pieces of information to stitch together to form a foundation for trend analysis. Secondary research from other authors of social and cultural history helped to form a fuller understanding of the why behind the trends related to the rise and fall of the doubleheader. One of the more profound cultural issues that affected the rise of doubleheaders, for which there is scant secondary research, is the changing nature of the ballpark spectator. Through my research, I have been able to sketch the outlines of exactly what types of people attended ballgames in the late nineteenth and early twentieth centuries, but this is one area of fertile ground for future research.

My research on Sunday baseball, notably the rise of Sunday doubleheaders in the 1910s, led to my quest for further knowledge on the general issue of doubleheaders. Early versions of my research on doubleheaders appeared as the articles "Evolution of the Sunday Doubleheader and Its Role in Elevating the Popularity of Baseball," published in *The Cooperstown Symposium on Baseball and American Culture, 2003–2004*, and "Holiday Doubleheaders," published in the 2004 issue of the *Baseball Research Journal*. There were two troublesome questions, though, that these two pieces of research failed to adequately bridge. Question 1: Why were two games of a Sunday doubleheader conducted on a single-admission basis, i.e., "two games for the price of one," while two games on a holiday typically were staged as separate-admission events? Question 2: Why did holiday two-game sets change to single-admission status so that all two-games-on-one-day events (along with Sunday and makeup doubleheaders) were conducted for just one admission fee? I had a general idea, as conveyed in the *Baseball Research Journal* article, that Sunday baseball was the reason, but it has taken me several years to more firmly substantiate that connection and put it into a broader perspective. Adding to the delay was that tracing the development of the first two-for-one doubleheaders was more challenging than first indicated and that the newest variations of the doubleheader, twi-night and day-night, turned out to be virgin territory for research.

Although I had managed to successfully employ a hunt-and-find approach using old-fashioned microfilm to research and write my book *Sunday Baseball*, this book on doubleheaders likely would not have been possible without the advent of digitized newspaper archives. Through the Boston Public Library and the Regina Library at Rivier College, I had access to archives of several digitized newspapers, and Widener Library at Harvard University provided access to microfilm for still more newspapers. While the ability to search terms is one distinct benefit of digitized newspapers, the ability to easily find numerous specific dates to record information is vital to discerning trends related to doubleheaders. Two comments are in order regarding some of this newspaper information. Reported attendance figures, especially prior to World War II, are notorious for their questionable accuracy; however, it is the relative comparison of attendance numbers among games that is important to the research analysis of doubleheaders, not the precise size of a crowd at a particular game. Judging the admission status of two games on one day is not a perfect science. The usual convention for newspapers was to use "morning" and "afternoon" labels on box scores for separate-admission matches and "first" and "second" labels for single-admission contests. Although highly accurate, this method is by no means foolproof. For important changes in a trend, multiple newspapers were viewed to ascertain similar reporting of admission status.

While this book provides primarily a social and cultural perspective on the history of the doubleheader, it also contains a statistical backdrop to reinforce the trends. Dave Smith at Retrosheet was very helpful in producing several aggregate runs of doubleheader numbers from the massive computerized database of major-league ballgames that his organization has compiled and makes publicly available online to all interested researchers. The information used here was obtained free of charge from and is copyrighted by Retrosheet. Interested parties may contact Retrosheet at www.retrosheet.org for more information. It is important to note that doubleheader as defined in the Retrosheet database is simply two games played on one day; there is no attempt to distinguish between separate- or single-admission status. This is another fertile area for additional research, to make a more exact determination of admission status for all two-games-per-day events. Additionally, sabermetrics-oriented researchers may wish to delve further into the analysis of doubleheader sweeps and splits and other statistical analyses, which are well beyond the scope of this book.

This history of the doubleheader is a unique addition to our knowledge of baseball history. While the concept of two games for the price of one is a disappearing element in major-league baseball today, this book offers both a new perspective and new information about the doubleheader to help sustain its memory as a legendary aspect of the game of baseball.

1

The First Doubleheader

A SURPRISE WAS AWAITING the early arrivals at the Agricultural Fair Grounds in Worcester, Massachusetts, on Monday, September 25, 1882. There to see the scheduled 3:00 P.M. baseball game between the Worcester and Providence clubs of the National League, the spectators discovered that a game between the two teams was already in progress.

To make up a game that had been postponed by rain on the preceding Friday, the owners of the Worcester ballclub took the unusual step of rescheduling the game for 1:30 P.M. as a prelude to the regularly scheduled mid-afternoon contest on Monday. In addition, the owners took the unprecedented move of charging a single admission fee for spectators to watch both games. The two Worcester–Providence games held on September 25, 1882, comprised the first single-admission doubleheader ever played in major-league baseball history.[1]

After the Friday, September 22, 1882, game had been rained out, the *Worcester Spy* reported the next day that the ballclubs "will play two games in this city Monday, the first at 1:30 and the second 15 minutes after the completion of the first." On Monday, the *Spy* reported that "the admission will be 50 cents, which will include both games." However, the *Spy* noted nothing exceptional about two games being played consecutively on the same day for the price of one admission.[2]

While the *Worcester Spy* was fairly pedestrian in its advance reporting of the September 25 doubleheader, the *Providence Journal* divulged more details: "Manager Wright has arranged for two games at Worcester on Monday afternoon, in order to complete the schedule as expeditiously as possible." It was Providence that wanted to play the postponed game, not Worcester, which was mired in last place in the National League. Harry Wright, among his many contributions to baseball following his leadership of the undefeated 1869 Cincinnati Red Stockings ballclub, can be considered to be the father of the major-league doubleheader. In 1882, Wright was the manager of the Providence team, which in late September was in second place in the National League standings. Wright needed to reschedule the postponed game of September 22 with Worcester before the season concluded on September 30 in order to play as many games as possible in his quest to wrest first place from the Chicago ballclub.[3]

Tuesday, September 26, ostensibly was a good day to play the postponed contest, since both Worcester and Providence did not have a game slated that day on the National League schedule. However, Wright was a pragmatic businessman as much as a baseball man. He had already lined up a lucrative exhibition game for Providence on September 26 at the Polo Grounds in New York City against the independent Metropolitan team. Worcester had also arranged an exhibition game for September 26, against the Rollstone ballclub in Fitchburg, about 10 miles north of Worcester. Both clubs were likely to generate a better financial result from these exhibitions than they would by playing the postponed league game.

It's unclear if Wright first proposed that the two teams play in the morning with a separate admission to make up the postponed game rather than in the early afternoon as a prelude to the regularly scheduled game. Worcester's incentive was to keep expenses low. A small attendance at a rescheduled game on Monday morning would have only exacerbated the club's poor financial situation, as expenses likely would have exceeded the intake from the few spectators that would have shown up to pay a 50-cent admission charge. Wright may have suggested the two-for-one approach as a way for Worcester to optimize its attendance for the day at minimal additional expense (an approach that would also enhance Wright's visitor's share of the gate). As it turned out, Chicago won four straight games from Buffalo to easily capture the 1882 pennant, rendering moot the makeup of the September 22 postponed match that became major-league baseball's first doubleheader on September 25.

The very first doubleheader was a split decision, as Worcester defeated Providence 4–3 in the first game while Providence beat Worcester 8–6 in the second game. "The patrons of yesterday's ball games were given their money's worth," the *Worcester Gazette* reported. "It is not often that one can see 17 innings of ball in one afternoon." Darkness prevented the completion of nine innings in the second game, a perpetual problem with doubleheaders well into the twentieth century.[4]

Worcester won the first game on the strength of the pitching and hitting of Frank Mountain. As the Worcester pitcher, Mountain scattered the nine hits made by the Providence club; as a Worcester batter, Mountain collected two of his team's seven hits in the game. The victory was just number 18 of the season for Worcester, which suffered a total of 66 losses during the 1882 season that concluded five days later. Worcester finished dead last in the standings of the eight clubs in the National League.

As became customary for the single-admission doubleheader in its early history, the Worcester team employed a new battery for the second game, with Lee Richmond and Doc Bushong coming off the bench to be the pitcher and catcher, respectively. Jackie Hayes, the catcher for Mountain in the first game, moved to center field for the second game, with Fred Corey moving from center to shortstop to relieve Frank McLaughlin. For Providence, though, Hoss Radbourne pitched both ends of the doubleheader, and Barney Gilligan caught both of them; the club's only substitute for the second game was Cliff Carroll replacing Tom York in left field.

An early impediment to employing the doubleheader concept was the general inability for most catchers to play two games in one afternoon. In the early 1880s, there were no catcher's mitts. Catchers caught the ball with two hands, and used their fingers to stop the serves of the pitcher, either barehanded or wearing just thin, lightly padded gloves on both hands with the fingertips cut off. Catchers were constantly under assailment, battling broken fingers and other assorted injuries to their hands. Playing two games in one day only exacerbated the challenge faced by the catcher to remain injury-free during the season.

Bushong was one of the pioneers in developing the catcher's mitt. His reasoning, as one historian described it, was to allow "the nonthrowing hand to absorb most of the shock, because he wanted to preserve his right hand for his postbaseball career in dentistry." By 1886 Bushong wore "a left-hand glove that attracted attention for its size and for being a conglomeration of ragged buckskin, strings, sponges, and cloth." But in 1882, Bushong, like all other catchers, was highly susceptible to injury, so he was paired with the team's premier pitcher, Richmond, for the second game of the doubleheader.[5]

The second game commenced at 3:30 P.M., 15 minutes following the conclusion of the first contest. Providence captured the victory in the second game as darkness descended on the baseball diamond that was formed on the infield of the half-mile horse track that ringed the interior of the Worcester Agricultural Fair Grounds. Spectators could sit in the wooden grandstand built for the race track, which paralleled the first-base line, or stand on the infield grass along the third-base line. Spectators and the Worcester ballplayers left the grounds to go to their local residences for dinner, while the Providence ballplayers took horse-drawn carriages to travel the mile and a half back to Union Station to catch a train to return to Providence to get some rest before the club's excursion the next day to New York City for the exhibition game with the Metropolitan club.[6]

A marker at the Weller Academic Center of Becker College on Sever

Street in Worcester, the present-day site of the Worcester Agricultural Fair Grounds, indicates the historical importance of the site. However, the marker does not honor the first major-league doubleheader played there, but rather the first perfect game ever pitched in major-league history there. Lee Richmond, the losing pitcher in the second game of the first-ever doubleheader, is honored on the marker as that perfect-game pitcher.[7]

Attendance figures for the September 25, 1882, doubleheader were not publicized, as the *Worcester Spy, Worcester Gazette,* and *Boston Globe* all failed to report an attendance figure the next day. The number of patrons likely was around 100 or fewer, based on the *Globe*'s attendance reports for Worcester's last two home games. At the September 28 game between Worcester and Troy, the *Globe* reported that "about a score of people" watched the game, while the next day's game was played before "the presence of about two dozen people." Those attendance figures may also have been generous estimates, given that the Worcester ballclub had already been booted out of the National League.[8]

While the Providence–Worcester game was being rained out on Friday, September 22, the National League held a meeting in Philadelphia for the purpose of summarily jettisoning the Worcester and Troy clubs from the league. In the words of the *Worcester Spy*, this action occurred "in order to let in the better paying cities of New York and Philadelphia." Attendance was meager at Worcester in 1882, as reflected in the team's finances divulged a few days following the doubleheader. The *Worcester Spy* reported remarks by Edward Goulding, the ballclub's treasurer, "that all local bills had been paid, and that the club's funds amounted to about $650, a sum about $800 short of what would be required to pay the players in full at the end of the season." In Goulding's opinion, raising the $800 to balance the books "could never be done." At the end of September 1882, the Worcester franchise faded from existence.[9]

Worcester was the smallest city to ever represent a ballclub in the National League. But despite its small size relative to other National League cities, Worcester possessed desirable characteristics to be a major-league city in the early 1880s. While other cities in New England specialized in textile or shoe manufacturing, which suffered ups and downs as the economy expanded and contracted, Worcester had a more stable economic base. As stated in *The New England League: A Baseball History, 1885–1949*, "Worcester developed a diversified economy rather than one having a one-industry dependence. Worcester became a center for metal trades after the opening of the Blackstone Canal in 1828 and the introduction of railroad lines in the 1830s that connected the city with Boston, Providence, and points north. The city became a supplier of machine parts and other metal goods needed by the textile and shoe industries." Small-business owners could thus be counted on to support the ballclub in Worcester, especially since former mayor Charles Pratt was its president.[10]

The National League was very New England–centric in the early 1880s, which allowed for low transportation costs to the other eastern ballclubs located in Boston, Providence, and Troy, New York (which, while located in the Hudson River Valley, was only a short distance from the Massachusetts border). However, natural rivalries among these four franchises, which would have sparked greater spectator interest, never truly developed, certainly in comparison to the robustness of the later rivalries that Boston had with the New York and Philadelphia clubs that entered the league in 1883.

As exemplified by the September 25, 1882, doubleheader, much of the early history of the doubleheader was intertwined with league protocol on the rescheduling of postponed games. Article V, Section 2, of the original National League constitution in 1876 was very lax in this regard: "If any game arranged according to the requirements of this rule be prevented by rain, or if a tie or drawn game be played, the visiting club shall not be required to extend its stay, or to again visit such city for the sole purpose of playing off such tie or drawn game, or game prevented by rain." This provision was changed at a league meeting in December 1879, when the ballclub owners authorized "compelling a club to remain over and play off postponed games" unless the club had an obligation for another series.[11]

In 1882 there were plenty of days on which clubs could reschedule postponed games. The eight ballclubs in the National League had an 84-game schedule that year, typically playing three or four games each week over a season that spanned from May 1 to September 30. For instance, when Worcester's game at Providence on May 23, 1882, was rained out, the two clubs played this postponed game on the following day, May 24, which had been an open date on the schedule. During the first seven years of the National League's existence from its 1876 inaugural year, most ballclubs had little difficulty in rescheduling postponed contests. If a postponed game couldn't be squeezed in before the end of the season, that game was just disregarded and the two teams simply had fewer wins and losses posted in the league standings.

The term "doubleheader" did not immediately take hold at the time of the inaugural 1882 event, but rather needed another fifteen years before implanting itself into the baseball lexicon. During the intervening period, the occurrence of two games for a single admission was simply called the combination of a postponed game and a scheduled game.

Paul Dickson, in *The New Dickson Baseball Dictionary*, defined a doubleheader as "a set of two games played in succession on the same day between the same two teams and to which spectators are admitted for the price of a single game." Dickson cites July 20, 1896, as the first usage of the baseball term, via the following *Cincinnati Enquirer* reference: "In case rain should stop today's or tomorrow's games, double headers will have to be played the next day as there is no open time in the new Pittsburgh series to play off any postponed games."[12]

There was sporadic use of the term before 1896 in baseball accounts, such as this reference in 1892 in the *Boston Globe*: "The game will no doubt be played in Boston on the next trip of the Orioles to the Hub, making a double-header." However, because its popular usage exploded following the July 1896 date cited by Dickson, there is no doubt that the above *Cincinnati Enquirer* reference helped to popularize the word in the baseball sense. The newspaper seems to have picked up the term from Frank Bancroft, the business manager of the Cincinnati ballclub, who borrowed it from another 1896 event (see below) to generate interest in attending the two-for-one affair during the tough economic times of the mid–1890s. "Bancroft is responsible for 'double header' being used to designate two games for one price of admission," the *Cincinnati Enquirer* reported two years later. "Bannie advertised his double attraction as a 'double header' and it was not long until every club in the league was using the term."[13]

Dickson also cites the etymology of the baseball term "doubleheader" as stemming from the railroad term of the same name in the late nineteenth century. In railroad parlance, a doubleheader is "attaching two locomotives to double the usual number of cars in each train" to increase the capacity of a single locomotive. Two engines, one behind the other, pulling a train is somewhat similar to two baseball games played consecutively on the same day.[14]

However, there are two reasons why the extension of the railroad term seems to be a false etymology. The 1896 citation is a full ten years following 1887 when the practice of playing doubleheaders to make up a postponed game became commonplace. The railroad usage of doubleheader was in general use by 1885, when the *New York Times* reported that ownership sent out doubleheader trains "under the general charge of one conductor and three brakemen, thus dispensing with the services of one conductor and one brakeman." Due to this cutback on the number of workers needed to be employed on doubleheader trains, a large number of labor strikes occurred in the 1880s and 1890s and were widely publicized in newspapers. Surely, long before 1896, baseball writers would have made the connection between doubleheader trains and two ballgames played on one day (and perhaps even applied it to the concept of the separate-admission two-game sets played on holiday dates). Even if there was a ten-year lag in the transfer from the railroad term, the railroad usage fails to account for the "two for one" aspect of the baseball doubleheader, where spectators pay admission for one game and view the second game for free. Therefore, other applications of the term "doubleheader" more likely led to the baseball variation.[15]

1. The First Doubleheader

Before its use as a railroad term in the mid–1880s, the first "doubleheader" was a type of fireworks that exploded at both ends. In 1870, the *New York Times* wrote about Chinese fireworks and the "[fire] crackers, rockets, bomb shells and double-headers peculiar to that celestial region." The two-headed firecracker spawned the usage of the word to describe a political ticket of two candidates who both had the credentials to be the main candidate, even though one was subservient to the other on the ticket. This usage expanded into many things that provided a "two for one" benefit. "The selection of Mr. Bliss was a double-header for the President," the *New York Times* reported on a decision by President Benjamin Harrison in 1892. "It was a slap at Platt and it was a compliment to the Union Leaguers."[16]

In 1896, the political usage of "doubleheader" took on a different meaning when the Democratic Party split over the issue of using silver, in addition to gold, to back the U.S. dollar. At the time, the nation was still enduring an economic depression that had begun in 1893, in which many people blamed the gold standard for contracting the money supply and causing deflation, i.e., a decline in the value of prices and wages. Some Democrats argued that backing money with silver in addition to gold would expand the money supply and help end the depression, although at the expense of inflation, which the Republicans abhorred. The silver interests were mostly based in the western and central states, while gold (or "sound money") interests dominated in the eastern states. Because the major-league baseball landscape in the mid–1890s stopped at the west bank of the Mississippi River, the silver issue was not nearly as mainstream in newspapers in New York and Pennsylvania as it was in newspapers in Nebraska and North Dakota.

Many Democratic political conventions held in states in the Midwest couldn't agree on whether their delegations should represent gold or silver. In many instances the conventions selected two delegations, referred to as a doubleheader, with one representing silver and the second gold. This is illustrated in the following 1895 headline and article about an Ohio convention:

> Brice and Thomas Lock Horns in a County
> Convention—A Double Header Results

Springfield, Ohio, Aug. 3—The preliminary fight between Senator C.S. Brice as the sound money candidate for re-election and John H. Thomas, as the opposing free silver candidate, [began] in the county convention here today. Both sides claim a victory, but the factions fought until confusion reigned supreme. After their separation, two sets of delegates were selected to the state convention and the fight will be continued before the committee on credentials and possibly in the state convention.[17]

Since the convention left it to someone else to sort out later which delegation should eventually be seated, these were truly "two for one" doubleheaders, i.e., two delegations for one placement.

William Jennings Bryan, the 1896 Democratic candidate for U.S. president, was influential in extending the doubleheader connotation from politics to baseball. Bryan hailed from Nebraska, where there was lively debate over the gold-silver issue. The Nebraska delegation at the 1896 Democratic National Convention was actually a doubleheader, which helped to provide credence to the term's resulting baseball usage given the highly publicized nature of the unseating of one delegation (gold) at the expense of the second one (silver).

At the convention held at the Chicago Coliseum, the Democratic National Committee had initially seated the Nebraska delegation backing the gold standard. However, silver interests dominated the credentials committee, which eventually ruled that the delegation backing silver should instead be seated. When the decision was announced from the podium on the convention floor, a raucous celebration resulted by the delegates, most of whom backed silver. Amid cheering and whistling, the silver delegation entered the convention floor at the same time that the gold delegation was leaving. As described by Bryan biographer Louis Koenig, "While thousands of witnesses roared approval punctuated with laughter and hisses, the Nebraska silver men chased their state's gold delegation from the floor into the galleries."[18]

On July 10, the day after Bryan's famous "Cross of Gold" speech, the Democratic National Convention in Chicago nominated the Nebraskan to be its presidential candidate in the November election. Interestingly, on the same day, the first doubleheaders of the 1896 baseball season were played, with two-game slates between Baltimore and Cleveland, Brooklyn and Pittsburgh, and Washington and Cincinnati. Suddenly, baseball writers began to use the term "doubleheader" in their accounts of these ballgames. The *Brooklyn Eagle* reported: "Although Foutz wanted the postponed game played off tomorrow, Mack insisted on the double header being decided this afternoon." The following day, the *Washington Post* ran a headline entitled: "Spiders Played the Orioles a Double Header and Lost the Second."[19]

Bryan was defeated in the 1896 election by Republican William McKinley. Although gold interests triumphed over silver ones in that election, the term "doubleheader" that had risen from the debate over that issue was the real winner. Cincinnati, which in July 1896 was battling with Cleveland and Baltimore for first place, received prominent coverage of its games in the nation's newspapers. That coverage expanded following the July 19 contest between Baltimore and Cincinnati when nearly 25,000 people crammed into Cincinnati's League Park to set a National League attendance record. Dickson's citation of the first reference to "doubleheader" occurred in the *Cincinnati Enquirer* the next day, which is an accurate beginning of the genealogy for the popularity of the term.

1. The First Doubleheader

The mid-season success of the 1896 Cincinnati ballclub, with some clever promotion by its enterprising business manager, enabled a Midwestern political term to enter the baseball lexicon of cities in all sections of the country. After the July 23 game between Boston and Cincinnati was rained out, the *Boston Globe* reported that "a double header is booked for tomorrow." When that two-game set was also rained out, the *Globe* reported: "There was enough water on the diamond at League Park for yacht races, when the time to call the first game of the double-header, scheduled for today, arrived." When the two clubs finally played two games on Saturday, July 25, more than 11,000 spectators jammed League Park and overflowed onto the field. Soon it was commonplace for newspapers across the country to use the term "doubleheader" to refer to the concept of two games played on the same day for a single admission.[20]

There is no doubt that the doubleheader did change the face of the game in the late nineteenth and early twentieth centuries. As the spectator base changed from businessman to wage earner, baseball fans chose to attend two games for the price of one, rendering the single weekday game an albatross for club owners to cope with to devise a workable economic model for the baseball business.

As "doubleheader" developed into a common baseball term in the

HOW WAS THAT FOR A DOUBLE HEADER?

Nineteenth-century newspaper cartoons, such as this one from the May 18, 1898, edition of the *New York Evening Journal*, depicted the baseball doubleheader in a literal fashion — with two heads — after the doubleheader term was popularized in 1896 following the nomination of William Jennings Bryan as the Democratic candidate for U.S. president. The months preceding the 1896 nominating convention featured political doubleheaders, with two delegates representing the gold and silver interests vying for just one seat at the convention.

latter part of the 1890s, it also began its journey to gradually transform into one word from its beginning as a two-word phrase. The one-word term "doubleheader" evolved into its final adjective-noun compound form from its original spelling as two distinct words, the adjective "double" preceding the noun "header," and an intermediate hyphenated version as "double-header." By the 1940s, the term was most often used in its one-word version.

The development of the one-word term "doubleheader" happened in much the same way as did the term "baseball" as well as the modern-day terms "online" and "website." All three of these terms linguistically began as two words, rapidly converted into a hyphenated form, and then morphed into a single-term compound word. The formation of solid compound words such as doubleheader typically follows a pattern, in which "many solid compounds begin as separate words, evolve into hyphenated compounds, and later become solid compounds."[21]

Accompanying the change in written form was likely a subtle change in speech pattern in how the term was pronounced verbally. Typically, when the adjective-noun combination is treated as one word, the emphasis is on the initial portion (denoted here by all caps), i.e., DOUBLEheader. When the combination is treated as distinct words, the stress is usually on the second portion, i.e., double HEADER. The classic example of this verbal convention is the pronunciation of greenhouse, the place where plants grow, compared to green house, a building painted green.[22]

For the first half-century of major-league baseball, doubleheaders were most often employed to make up postponed games, after the concept pioneered in Worcester in 1882 gained general acceptance by ballclubs in 1887. The rescheduling of a postponed game was the most basic level of the following three-tier taxonomy of doubleheader applications:

- Level 1—Makeup of a postponed game.
- Level 2—Elimination of a low attendance date by rescheduling a weekday game.
- Level 3—Optimization of attendance on the club's best attendance day of the week.

A Level 1 doubleheader was sometimes called a natural doubleheader, because its genesis was a naturally occurring event (rain or a tie game). A Level 2 doubleheader was often pejoratively called a synthetic doubleheader, because its genesis was a man-made occurrence. Level 3 doubleheaders were usually Sunday and holiday doubleheaders.[23]

Ballclub owners in the 1880s weren't necessarily averse to scheduling two games on one day. Holiday schedules on Decoration Day and Independence Day often called for two games (as did Labor Day following its establishment as a national holiday in 1894). This scheduling was similar to the better theaters of the time that conducted performances of a play or opera twice on one day, for separate admissions, first at a 2:00 P.M. matinee and then at 8:00 P.M. in the evening.

Because these holiday baseball affairs had separate admissions for morning and afternoon games, they are not considered true doubleheaders. In this book, the use of the term "doubleheader" is geared to just single-admission, two-game events; separate-admission events for two games on one day are generally referred to as "two-game sets." This distinction is important in order to understand the historical development of the true doubleheader, especially since baseball writers often used "doubleheader" interchangeably for both types of admission arrangements.

It is sometimes difficult to discern from newspaper accounts whether the two games played on a day were for a single admission—and thus considered to be a doubleheader—or for separate admissions. Baseball writers did not always find the distinction important, especially during the nineteenth century, and attendance figures were often only sporadically reported. Gradually, the convention evolved to report separate-admission, two-game sets as "morning" and "afternoon" events, with box scores usually containing these labels as a heading. Two games for a single admission were typically reported as "first" and "second" games, with similar headings over the box scores. This convention was by no means 100 percent accurate (particularly during the period when holiday two-game sets transformed into doubleheaders), but it does yield a high probability to the games' admission status.

While the Worcester–Providence doubleheader in 1882 was the first time that major-league ballclubs charged a single admission for patrons to watch two games on the same day, it was not the first time that major-league ballclubs engaged in the playing of two games on the same day. During the inaugural National League season in 1876, Hartford and Cincinnati played a morning-afternoon, separate-admission, set of two games on September 9. In 1878, Providence made up a tie game with Indianapolis as part of two games on August 9. During 1880, Worcester participated twice in two-game sets, on August 16 at Cleveland and, curiously, against Providence at Worcester on October 1.

These were the forerunners of the holiday two-game set, which became a National League scheduling staple in 1883. The doubleheader and the holiday twosome paralleled each other as separate concepts for several decades before they eventually merged together in the 1920s.

2

Holiday Two-Game Sets

IN THE EARLY 1880s, the conventional approach to conducting two ballgames in a single day was to play separate-admission games, one in the morning around 10:30 A.M. and the other in the afternoon around 3:30 P.M., rather than a single-admission doubleheader. After several ballclubs had used the separate-admission approach in 1880 to make up a postponed game via a morning game in advance of the regularly scheduled afternoon contest, it was a natural extension for clubs to consider playing two games on a holiday date in 1881. Two national holidays fell within the baseball season in the early 1880s, Independence Day on July 4 and Decoration Day on May 30.

Independence Day, commonly called the Fourth of July, is the oldest of the national holidays and commemorates the date that Congress formally approved the Declaration of Independence in 1776. The holiday dates back to 1777, when the *Pennsylvania Evening Post* reported that, in Philadelphia, "yesterday, the 4th of July, being the Anniversary of the Independence of the United States of America, was celebrated in this city with demonstrations of joy and festivity." The earliest Independence Day holidays were marked by public speeches, formal dinners, discharge from cannons, and the lighting of fireworks.[1]

John Adams, a founding father and signer of the Declaration of Independence, wrote a letter in 1776 that, in retrospect, seemed to establish the tradition of playing baseball to celebrate the signing the Declaration of Independence. "I am apt to believe that it will be celebrated by succeeding Generations, as the great anniversary Festival," Adams wrote to his wife Abigail, in a letter that would be reproduced in numerous newspapers during the nineteenth century. "It ought to be solemnized with Pomp and Parade, with Shows, Games, Sports, Guns, Bells, Bonfires and Illuminations, from One End of this Continent to the other from this Time forward forever more."[2]

Decoration Day, now called Memorial Day, commemorated those soldiers who died in the Civil War. The holiday dates back to 1868, three years following the end of the Civil War, when General John Logan, national commander of the Grand Army of the Republic, issued an order establishing May 30 to be observed "for the purpose of strewing with flowers or otherwise decorating the graves of the Comrades who died in defense of their country during the late rebellion." In 1873, New York was the first state to recognize Decoration Day as a legal holiday; Pennsylvania and the New England states soon followed (e.g., Massachusetts in 1881).[3]

The Independence Day and Decoration Day holidays were plum attractions for ballclubs, since they usually drew the largest crowds of the season, often three to five times the normal attendance of a weekday game. "The seating capacity of the grounds was to be taxed to its utmost, crowds of people surging in at the several entrances," the *Chicago Inter Ocean* reported on the crowd at a holiday game in 1881. "Almost the entire field was covered with people when the players stepped onto the field at little before 3 o'clock." All these additional 50-cent admissions made holiday dates a very lucrative aspect of ballclub finances in the National League.[4]

Attendance swelled for holiday games because it was the only time that most working people could attend a ballgame, since they typically labored ten hours a day for six days a week and rested on Sunday. Because Sunday baseball was prohibited in the National League until the 1892 season, mill workers and other laborers usually packed the ball grounds for a holiday game to augment the coterie of middle-class, small-business owners who were the predominant attendees at weekday games.

Patrons of ballgames held on Monday through Saturday needed to have the flexibility in their work schedules to find the time to attend an afternoon contest, since baseball was then played exclusively during the daytime. Baseball owners appealed to middle-class patrons to fill seats in their ballparks, not only because the middle class had the time and money to attend games but also because they helped deem baseball as respectable recreation. Workers in the burgeoning industries of America generally were excluded from the opportunity to observe a ballgame. As one historian wrote, "The result of an onerous work load was that it was difficult for craftsmen and almost impossible for unskilled personnel to attend a ball game unless they worked unusual hours like a baker, took time of from work, were unemployed, had a rare holiday, or lived in a city that permitted Sunday baseball." A holiday was a rare occasion that working people could attend a ballgame played in a National League city.[5]

In the competing American Association, holiday dates were less essential to ballclub finances because Sunday baseball was played in many cities (and all clubs played road games on Sunday whenever possible). Sunday baseball enabled working people to more easily attend games during the season, which often attracted similarly sized crowds as the holiday games in the American Association. In the American Association, revenue from Sunday baseball (both the home team's and visitor's share of the gate) was viewed as the most vital economic component, whereas in the National League revenue from holiday games was considered prime.

Due to the financial importance of holiday games, the National League generally parceled out holiday dates equally among its clubs. With eight teams playing four games on each of two holidays, it was easy to arrange for each club to have one holiday home date each season. During the three years 1880 to 1882, the National League schedule was devised to have single games on Decoration Day played at the home sites of the four eastern clubs and single games on Independence Day played on the home grounds of the four western clubs. This geographic pattern of allocating playing sites for Decoration Day and Independence Day games had been originally established in 1876, the inaugural year of the National League. That year, the clubs in Boston, Hartford, Brooklyn, and Philadelphia hosted single games on Decoration Day and the clubs in Chicago, Cincinnati, Louisville, and St. Louis hosted single games on Independence Day.

The rationale for the original holiday allocation in 1876 was that Decoration Day was primarily celebrated as a holiday (legal or otherwise) only in northeastern cities. States that were part of the seceding Confederate states, and states that were slave states before the Civil War began in 1861, were slower to adopt Decoration Day as a state holiday, since the intent of the holiday was to honor Union soldiers killed in action during the Civil War. Understandably, in 1876, Decoration Day was not a major initiative in St. Louis and Louisville, located in the former slave states of Missouri and Kentucky, respectively, nor in Cincinnati, which is situated just across the Ohio River from Kentucky.

To illustrate this dichotomy, the *Philadelphia Inquirer* published dispatches from major cities across the country about their Decoration Day holiday activities in 1876. There were long accounts from Washington, New York, Chicago, and the New England states, but just short items from other cities. From Cincinnati: "The decoration of soldiers' graves at Spring Grove Cemetery occurred with the usual ceremonies today, but except the closing of the post office and other national offices, there was no suspension of business." In St. Louis: "Although the day was not observed as a holiday, several thousand people were on the ground" at a ceremony at National Cemetery. While some modern-day observers attribute this lack of holiday celebration to lingering hostility between the North and the South (which would be the case for states in the Deep South where separate Confederate Memorial Day holidays were established), in the border states of Kentucky and Missouri, it was more simply the case that there were just not that many graves of Union soldiers to warrant a broad-based holiday.[6]

2. Holiday Two-Game Sets

From the standpoint of the development of the holiday two-game set in the major leagues, the important point is that the precedent was established in 1876 that Decoration Day was reserved on the schedule for ballclubs located in the eastern states and that Independence Day was reserved for ballclubs in western locales. The American Association adopted an identical holiday scheduling format when it commenced business in 1882, as Decoration Day games were held that year in Baltimore, Philadelphia, and Pittsburgh with Independence Day games hosted by Cincinnati, Louisville, and St. Louis. Even after Decoration Day was celebrated more widely outside of the eastern states, this geographic allocation pattern remained in place as the foundation of holiday scheduling for two decades because of its impact to the overall schedule. Lengthy road trips were common in those days, sometimes as long as four weeks, so shuttling western teams east for Decoration Day games, or eastern teams west for Independence Day games, was no small matter in those days of inefficient railroad travel.

The first holiday two-game set in major-league baseball history was staged in the National League on Independence Day in 1881. Two cities, Buffalo and Detroit, hold the distinction of staging the first holiday twosomes, as Detroit hosted Worcester on July 4, 1881, and Buffalo hosted Troy the same day. There was little newspaper fanfare about the novel holiday arrangements, however, since the nation was in a somber mood with President James Garfield on his deathbed after being shot by an assassin. Detroit won both of its holiday games with Worcester. Similarly, in Buffalo, Mickey Welch pitched and won both games for Troy, as the *Buffalo Express* reported, "In the afternoon contest the stands were filled to sardine compactness and the assemblage was very enthusiastic." In the years before the overhand delivery was legalized in 1884, pitching two games in a single day was a common occurrence.[7]

The two-game slates in Detroit and Buffalo were efforts by ballclub owners located in the league's mid-sized cities to improve their club finances by attracting larger crowds on a day that most working people had off. Worcester and Troy, the league's two smallest cities, were certainly amenable to rescheduling their July 5 games with Detroit and Buffalo to gain a much larger visitor's share of the gate from the morning game on July 4 than they likely would have received from the scheduled game on July 5. Detroit had witnessed this firsthand at its Decoration Day game at Worcester earlier in the season, when the attendance at the Agricultural Fair Grounds was "the largest ever known, the turnstile count showing 3652 persons" compared to just a few hundred at the subsequent game on June 1 between the two clubs. Attendance was robust at all four Independence Day holiday sites in 1881. As one newspaper reported, "There were good crowds at the Western games: 8500 in Chicago, 5000 in Cleveland, 1500 at the first game in Buffalo and more in the afternoon, over 2000 at the morning game in Detroit, and over 3600 in the afternoon."[8]

Worcester and Troy, the two visiting teams at the 1881 Independence Day two-game sets, both sought to stage a similar two-game match for their Decoration Day home dates in 1882 with the Cleveland and Chicago ballclubs, respectively. The contests between Cleveland and Worcester had to be scuttled, though, when Cleveland's May 28 game at Buffalo was rained out and Buffalo insisted that it be made up on May 29. This caused Cleveland to miss its train connections to get to Worcester for the 10:30 A.M. first game on the May 30 holiday; the Cleveland club made the long train ride from Buffalo to Worcester barely in time for the 3:30 P.M. second game. A large advertisement on the front page of the *Worcester Spy*, announcing the two games on the holiday, went for naught.[9]

The holiday twosome in Troy went on as planned, the first time that major-league ballclubs played two games on Decoration Day. Not only were separate games played in the morning and afternoon between Troy and Chicago, but the games were also staged at separate venues. The afternoon game was played on Troy's regular grounds in West Troy, after the morning game had been played five miles down river near Albany, at the Greenbush grounds. The attempt to increase overall attendance for the day by staging the morning game at a different location than its regular grounds didn't pay off spectacularly for Troy. Fewer than 700 people witnessed the morning contest at the Greenbush grounds. Four times as many showed up at the afternoon game in West Troy, where the *Troy Daily Times* reported the attendance to be 2,878. Some of the afternoon crowd may have been inspired to attend by this *Albany Morning Express* report: "The witching announcement that 50 good-looking girls from a leading collar shop here have expressed their intention to attend in a body the Decoration Day game in West Troy will doubtless secure a goodly representation of our lahdedah youths."[10]

Boston and Providence did not join Worcester and Troy in arranging for two-game sets on Decoration Day in 1882. While there was demonstrable demand for one game on the holiday, especially in the league's larger cities of Chicago and Boston, there was a legitimate question whether two games on one day would simply divide existing one-game demand between the two games or actually increase total attendance for the day. For their solo matchups on Decoration Day in 1882, Boston drew 6,000 spectators for its game with Buffalo (who arrived just half an hour before game time) while 7,000 people attended the Providence game with Detroit.[11]

Chicago was the first of the league's larger-sized cities to tackle this issue, with its Independence Day two-game set with Troy in 1882. This match was one of four in the western cities that year as all eight teams in the National League played two games on a holiday for the first time. "If the numerous letters and telegrams received, asking for reserved seats, are any indication, there will be a very large attendance at both morning and afternoon games," the *Chicago Inter Ocean* reported about the advanced ticket sale for the holiday two-game set. One economic by-product of the working-class population wanting to watch a holiday baseball game was the increased sales of reserved seats to the ballclub's usual weekday attendees, which thwarted any fears of a club's treasurer that holiday attendance would be predominantly the laboring class. While only a few thousand attended the morning game in Chicago, 8,000 people flooded the stands for the afternoon contest and spilled over onto the field.[12]

Boston became a believer in the two-game concept for holiday dates at its 1882 Independence Day match in Detroit, where 3,500 people reportedly saw the morning game and another 6,000 attended the afternoon contest, "filling the field so that a hit within the crowd only went for two bases." Boston collected seven doubles, to Detroit's two, to lambaste the host club in the second game, 14–1, whereupon "the hoodlum element of the crowd attempted to mob Hawes, his umpiring being bad."[13]

The first Independence Day two-game set in Chicago was prominently advertised in the July 4, 1882, edition of the *Chicago Inter Ocean*. The willingness of larger cities like Chicago to stage two games on a holiday, with separate admissions for morning and afternoon games, accelerated the general acceptance of the holiday two-game concept from just a small-city technique in 1881 to one used by all major-league ballclubs in 1883.

The holiday two-game sets in 1881 and 1882 in the National League were all ad hoc arrangements, with a postponed game or a game moved from another date serving as the basis for the morning game, which was the prelude to the planned afternoon game. The first scheduled holiday two-game sets occurred in 1883, when both the National League and the American Association made such arrangements in their initial schedules released in March. While the existing geographic pattern for allocating holiday dates was the foundation underlying the 1883 holiday schedule, it was not the only criteria—politics also played a role.

When the National League expelled Worcester and Troy from its ranks after the 1882 season to create room for ballclubs in New York and Philadelphia to rejoin the league (after a six-year absence following the expulsion of their predecessor clubs after the 1876 season), the league offered the two new franchises home dates for both holidays in 1883. The rationale seemed to be to jump-start the finances of the new ballclubs located in two of the country's largest cities, which would benefit the league in general as well. The Independence Day games played in New York and Philadelphia in 1883 were some of the very few Fourth of July games hosted by eastern cities over the next dozen years in the major leagues.

Decoration Day dates in 1883 were given to the four eastern cities, as usual. To make room for New York and Philadelphia on the Independence Day schedule, the league had to send two western clubs to play in New York and Philadelphia and thus go without a holiday home date that year. The league awarded Independence Day games to Chicago and Detroit, and relegated Buffalo and Cleveland to second-class status by withholding holiday dates from those two ballclubs.

In addition to Troy's use of alternate locations for a holiday two-game set in 1882, another technique used to differentiate the two games of a holiday match was to have the home team play one team in the morning game and a different team in the afternoon game. This arrangement helped the Boston and Providence clubs in the National League overcome their attendance concerns of playing two games in one day, by appealing to a common body of people to attend both contests and negating any disinclination by having the same opponent for both.

On Decoration Day in 1883, Boston and Providence hosted two-game sets where their respective opponents, Cleveland and Buffalo, shuttled by train between the two cities, which are located 40 miles apart. After a morning game in Boston, Cleveland took the train to Providence for an afternoon match there. Likewise, Buffalo played a morning game in Providence and took the train to Boston for an afternoon contest at the South End Grounds. The maneuver seemed to work, as attendance in Boston and Providence for both games in 1883 exceeded that of their single holiday games the previous year. In Providence, more than 10,000 attended the contests, 2,800 in the morning and 7,500 in the afternoon. The *Boston Globe* didn't publish actual figures, but made it clear that multitudes attended both games. "A crowd that occupied every seat on the South End Grounds assembled yesterday morning," the *Globe* reported. In the afternoon, "the spectators began to gather by 1:30, and the [trolley] cars were replete with them, in some cases affording the poor conductors only the precious foot-hold the brake could give."[14]

While the New York ballclub of the National League hosted Detroit for two games on Decoration Day in 1883, the Metropolitan club in the American Association, also located in New York City, hosted a Decoration Day two-game set as well that year. But the Metropolitan set was unusual for two reasons. First, the club played two different opponents that day, as Boston and Providence also did in the National League. More unusual, though, was that Metropolitan's games were played simultaneously with, and directly adjacent to, the games played by the New York team of the National League.

The unusual set of games was possible because John Day owned both the New York–based franchises that competed in the National League and the American Association. The Metropolitan club had been formed in 1880 by the partnership of Day, "a wealthy young merchant and Tammany politician who preferred to think of himself as a baseball player," and Jim Mutrie, "a man without Day's financial means but with a greater understanding of baseball." Day acquired the New York franchise in the National League when the league wanted to expand into the nation's largest city for the 1883 season.[15]

At the Decoration Day games in 1883, the two teams played their games on opposite ends of the Polo Grounds. "The ground was divided by a canvas fence running from One Hundred and Tenth to One Hundred and Twelfth street, by which two games were played at once," the *New York Times* described the holiday playing scene. In the morning games, the New York National League club played Detroit on the Fifth Avenue side of the Polo Grounds, while Metropolitan of the American Association played Cincinnati on the Sixth Avenue side. Day actually scheduled five games at the Polo Grounds on that Decoration Day. While the Metropolitan team waited for its afternoon opponent, Columbus, to arrive from its morning game in Philadelphia (where Cincinnati traveled for its afternoon match), and the two National League clubs rested, Yale and Princeton played a college game on the Fifth Avenue side of the Polo Grounds. New York and Detroit then played the second game of their holiday set. The *Times* reported that more than 10,000 people watched the five games played at the Polo Grounds on that holiday.[16]

Boston and Providence served as the traveling opponents for the Independence Day two-game sets in New York and Philadelphia in 1883. Transportation challenges surfaced as one disadvantage to the different-opponent strategy of holiday sets, when Providence forfeited the morning game at Recreation Park in Philadelphia. "The Providence nine did not arrive on the ground until eleven o'clock," the *Philadelphia Inquirer* reported. "As they were to play in New York in the afternoon, they were compelled to leave at the close of the seventh inning, when the score stood 11 to 9 in their favor." The New York–Philadelphia double switch was quickly abandoned as a feasible holiday strategy.[17]

In 1884, New York and Philadelphia went without holiday dates in the National League, as Chicago and Cleveland secured both Decoration Day and Independence Day dates on the schedule. Boston and Providence continued to employ the different-opponent strategy on Decoration Day in 1884, with New York and Philadelphia serving as the traveling opponents, to the delight of huge crowds in both cities. In the American Association, John Day lined up two opponents for his Metropolitan ballclub on Decoration Day, trading off with the new Brooklyn club in the league rather than with the Athletic club in Philadelphia. In addition, Baltimore and Washington used the different-opponent strategy in the American Association.

New York and Philadelphia also served as alternating opponents for Boston in a second holiday match in Boston that year, a holiday that was distinct only to Boston among National League cities—Bunker Hill Day on June 17—celebrating a battle during the Revolutionary War.

Another transportation snag, though, signaled an end for the different-opponent strategy for holiday matches. Boston and Providence once again deployed this approach for Decoration Day in 1885. After Chicago had played a morning game in Providence, rainy weather caused its train to be late arriving in Boston and delayed the start of the afternoon game there by nearly an hour. The Chicago-Boston contest ended in the fourth inning due to the rain and thus did not constitute a complete game to count in the standings.

The demise of the different-opponent strategy came after Brooklyn and Metropolitan switched opponents on Decoration Day in 1886 (which was played on May 31 since the 30th was a Sunday, the general rule for holidays falling on a Sunday). Providence left the National League after the 1885 season and Metropolitan left the American Association after 1887, which resulted in fewer proximate league cities to efficiently conduct such a strategy.

However, the 1886 Decoration Day two-game set in Brooklyn was very telling for another reason—the attendance. As the *Brooklyn Eagle* reported, Brooklyn's contests with Cincinnati and Louisville on the holiday were "played before the largest assemblage of spectators ever seen on the Washington Park ball grounds, over thirteen thousand people witnessing the two games played there on Decoration Day." Clearly, playing two games on a holiday did not dissipate the overall attendance, compared to a single game, and in most cases resulted in a vastly greater number of spectators.[18]

The new challenge for a holiday two-game set was to generate greater attendance at the morning game, since huge throngs could be relied on to attend the afternoon contest. The morning game nearly always drew less than one-half the size of the attendance of the one in the afternoon. For instance, at the Decoration Day match in Brooklyn in 1886, reported attendance at the morning game was 4,000 people, which was less than half of the 9,000 people that saw the afternoon contest. In Boston 3,000 were at the morning game on Decoration Day, while the afternoon match attracted 7,600. At the Polo Grounds in New York, attendance at the morning game was 7,000, with a reported 20,000 crashing the gates for the afternoon contest. "For three hours a steady stream of human beings passed into the inclosure. The grand stand seats were all sold after the doors were opened, and the spectators were forced to take to the field and stand in the sun," the *New York Times* reported. "Among the spectators were a number of persons from suburban cities and towns, who, after taking a look at the tomb of Gen. Grant in Riverside Park, flocked to see the ball game." Soon, the challenge of attracting crowds to the morning game took care of itself. With such large crowds at the afternoon match, more people began to attend the morning contest as the more realistic way to actually see a game on the holiday, rather than be squeezed among the crowd at the afternoon game, or worse, being left outside the gate by not being able to purchase a ticket.[19]

Attendance became so large for holiday two-game sets that the holidays attained even greater political importance in the development of league schedules. It was no longer sufficient to get an equitable allocation of the number of holiday home dates; obtaining holiday opponents that would maximize attendance became a more significant factor. For instance, in 1888, the *New York Times* reported the displeasure of owner John Day about the holiday scheduling for his New York club. "On Decoration Day the Pittsburg nine—a club that does not draw well—is scheduled to play here, and on the Fourth of July the Giants are booked to play in Detroit," the *Times* wrote. "On the whole, as Mr. Day remarked, the Philadelphia Club got all the plums, and it is surprising to him that Manager Wright, in his effort to eclipse all past performances, even allowed the tree that bore the fruit to remain." Harry Wright did manage to finagle good holiday attractions for his Philadelphia club, hosting Detroit, the defending National League champion, on Decoration Day and playing at Chicago on Independence Day.[20]

Up until 1888, holiday scheduling could be relatively simple, as each franchise in the National League and American Association could be allocated one holiday date, since there were eight clubs in each league to divvy up the eight home dates for Decoration Day and Independence Day. The addition of a third legal holiday during the baseball season changed all that. By 1887, several states began to celebrate Labor Day, the first Monday in September, as an official state holiday, notably New York and Massachusetts; Pennsylvania followed suit by 1889. Since it was "inevitable that some teams would get two holiday dates during a year, while others would get just one," the introduction of the Labor Day holiday elevated holiday scheduling politics several notches.[21]

3

Emergence of the Doubleheader

AFTER THE FIRST-OF-ITS-KIND doubleheader played in 1882 by the Providence and Worcester clubs of the National League, it took five years for the doubleheader concept to take root in the major leagues. Until 1887, the holiday-style scheduling pattern of morning and afternoon games with separate admissions was the preferred approach for playing two games on one day when necessary to make up a postponed game. Late in 1886 the idea of the doubleheader was popularized and in 1887 more ballclubs began to employ the concept to make up postponed games.

No National League club emulated the doubleheader concept in 1883 or 1884, even though the playing schedule had been expanded by 14 games in 1883 and by another 14 games in 1884. Ballclubs were able to make up postponed games through open dates for the most part, despite the fact that the playing season was extended by less than two weeks during that period to accommodate the expansion from an 84-game to a 112-game schedule. In addition, there were a few separate-admission two-game sets played during that period, such as the Cleveland–Philadelphia match on September 14, 1883, and the Buffalo–Detroit match on August 8, 1884.

The next doubleheaders on record, while technically two games for a single admission, occurred when the first contest ended in a forfeit. With a sizeable audience in the stands, quick-thinking managers hastily arranged to replay a postponed game to retain the day's gate receipts.

For example, on August 11, 1884, in the first inning of a game between Chicago and Buffalo at Chicago's Lakefront Park, Chicago manager Cap Anson disputed an umpire's decision to call Mike Kelly out at first base when Chicago runner George Gore tackled the Buffalo second baseman to prevent him from throwing Kelly out to complete a double play. When the umpire declined to reverse his decision, Anson refused to go on with the game, which caused the umpire to forfeit the game to Buffalo. Having played two games on one day in Detroit just three days earlier, the Buffalo manager probably suggested playing a postponed game to quell the 2,000 spectators in the stands at Chicago. "After waiting an hour the nines again came on the field and played a postponed game," one newspaper recounted the situation, "which was called at the end of the ninth inning on account of darkness," with the score deadlocked in a 6–6 tie.[1]

Two weeks later, another doubleheader spontaneously materialized at a Union Association game between Boston and Wilmington on August 25. When Wilmington, a replacement team taking the place of the disbanded Keystone club of Philadelphia, failed to show for the 3:30 P.M. starting time in Boston, the umpire declared the game forfeited to Boston. While half the crowd accepted a refund, the other half stayed to watch an impromptu match to be played between the Boston Unions and a picked nine from the stands. As Boston manager Tim Murnane was organizing the exhibition, "some carriages came tearing up to the grounds and the Wilmingtons rushed on to the grounds." The ballclub had missed its train connection in New York and a telegram notifying Boston went astray. The two teams hastily agreed to play a Boston–Keystone postponed game, which lasted just six innings before darkness halted the action with Boston ahead, 6–0. After accumulating two losses in one day in Boston on August 25, the overmatched Wilmington club went on to compile a dismal 2–16 record in its brief foray in the Union Association before disbanding in mid–September.[2]

The first true application of the doubleheader concept following the Worcester–Providence experiment of 1882 occurred on October 4, 1884, in the American Association, when Indianapolis played at Baltimore. "On account of rain the game scheduled for the 3rd was postponed until the 4th, when by agreement two games were played, the payment of one admission giving the spectators a double treat," *Sporting Life* described the arrangement. "The first game was started at 1:30 P.M., when about 500 people were present," the *Baltimore Sun* reported. "It was over at 3:30 and the second game was started a few minutes before 4 o'clock." Those few spectators that viewed both contests received slightly less than two-for-one value, however, since the second game ended after six innings due to darkness. As demonstrated in all three doubleheaders conducted in 1884, completing nine innings in the second game of a twin bill was a persistent problem in the nineteenth century when trying to squeeze two contests into a late-summer afternoon in that pre-daylight-saving-time era.[3]

Billy Barnie, manager and part-owner of the Baltimore club, was no doubt the man behind the idea to play two games for a single admission on October 4. Barnie, an optimistic man of many words and a lot of bluster, was not only "one of the most universally liked men ever connected with professional baseball" but also a businessman who was appreciated for his "attention to the cost of running a franchise in a time when a manager's title encompassed the responsibilities of today's general manager." Barnie was a promoter, along the lines of P. T. Barnum, who understood that a little showmanship could go a long way toward attracting a crowd. Exactly what encouraged Barnie to stage a single-admission doubleheader in 1884 is unclear. A possible catalyst may have been his attendance at a local Baltimore theater that often offered two shows for the price of one admission, which the theater industry called a "double bill." Albaugh's Holliday Street Theatre and Kelly's Front Street Theatre both advertised the availability of a double bill in the *Baltimore Sun* that year.[4]

In 1885, the doubleheader concept took a step forward when John Day, owner of both the New York club in the National League and the Metropolitan club in the American Association, arranged several dates for both teams to participate in a two-for-one spectator event. "There will be two games at the Polo Grounds to-day," the *New York Times* reported about the novel concept on August 25 that year. "The Metropolitans will play the Baltimores, beginning at 2 o'clock, and immediately after the New Yorks will cross bats with the Providence nine. Fifty cents admission will entitle a person to witness both games." When the original August 25 two-for-one event was rained out, the four clubs took the field the following day to engage in Day's inaugural interleague doubleheader, with the home teams winning both games. "There were two games of baseball on the Polo Grounds yesterday, and the patrons of the sport had an opportunity of witnessing four hours of steady playing," the *New York Times* reported. "The day was raw and chilly and anything but pleasant for the spectators. In spite of this drawback over 3,000 spectators sat four hours and witnessed both games."[5]

A second interleague doubleheader was staged two days later on August 28 when the Athletic club of Philadelphia met the Metropolitans in an American Association game and Boston took on New York in a National League contest. However, in this twin bill, the *New York Times* treated the National League game as the decided top billing, adding an addendum to its coverage: "Previous to the New York–Boston game on the Polo Grounds yesterday, the Metropolitans crossed bats with the Athletics." Five more doubleheaders were conducted on the Polo Grounds in September, making a total of seven such interleague combinations that year.[6]

Like its forfeit-initiated and darkness-shortened forebears in 1884, Day's interleague doubleheader was also not a completely legitimate two-for-one affair for the spectators. The usual admission fee for the Metropolitans' American Association games was 25 cents, half the standard admission fee to the Giants' National League games. By paying 50 cents to attend the interleague doubleheaders at the Polo Grounds, fans of the National League ballclub actually received just a one-and-a-half-for-one value. To the extent that early arrivals for the National League game saw a few innings of the American Association game, Day didn't lose much at all. Those spectators who came to primarily watch the American Association game paid twice the usual price, so Day gained even if they stayed to watch the entire National League game.

After the Metropolitan franchise was formed in 1880 by the partnership of owner Day and manager Mutrie, it operated as an independent club for a few years. It played numerous games with the Atlantic club in Brooklyn, managed by Billy Barnie, before going "big league" by joining the American Association for the 1883 season. Day also acquired a franchise in the National League at the same time, as both leagues were ravenous to have a New-York-based ballclub. Each team played several simultaneous games at the Polo Grounds in 1883, which were held on opposite ends of the grounds, but the concept was not well received by spectators. After the Day-owned, Mutrie-run, Metropolitan club copped the American Association pennant in 1884, Day transferred Mutrie and the best ballplayers from the Metropolitans to the New Yorks (as the National League team was then called) for the 1885 season. In 1885, Day was looking to sell the Metropolitans and focus on his National League club.

Day seems to have planned to have two doubleheaders in late August 1885, since August 25 and 26 were the only conflicting home dates for the two New-York-based clubs on the National League and American Association schedules. The National League team was slated to play its last home game on September 4 and then embark on an extended road trip for the remainder of the season, while the Metropolitans had a lengthy homestand. With many of his wealthy customers likely away from the city during the heat of late August and staying at resort locations such as Saratoga, New York, Day and Mutrie could easily have concocted the twin bill idea as a promotion to encourage attendance at the National League game, which was the second contest of the doubleheader. Interestingly, the visiting team in the American Association games scheduled for August 25 and 26 was Baltimore, managed by Billy Barnie, the instigator of the October 1884 doubleheader. As old pals, Barnie and Mutrie could have exchanged thoughts about the doubleheader concept in the off-season, allowing Mutrie to convince Day of the soundness of the idea.

Five more interleague doubleheaders were staged in September 1885, when the New York club of the National League transferred several games that they were scheduled to play in other cities. Games were moved from Providence and Buffalo to New York in hopes of capturing a larger attendance than could be garnered in either Providence or Buffalo. On September 10,

Louisville played the Metropolitans in the opener of a doubleheader, as Providence played New York in the second game (there was another twin bill among the four clubs on September 12, but the National League game was declared to be an exhibition contest while the American Association game was played as a regular-season game). On September 23–26, four games originally slated to be played in Buffalo were played in New York, which served as the second game of a doubleheader with the Metropolitans as the opening act. Since Day was on the verge of selling the Metropolitan ballclub, he didn't especially care about the financial impact to the Metropolitan club and may have thought that the twin bills would attract some attention and assist in securing a good price for the ballclub.

Buffalo was the only ballclub in either the National League or American Association in 1885 to expand on Day's concept and play a doubleheader at its own ball grounds to make up a postponed game. On September 12, Buffalo slated a doubleheader against Detroit, which prompted the *Buffalo Express* to report: "Don't forget that two full games, 18 innings, can be seen at Olympic Park this afternoon for 50 cents, the usual price of admission. A dime will admit youngsters to the four hours of fun." The two clubs got in 17 innings of baseball that day, nearly two complete games, as the second game was concluded by darkness after eight innings.[7]

When the 1885 season entered its final days in early October, Buffalo also played doubleheaders with Providence on October 7 and 10. However, both of these twin bills fell far short of a two-for-one value. The two games on October 7 were restricted to five innings each, in order to complete both of them before darkness descended on the ball grounds. Similarly, the first game of the

Advertisement for one of John Day's interleague doubleheaders at the Polo Grounds in New York City during the 1885 season. These events featured two ballgames—one between American Association clubs and the second between National League clubs—for the price of one National League admission. Being sandwiched between ads for two theaters in the amusements section of the *New York Times* didn't exactly depict the two-for-one doubleheader as a highly accepted cultural phenomenon.

October 10 doubleheader (which was played at a neutral site in Elmira, New York) was limited to six innings, while the second contest ended after five innings. For their single admission to these doubleheaders, patrons essentially viewed the equivalent of just one game, with an extra inning or so, not two contests worth of baseball.

After the 1885 season, Buffalo faced a similar fate as Worcester did in 1882. Buffalo was also forcibly expelled from the National League to enable another city to enter the league that might draw larger attendance to its ballgames. "Yesterday at the conclusion of two five-inning games between the Providence and Buffalo teams, the National League said good-by to Buffalo, not only for the season of 1885 but perhaps—forever," the *Buffalo Express* reported. "The day was raw and cheerless and the farewell was of the same sort." Providence, the visiting team in both the 1882 inaugural doubleheader and many of the ones in 1885, was also driven out of the National League after the 1885 season.[8]

Doubleheaders were not well received by most major-league ballclubs in 1885, due to the overt promotionalism of John Day. The extent of accepted promotion in those days was Ladies Day, which allowed a woman accompanied by a male to enter the game free (but of course the man had to pay). Doubleheaders were perceived as unseemly or desperation moves on the part of the ballclub owners that conducted them, since they almost exclusively involved teams at or near the bottom of the league standings. Then there was that f-word. "Those attending the first game were allowed to remain over for the second game free of charge," one newspaper reported in 1885 about the doubleheader's giveaway status. Since patrons paid to see ballclubs play one championship game for the majority of the season, allowing them to see a game for "free" ran counter to the economic instincts of the club owners. When it came to postponed contests, clubs were inclined to forego playing a postponed game if it couldn't be squeezed in on an open date in the regular schedule, rather than cheapen the concept of the championship game by rescheduling the postponed game to be part of a doubleheader.[9]

Besides an aversion to in-season doubleheaders, there was little desire by National League teams to make up postponed contests following the conclusion of the season, as clubs in the American Association often did. For instance, the *Boston Globe* reported in October 1885 that "it is probable that the St. Louis–Detroit postponed games will never be played off." The *Globe* also reported that Harry Wright, now the manager of the Philadelphia team in the National League, had telegraphed the *Globe* to inform the newspaper that his club's postponed games with St. Louis and Providence would not be played that season since Wright had already lined up postseason exhibitions with three clubs of the American Association immediately following the end of the National League season. It was simply inevitable that teams would have a few games left unplayed at the end of the season. Season-ending league standings were often printed with a column entitled "Games to Play," with clubs listed with anywhere from one to four postponed games left unplayed.[10]

The John Day and Buffalo doubleheader events in 1885 might have been ignored as much as the 1882 Worcester experiment was if both major leagues hadn't expand their schedules for the 1886 season. The National League schedule expanded to 126 games without increasing the length of the playing season. The American Association schedule expanded to 140 games, adding two weeks to the beginning of the season with an April 17 start date. There were now far fewer open dates on the calendar in which to make up postponed contests. This was compounded by the National League's prohibition of Sunday games that limited the league to just six playing days each week, rather than the seven that were available in the rival American Association where Sunday baseball was played in several cities.

In 1886 a heated pennant race between Chicago and Detroit in the National League contributed to the doubleheader becoming an acceptable scheduling technique by the end of the season and its being popularized league-wide in 1887. With the new 126-game schedule in the National League in 1886, the close battle between Chicago and Detroit for first place created a new urgency to make up postponed contests. Heading into mid–September, both teams had several postponed games on their dockets with little time in which to make them up before the season ended on October 9. Chicago was in first place, and second-place Detroit had more postponed games than did Chicago.

Both ballclubs initially used the holiday-style separate-admission arrangement to make up their postponed contests. On their final western swings before heading east, both teams played morning-afternoon two-game sets in Kansas City; Detroit split its two games while Chicago won its two. Detroit had renewed hope for the pennant when Chicago dropped its morning and afternoon matches in Philadelphia on September 25. During the final week of the season, Detroit took both games of a morning-afternoon twosome in Washington on October 5.

Coming into the final day of the 1886 season, October 9, there was talk of the two ballclubs each making up one of their several remaining postponed games on Monday, October 11, the one-day grace period that the National League then allowed to play postponed games (since October 10 was a Sunday), if such games would impact the pennant race. Boston agreed to play Detroit on that date. Chicago, still in first place, suggested that it'd play St. Louis, the league's last-place club, on that date, if necessary.

On October 9, both ballclubs had the same number of losses (34), but Chicago had two more wins than Detroit did (89 to 87). Chicago had one game in Boston that day, while Detroit agreed to play two games, not as separate admissions but rather as a doubleheader, against Harry Wright's Philadelphia team. "The league championship season closed here to-day with two games between Detroit and Philadelphia," the *Chicago Inter Ocean* blandly reported on the novel end to the 1886 season. "The first game began at 2 o'clock ... after an intermission of fifteen minutes the second game was begun." Playing off any remaining postponed games turned out to be moot, as Chicago defeated Boston and Detroit lost its twin bill with Philadelphia. Chicago comfortably won the 1886 pennant, while Detroit struggled through a second game in Philadelphia that lasted just six innings before darkness expunged Detroit's pennant hopes as, in the opinion of the *Philadelphia Inquirer*, "nearly nine thousand persons witnessed two of the prettiest games ever played on the local grounds."[11]

History tends to favor the surviving entity. Such is the case with the doubleheader, since the National League survived and the American Association didn't (merging with the National League after the 1891 season). In a 1947 article in *Baseball Magazine*, baseball writer Dan Daniel marked the inaugural doubleheader as the October 9, 1886, match in Philadelphia, "You can see them on the field that October afternoon sixty-one years ago, some of them wearing walrus mustaches, some sideburns, all decked out in the strange-looking uniforms of their day, with tight pants and squarish caps," Daniel wrote. "There they are, fighting through the long afternoon of a day that was to become historic in the box-office annals of the major leagues." The Providence–Worcester doubleheader in 1882, the Indianapolis–Baltimore doubleheader in 1884, the Buffalo doubleheaders in 1885, and the several previous ones in the American Association in 1886 all escaped Daniel's research.[12]

The truth is that Harry Wright of the Philadelphia National League club didn't recast his memories of managing Providence in that inaugural 1882 doubleheader at Worcester into the October 9, 1886, doubleheader with Detroit in Philadelphia. Several ballclubs in the American Association had deployed the doubleheader concept in 1886 weeks before Wright used it in the National League on October 9, including the Athletic ballclub in Philadelphia that was owned and managed by Billy Sharsig. In many ways, Sharsig, Barnie, and the other ballclub owners in the American Association were largely responsible for the emerging popularity of the doubleheader in the major leagues.

On August 25, 1886, Sharsig and Barnie agreed to have their ballclubs play a doubleheader in Philadelphia. Sharsig, who had a promotional bent like Barnie, arranged for newspaper advertisements to promote the match, between the sixth- and eighth-place clubs in the standings, as "two great championship games for one price of admission." While the use of "great" was clearly an exaggeration on Sharsig's part, two ballgames for 25 cents attracted many to the Jefferson Street ball grounds. "The Athletics and Baltimore played two games yesterday afternoon, one a postponed game and the other a regularly scheduled," the *Philadelphia Inquirer* reported. "The Athletics won two games from Baltimore in Philadelphia yesterday in the presence of nearly 7,000 persons," according to the *Baltimore Sun*. Those two contests were the first of four doubleheaders during the 1886 season in the American Association, while there was just one in the National League, on October 9 in Philadelphia.[13]

Two weeks after the August 25 doubleheader in Philadelphia, Pittsburgh staged a doubleheader on September 8 with first-place St. Louis, which attracted 11,000 spectators, an unheard of number for a weekday game. "The crowd extended around the field and encroached so much upon the players that a rule was made that no hit should count for more than two bases," one newspaper reported the impact of the overflow crowd. This twin bill helped to build the case that the "free" second game was good for business. After Pittsburgh hosted a second doubleheader, on October 5 against Barnie's Baltimore ballclub, Sharsig's Athletic club conducted another one on October 15, the last day to make up postponed games in the American Association that season. Sharsig had also scheduled a twin bill on October 14 against Baltimore, but following a lengthy first game the second contest ended after the second inning.[14]

At his death in 1902, Sharsig was hailed as a man who was not only "the inspiring genius of the Athletics ... devising ways and means to raise the financial wind" but also for being part of the American Association, which was responsible for baseball's popularity, not the National League. The men in the American Association "knew that base ball was the afternoon diversion of the masses, and they appealed to the masses by charging popular prices."

> BASEBALL TO-DAY (WEDNESDAY)
> Athletic Grounds, 26th and Jefferson Sts
> TWO GREAT CHAMPIONSHIP GAMES
> For One Price of Admission
> First Game Commences at 2:30 P.M.
> Eighteen Consecutive Innings, with Change of Batteries
> ATHLETIC vs. BALTIMORE
> ATHLETIC vs. BALTIMORE
> Athletic Battery, First Game Atkinson & Milligan
> Baltimore Battery, First Game McGinnis & Dolan
> Athletic Battery, Second Game Hart & O'Brien
> Baltimore Battery, Second Game Conway & Fulmer
> ALL FOR 25 CENTS

Reproduction of an early advertisement for a single-admission doubleheader between the Baltimore and Athletic (Philadelphia) ballclubs in the American Association in the August 25, 1886, edition of the *Philadelphia Inquirer*. This doubleheader paved the way for the season-ending, two-for-the-price-of-one match between the Detroit and Philadelphia ballclubs in the National League, which led to the popularization of the doubleheader during the 1887 season.

The National League, on the other hand, in the 1880s, prohibited Sunday games, forbid the sale of liquor at the ballpark, and kept admission prices high to keep out "the common element." Of the men that formed the American Association, "not one contributed more to its success than did Billy Sharsig. Like the lamented Harry Wright he loved the game for the sake of the game ... other men, shrewder, less scrupulous possibly, have reaped large harvests from what Billy Sharsig helped to sow in the early 1880s."[15]

Sharsig was also a pioneer of Sunday baseball in the East, when he arranged for the Athletics to play home games on Sunday in 1888. Sharsig merely "looked across the Delaware River, saw Gloucester, New Jersey, at the other end of the ferry that crossed the river and built ball grounds in another state to stage Sunday games." Gloucester was a popular beach resort and horse-racing venue, so adding baseball to the Sunday menu was a natural to evade the restrictive Pennsylvania laws.[16]

But it was Harry Wright's imprint on the doubleheader—by

Billy Sharsig, owner of the Athletic ballclub (Philadelphia) in the American Association, was an early promoter of the two-for-one doubleheader concept, along with Billy Barnie of the Baltimore ballclub. Sharsig never received credit for his promotional efforts that led to the rise of the doubleheader because the American Association ceased to exist after the 1891 season when its remnants merged into the National League. (National Baseball Hall of Fame Library, Cooperstown, New York)

allowing such an event in an important situation as Detroit challenging for the pennant on the last day of the 1886 season—that gave the concept more credibility in the National League than any of the actions that occurred that season in the American Association. One of the prime reasons for the failure of the American Association to gain credit for the doubleheader's popularity was the fact that several of its twin bills involved last-place Baltimore, a plight that plagued the early efforts of Worcester and Buffalo in the National

League. There was also that longstanding resistance to the American Association's policies regarding Sunday baseball, liquor sales, and 25-cent admission prices. In this way, Wright had a large hand in enhancing the popularity of the doubleheader.

When Boston and Chicago adopted the doubleheader concept in 1887, the National League firmly embraced it as an acceptable method to make up postponed games. As the only two ballclubs that had been members of the National League since its inception in 1876, and thus were leaders in the league, Boston and Chicago demonstrated that the doubleheader could be a money-making proposition in addition to being a spectator-friendly event.

While part of the owners' desire to play morning-afternoon two-game sets rather than doubleheaders may have been to preserve the integrity—or marketability—of the "championship" game concept, more important was the perceived economic benefit of being able to charge two admissions. However, at the September 8, 1886, two-game set in Chicago between New York and Chicago, only about 1,000 people paid to watch the morning game while the afternoon contest attracted 3,000 spectators. As this example shows, even a top-caliber team like Chicago that was on its way to winning the pennant was very likely to draw a far smaller crowd for a makeup morning game than for the regularly scheduled afternoon match.[17]

Small businessmen, the primary audience for National League ballclubs, could often arrange their schedules to attend a 3:30 P.M. game, but getting to a 10:30 A.M. contest was far more difficult, especially one that materialized overnight (i.e., a rained-out game in the afternoon turned into a makeup one the following morning). This differed from the holiday two-game sets, when most potential spectators had the day off from work and therefore could more easily make arrangements to attend a morning game.

The gentlemanly aspect of the frequent spectator at the ball grounds, which the National League clubs desired to attract, was the subject of a *Boston Globe* article in 1885. "A gentlemen who is a great admirer of the national game, and attends as many of the League contests as his business will permit, remarked the other day on leaving the grounds that he had noticed a number of people who always seem to be there. He was exactly right, for there are a goodly number of base ball enthusiasts, or cranks, whose faces are almost as well known on the grounds as the players themselves." The *Globe* added, however, that in order for these gentlemen to enter the ball grounds, they had to approach the ticket office "where you must run a gauntlet of urchins under their fire of 'Gimme ticket mister' or 'Take me in.'"[18]

One of the Boston cranks was Arthur Dixwell, a member of the idle rich; because his father was a rich banker, Arthur never had to work a day in his life. He never married and spent a good deal of his time following the Boston ballclub. "There may have been earlier baseball rooters, but there were not any firmer ones," the *Boston Globe* wrote at Dixwell's death in 1924. "Dixwell was a regular attendant at the baseball games back in the '80s and he accompanied the Boston team on some of its trips." Other well-heeled cranks of the Boston club were Thomas Lawson, head of Amalgamated Copper Company, George Appleton, Dr. Pope, and A.A. Phipps. These men were driven to the ball grounds by a driver of a carriage, not by riding the horse-drawn trolley.[19]

With Wright vouching for the credibility of the doubleheader, from the championship contest perspective in 1886, the ballclub owners soon became more accepting of the economic potential of the doubleheader in 1887. The benchmark attendance for a doubleheader was not double the average crowd for weekday game, but rather the more easily obtained average weekday crowd plus the expected level for a morning game during the workweek. As shown in the example above of the New York–Chicago two-game set in September 1886, this threshold could be as low as one-and-a-quarter to one-and-a-third the size of the average weekday crowd.

Boston's first experiment with a single-admission doubleheader in 1887 demonstrated that there could be an ancillary economic benefit to the twin bill—increased sales of reserved grandstand tickets. Typically, patrons paid 50 cents as the admission fee to the grounds, and then needed to pay an additional 50 cents to sit in a reserved seat under the grandstand roof. Otherwise, they normally had to sit on the bleachers flanking the left- and right-field foul lines unless an empty seat could be located in the back of the grandstand. The additional 50 cents for a reserved seat typically inured completely to the home club and wasn't shared with the visiting team, as were the receipts from the basic 50-cent admission fee. Many patrons paid $1.00 to see the Washington–Boston doubleheader in order to sit in the grandstand, effectively paying twice to see two games.

Boston staged its first doubleheader on August 20, 1887, against Washington. "The Bostons and Washingtons will play two games on Saturday," the *Boston Globe* reported the day before. "There will be one admission charged. Fifty cents will entitle a man to see both games." On the day of the doubleheader, the *Globe* reported: "The entire grandstand will be reserved for today's games. Reserved seats can be obtained at Brock's Cigar Store, Water Street, up to 1 o'clock. After that they can be had at the grounds." Washington won both games that afternoon, as Jim Whitney pitched both games to become the first pitcher to win two nine-inning ballgames in a single-admission doubleheader.[20]

Chicago hosted its first doubleheader on September 10, 1887, after its game with last-place Indianapolis on September 9 was rained out. "Rain checks were issued for the first time this season and they will be good for to-day, when two games will be played," the *Chicago Inter Ocean* reported.

"The first game will be called at 1:30 o'clock and Baldwin and Daly will be the battery. At 3:30 the second game will be called with Clarkson and Flint in the points." The Chicago ballclub advertised the match to emphasize "one admission only for both games." As Billy Sharsig had done with his doubleheaders in the American Association, a new battery for the second game was a key element to convince spectators that they would see a completely different ballgame in the second contest of the doubleheader. About 1,500 were in the stands at the start of the first game, whereas 4,000 had assembled by the start of the second one.[21]

Because of the good success with this experiment of a single-admission doubleheader, Chicago arranged for several others, to get in as many ballgames as possible in the team's quest for first place held by Detroit. The club stepped over league bounds with its scheduling of doubleheaders with Boston on September 23 and 24, as Detroit cried foul. Three of the four games played during those two days were tossed out by the league. However, legitimate doubleheader scheduling was executed with Pittsburgh on September 28 and 29.

One commonality of this first major wave of doubleheaders in major-league history was their occurrence during the last series played with a particular ballclub. For example, the August 20 game in Boston was the last time that Washington was slated to appear in Boston that season. In other words, the doubleheader was employed only as a last resort when a postponed game could not physically be rescheduled before the end of the regular season. This began to change in 1888 when the National League expanded its playing schedule to 140 games, from the 126-game schedule used in 1886 and 1887.

4

Lure of the Doubleheader

A PIVOTAL YEAR IN the history of the doubleheader was 1888, when the National League expanded its schedule to 140 games, 14 more games than had been slated during the previous two seasons. If not for the doubleheader concept of a single admission for two games in one day, the playing season could not effectively have been expanded beyond 126 games.

The existence of the doubleheader concept to make up postponed games, i.e., a Level 1 doubleheader as defined in Chapter One, was an essential ingredient to permit ballclubs to complete their full complement of games in the expanded 1888 schedule. Only 12 playing dates were added to the schedule, which began on April 20 (then the earliest in National League history by more than a week) and ran through October 13. These extensions added pressure to the existing lack of slack in the 1887 schedule, when ballclubs had just 14 open dates when they could travel or reschedule postponed contests.

Moving the starting date for the 1888 season into mid–April and the ending date into mid–October also presented challenges to the completion of the schedule. The additional days in April, a notoriously rainy month, increased the likelihood that games would be postponed. The additional days in October were even less optimal due to the chilly weather, late-afternoon sunsets, and uncompetitive games since most clubs were out of pennant contention by that point in the season. The early sunsets in October also affected the ability to complete both games of a doubleheader to make up a postponed game from earlier in the season.

In 1888 ballclubs began to make up postponed games as part of a doubleheader during the summer rather than wait until the end of the season. Detroit and Pittsburgh hosted doubleheaders on July 13 to make up the postponed games of July 12 rather than wait for their opponents to return in September. These twin bills initiated the practice of using mid-season doubleheaders to make up a postponed game rather than having them bunch up in September and October as occurred in 1886 and 1887. The longer daylight hours in summer also eliminated concern about the second game's possible early curtailment by darkness, which often occurred in September and October doubleheaders. Warmer weather also provided better conditions for spectators, which might attract more paying customers to the doubleheaders.

In 1889 the 140-game National League schedule tested the limits of scheduling by contracting the season by 12 days. By eliminating the unpopular October extension and half of the April extension, the 140 games for each ballclub were crammed into 165 days from April 24 to October 5. However, teams could only possibly play on 142 of the 165 days during this period because the National League still banned Sunday baseball. With two games on each of the Decoration Day and Independence Day holidays (and a few twosomes slated for Labor Day), ballclubs had only four or five days available to use as travel days or to reschedule postponed contests. The result was a 50 percent increase in the number of doubleheaders played in 1889.

Starting the playing season before May 1, which was a persistent scheduling challenge for decades due to rainy springs in the Northeast, first became a problem in 1889. While all four Opening Day games on April 24 were completed, only six of the 12 scheduled matches during the next three days could be played. Ballclubs began to reschedule postponed games in doubleheaders even earlier in the season, led by Chicago hosting a twin bill with Cleveland on June 5. "There was a very large attendance at the double game yesterday; there must have been 4,000 people at least in the seats," the *Chicago Inter Ocean* reported. "The crowd was amply repaid for the long sitting by witnessing eighteen innings of the best base-ball that has been put upon the Chicago Ball Park for many seasons." Cleveland won both contests, "the second game followed five minutes after the close of the first one." The *Inter Ocean* ran separate articles for each game, as was the custom at the time to treat each part of a doubleheader as a separate event even if only one admission was charged for spectators to watch two games.[1]

With three major leagues competing for spectator dollars in 1890, all three—the National League, Players League, and American Association—began to stage doubleheaders in June to make up postponed games. Better weather in 1891 created fewer postponed games, so that twin bills within the two remaining major leagues—the Players League having folded after just one season—didn't begin until August. However, these earlier-season doubleheaders still couldn't avoid numerous postponed games to be played off in September. For example, in 1889 Cleveland played three consecutive twin bills at Boston on September 12, 13, and 14. In 1891 the New York Giants played eight doubleheaders in September 1891 following a Labor Day two-game set on September 7, which comprised more than half of its remaining games for the season.

These mid-season twin bills, played in warm weather with no fear that sunset would shorten the second game, helped to elevate the concept of the doubleheader from schedule-stretcher to attendance-generator. The doubleheader began to transform the attendance expectation that ballclubs could aspire to for weekday games Monday through Friday, especially in the final weeks of the season in September and October.

By 1891 doubleheaders routinely attracted about twice the number of spectators to a weekday game. For example, when Brooklyn and Boston played a twin bill on Wednesday, September 23, 1891, attendance at the South End Grounds numbered 2,956. The day before, a single game between the two clubs attracted just 1,078 spectators. A single sentence in the *Boston Globe* seemed to have significant influence at the gate: "The Boston and Brooklyn teams will play two games this afternoon for one price of admission, commencing at 2 o'clock." Attendance at the next day's game with Philadelphia, which began at the usual 3:30 starting time, reverted to the more typical weekday crowd with 1,501 paying customers.[2]

While Boston was near the top of the league standings, other clubs lower in the league standings also experienced similar attendance patterns for doubleheaders. For example, a twin bill with Cleveland in Philadelphia on Wednesday, September 16, attracted a crowd of 2,710 in comparison to the attendance of 1,515 at Monday's game (with Cleveland) and 1,491 at Thursday's game (with Cincinnati).[3]

This doubling of the usual weekday-game attendance by staging a doubleheader far exceeded the previous economic standard for doing so—the combination of an expected morning-game attendance plus the usual weekday afternoon crowd—which had first promulgated doubleheader usage to make up postponed games. Ballclubs thus sought ways to avoid playing games on some poorly attended weekday dates in order to convert that day's game into the second game of a twin bill on a more auspicious date. While some methods to reschedule games to accomplish this result were above board and others more devious, these two-for-one matches were the initial vestiges of the Level 2 doubleheader.

Eliminating a Monday game in a Sunday-playing city to a stage a Sunday doubleheader was one overt way that clubs in the American Association got rid of a poorly attended weekday contest. For instance, in 1890, St. Louis moved up its Monday, September 29, game with Baltimore to create a doubleheader on Sunday, September 28. In 1891, Milwaukee, the replacement for the defunct Cincinnati club, canceled its Tuesday, September 15, match with Philadelphia to stage a twin bill on Sunday, September 13.

Postponing a game after minimal bad weather, a prerogative of the home team, was a more devious way to concoct a doubleheader. For instance, Washington canceled its match with Boston on April 15, 1892, after a morning rain storm. As the *Boston Globe* wrote, Boston "was not pleased with the decision of the management of the home team, as the sun came out strong about 2 o'clock and the games in Washington are not called until 4:30."[4]

The National League slowly adopted rules to handle the playing of doubleheaders. By 1891 the league's constitution had been amended to say: "But two games shall not be played on one day without prior consent of two-thirds of all league clubs." As with many rules of the day, franchise owners were sometimes lax in their rigid enforcement of them. When New York dropped two consecutive doubleheaders to Boston late in the 1891 season when Boston and Chicago were in a neck-and-neck battle for first place, Chicago owner Jim Hart cried foul after Boston finished in first place at the end of the season. Hart actually alleged, in polite terms, that New York threw some or all of the games to steer the pennant to Boston, using the doubleheader rules as a pretext.[5]

"I can not but feel that there has been either downright dishonesty on the part of the New York club or gross incompetency on the part of those in control of the team," Hart was quoted by a Chicago newspaper in regard to New York's five losses to Boston without playing star ballplayers such as Amos Rusie, Buck Ewing, and Roger Connor. "If the New Yorks were so badly broken up as they claim, why did they consent to play two extra games in Boston, one of which should have been played in New York instead of Boston? I would also like to know why it was necessary to be so secret in obtaining the consent of two-thirds of the league clubs for those games. It seems to me that common courtesy would demand that the consent of the Chicago club be at least invited?"[6]

The National League denied Hart's formal protest regarding the playing of the New York–Boston doubleheaders on September 29 and 30, and awarded Boston the pennant. "In this case the usual custom was observed, Boston having obtained the necessary consent of six clubs," the league's decision was worded. "The double games were arranged according to the rules governing postponed games and were entirely legal and in accordance with the league constitution."[7]

However, as the *Philadelphia Inquirer* had editorialized three weeks prior to the official league ruling, "A new rule regarding the playing off of postponed games is necessary." There were many questions to address. Could an immediate makeup of a postponed game be mandated? How optional was it to make up the postponed game in a series later in the year? Could the postponed game be transferred to the visiting club's site if necessary? Or desirable to achieve a greater attendance?[8]

The National League did create greater definition to the use of the two-for-one concept for the 1892 season, partly to avoid another distasteful situation like the New York–Boston doubleheaders at the end of the 1891 season but also to enable the league to expand its 140-game playing schedule. The National League—now a 12-club league after vanquishing and absorbing remnants of the competing Players League and American Association—decided to play a 154-game schedule in a split-season format with 77 games in each of the first and second halves (the winners of the two halves to play each other for the pennant). To accommodate the additional 14 games, the 1892 season began on April 12 and ended on October 15.

In an effort to avoid bunching up games via doubleheaders at the end of each half of the 1892 season, the ballclub owners amended section 45 of the league constitution to provide for "clubs to play off postponed games the day after the scheduled date of the postponed games." At least that is what ended up being printed in the constitution; the words "or any subsequent series" that had been agreed upon at the owners' meeting failed to find their way into print. The intention was to have ballclubs play off postponed games as early as possible, but the printing error caused a wave of confusion at the beginning of the 1892 season.[9]

While all six Opening Day games on April 12 were played, bad weather immediately set in and forced the postponement of two of the three contests slated for April 13 and all six matches scheduled for April 14. When Chicago's game at St. Louis was one of the postponements on April 13, the *Chicago Inter Ocean* reported, "Under the new constitution, section 45, the postponed and regular schedule games will have to be played to-morrow if the weather permits." However, National League president Nick Young disagreed with Chicago's interpretation of the rule change, mindful of the verbal agreement as to the rule's intent, and seemingly unaware of the printer error that Chicago tried to enforce. It was a moot point, since rain washed out the April 14 contest in St. Louis. When rain also washed out Chicago's game at Cincinnati on April 18, the *Inter Ocean* was a bit more cautious about the rescheduling, noting that "indications point to a double contest to-morrow." Indeed, Cincinnati did opt to play a twin bill on April 19, in which Chicago lost both games.[10]

Brooklyn challenged the new doubleheader rule two weeks later when rain postponed its game in Pittsburgh on May 2. "The rule adopted at the convention contained the words 'or any subsequent series,'" the *Brooklyn Eagle* reported, "which admitted an option to play such postponed games the day after or a week or a month after." The Pittsburgh club, steadfast in its right to schedule a doubleheader, announced that it would claim a forfeit if Brooklyn failed to show for the first game of the twin bill slated for May 3. "It is absurd, as I take it, to say that one club has a right to force another to play two games the same afternoon for one admission," Brooklyn manager John Montgomery Ward contended. But when Ward saw 3,000 spectators at the Pittsburgh ball grounds on a Tuesday afternoon, he relented and

Brooklyn played both games of the doubleheader. Three weeks into the 1892 season, the concept of playing off a postponed contest as soon as practicable was firmly in place.[11]

Even though there were actually more open dates on the 1892 schedule than in 1891—because the National League sanctioned the playing of Sunday baseball in 1892, resulting in St. Louis, Cincinnati, and Louisville playing several Sunday home games—doubleheaders proliferated in 1892. The April 19, 1892, doubleheader between the Chicago and Cincinnati teams was the earliest one played at the time, but set the stage for four twin bills to be played on April 23 and a flurry of doubleheaders staged throughout May and June. As clubs desperately tried to play as many postponed games as possible before the first half of the season ended, the Philadelphia and Washington clubs decided to play two postponed contests at a neutral site. On June 30, the two teams staged a doubleheader in Pittsburgh; however, bad weather limited the crowd to just 200 people as the two clubs split the two games.[12]

The prevalence of doubleheaders during the 1892 season—clubs played three to six each year in the late 1880s and early 1890s—began to put pressure on club rosters. During the late 1880s, pitchers usually worked every other day, or with two days rest, so it was not unusual for a pitcher to work both games of a twin bill. For example, in a September 12, 1889, doubleheader between Boston and Cleveland, John Clarkson of Boston pitched nine innings in each game, and won both games. "Clarkson did a grand day's work," the *Boston Globe* reported, "pitching the 18 innings without a let up and doing as well in the last as he did in the first inning." During this era, however, the bigger roster concern was the catcher, since catchers used limited protective gear and were often injured. Most catchers, therefore, could only be expected to work one of the two games of a doubleheader. While Clarkson pitched both ends of that September 1889 doubleheaders for Boston, his regular catcher, Charlie Bennett, played in just the first game, as Charlie Ganzel caught the second game.[13]

In 1893 the pitching distance was lengthened due to the elimination of the pitcher's box, whose front line was 50 feet from home plate, and replaced with the pitcher's plate that was 60 feet, six inches, from home plate. Following this rule change, pitchers didn't work as often and clubs needed deeper pitching staffs to cope with the escalating number of doubleheaders played during a season to make up postponed games. Due to the change in pitching distance in 1893, Amos Rusie, on October 4, 1892, was the last man to pitch nine innings in both games of a single-admission doubleheader and win both games before the storied feat of Joe McGinnity in 1903 when he won three complete-game twin bills in one month.[14]

Changes in catching equipment helped to foster the doubleheader concept during the 1890s. In the mid–1880s, catchers were constantly injured because they caught with their fingers using lightly padded gloves on both hands with the fingertips cut off. To extend their playing days, catchers gradually increased the padding in the left-hand glove to use in stopping throws and kept the right-hand glove unpadded to be able to throw the ball. "In order to make mitts effective, catchers first had to discard the traditional two-handed catching method," Peter Morris wrote in *Catcher: How the Man Behind the Plate Became an American Folk Hero*, "and learn instead to do most of the stopping with his left hand protected by a thickly padded glove." In 1888, Buck Ewing popularized the padded catcher's mitt, using a mitt that "looked for all the world like a big boxing glove crushed flat by a road roller." The acceptance of the catcher's mitt lessened the chance of injury to the catcher and enabled more catchers to play both ends of a doubleheader.[15]

Changes in the substitution rule at this time also assisted the increased scheduling of doubleheaders. Before 1889, substitutes could only enter the game in the case of a debilitating illness or injury to a player and had to be approved by the opposing team's captain. At the National League meeting in November 1888, ballclub owners agreed to a rule change governing substitutes: "One player, whose name shall be printed on the score card as an extra player, may be substituted at the end of any completed inning by either club, but the player retired shall not afterwards participate in the game." By 1892, the substitution rule had been expanded to allow multiple substitutes in a game, thus providing further options for teams to deal with an ailing, or ineffective, catcher or pitcher, especially in the second game of a doubleheader.[16]

For the 1893 season, the National League ditched the unpopular split-season format of its schedule and returned to the conventional full-season pennant race. Economic concerns due to the dismantling of the failed American Association forced ballclub owners to decrease the number of games to 132 per club, implement a player salary cap, and reduce the roster size in addition to the lengthening of the pitching distance to generate more offense and thus increase spectator interest. The success of these moves was hindered, however, by a long economic depression. Many historians consider the four-year economic depression from 1893 to 1897 to have been more devastating than the more famous Great Depression of the 1930s.

In 1893, the depression snuck up on most Americans, as "no frantic newspaper headlines announcing the failure of a great bank or the sudden collapse of stock-market prices signaled the beginning of the Panic of 1893." Dozens of railroads went bankrupt, crippling not only their investors but also businessmen that relied on this mode of transportation to ship goods or simply travel from one location to another. "For the year ending June 30, 1894, over 125 railroad companies went into receivership ... involving about one-fourth of all railroad mileage and capitalization," economist Charles

Hoffman wrote in *The Depression of the Nineties*. "Railroad reorganization on such a grand scale was one dimension of the intensity of the depression." Violent strikes were another dimension of this depression, most notably the 1894 Pullman Strike.[17]

Fortunately, the National League had adopted Sunday baseball and embraced the doubleheader concept, measures which, along with the few holiday dates available each year, became the basic economic drivers of major-league ballclubs in the 1890s. However, many clubs struggled to attract sufficient attendance, especially to weekday games.

The electric trolley helped franchises stave off the negative financial effects of the economic depression on game attendance, by making it easier for spectators to get to the ball grounds than they could using the old horse-drawn trolleys. After the first electric railway was constructed in 1887 in Massachusetts, the concept quickly spread to Boston and New York and other cities across the country. "During the decade between 1890 and 1900, not only was practically all the existing horse railroad mileage converted to trolley, but the total street railway mileage was tripled," one historian described the impact of the electric trolley.[18]

The increased efficiency of transportation and wider service area created by the electric trolley enlarged the potential patronage for ballgames. But the electric trolley also signaled a change in the nature of spectators at ballgames in 1890s. The electric streetcar not only brought about major modifications to transportation patterns but also to housing and work conventions. Downtown areas changed dramatically and, suddenly, businessmen were not as likely to spend an afternoon at the ballpark. As the result of expanding streetcar lines, "For the first time in the history of the world, middle-class families in the late nineteenth century could reasonably expect to buy a detached home on an accessible lot in a safe and sanitary environment," outside the city center, Kenneth Jackson wrote in *Crabgrass Frontier: The Suburbanization of the United States*. "The growth of downtown drove middle- and upper-middle class families from the center to the periphery," Robert Fogelson wrote in *Downtown: Its Rise and Fall, 1880–1950*. "For professionals and businessmen the suburbs offered a haven from the workplace, an idyllic setting in which they would do a little gardening in the morning and, after returning from a hard day downtown, dine with the family and maybe sit outdoors, reading a paper and smoking a cigar under their own semi-rustic vine and fig tree."[19]

These citizens exiting to the suburbs had been the core of ballpark attendance: working in the city, going to the game in the late afternoon, and returning to their home in the city for dinner. When these factory managers, small-business owners, and lawyers moved to the suburbs due to inexpensive home prices and cheap, convenient streetcar service, they stopped attending ballgames as often. In his book *Streetcar Suburbs*, author Sam Warner estimated that 15 percent of the urban population was comprised of the central middle class—the typical spectators at a ballgame. Warner believed five percent were wealthy and 20 to 30 percent were associated with the lower middle class. This latter group was the new source of spectators for weekday ballgames, with the increasingly available half-holiday on Saturday attracting spectators from the 50 to 60 percent of the population that were common laborers.[20]

As consolidation of many industries began to occur in the later part of the 1890s, the small-business owner became less of a factor in the economy of a city. "Advancement no longer required opening a business," Charles Morris wrote in *The Tycoons: How Andrew Carnegie, John D. Rockefeller, Jay Gould, and J.P. Morgan Invented the American Supereconomy*. "Exponential growth in the range and reach of white-collar occupations meant that an ambitious young man could often achieve status, power, and a good income over the course of a career with a single firm."[21]

Prior to the emergence of the giant corporation, entrepreneurship was the general path to financial success. This approach required starting a small business, which in the late nineteenth century usually meant operating in a partnership in concert with investors rather than under a corporate charter from the state (sole proprietorship was another option if the business could be self-funded). Under the partnership structure, the small-business owner assumed unlimited personal liability for the risks of operating the business with the partners. In addition, as noted in Jack Beatty's book *Colossus: How the Corporation Changed America*, the partnership form of company ownership "constrained firms' ability to raise capital" to expand operations and, more importantly, "included procedures for terminating the arrangement should one of the partners wish to withdraw" or, even worse, die, "which could have potentially disastrous consequences if assets had to be liquidated to pay off the decreased partner's heirs."[22]

Limited liability through a corporate structure was at first only available to companies involved in public works, such as water companies and railroads. By the mid–1850s, northern states, fearful of losing business to other geographic areas of the country, loosened the legal grip on incorporation, setting the stage for large companies like Carnegie's U.S. Steel and Rockefeller's Standard Oil to dominate commerce. The expansion of business incorporation affected baseball spectatorship in nearly all major-league cities, as small-business owners—once the predominant target of patronage by ballclub owners—either were swallowed up in the consolidations of Carnegie, Rockefeller, and other business brethren or were forced out of business. "Most companies were highly competitive" in the post–Civil War economy, Beatty wrote, but "by 1904 one or two giant firms controlled at least half the output in seventy-eight different industries."[23]

The corporation changed American society in many ways, but one that greatly affected baseball was the stifling of small-business startups. Ambitious young men could now secure employment as managers of large corporations and be paid salaries rather than needing to strike out on their own to start businesses. They didn't have ownership interests in their employers, but they could make decent livings. Unfortunately, less freedom over time at the corporation made it more difficult to get away from the office to see a ballgame in the afternoon. Large industrial corporations also created a potentially new, though not well-heeled, group of spectators for baseball games—the laborers in the various mills and factories of the corporation.

Community had been the cornerstone of the business model of ballclub owners since the founding of the National League in 1876. "In assuming that the prospective fans of a franchise would care more about its destiny because it was associated with their city, the owners of early baseball clubs were concluding that among the benefits of their possession of the franchise was an important reservoir of civic and territorial goodwill," Edward White wrote in *Creating the National Pastime: Baseball Transforms Itself 1903–1953*. "Partisanship was tied to local affiliation, to sense of place, to regional and civic pride. It was a manifestation of the persistence of a 'village mentality' among even peripatetic Americans." However, by the late 1890s, the nature of a city's "community" was radically changing, and thus, by necessity, so did the typical spectator at the ballpark.[24]

By the late–1890s, the mix of spectators at the ballpark had become more diverse than the largely gentlemanly crowds of the 1880s. The reporting of the *Boston Globe* demonstrated this during the Boston club's run for the National League pennant in 1897. At Opening Day in 1897 at the South End Grounds, the *Globe* noted: "Most of the old standbys were on hand to see the opening. Congressman Moody of Haverhill stopped off on his way to Washington ... Tom Lovell, John Morrill, George Appleton, Jimmie Connelly, Tom Pettitt, Dr. Merrill, Michael Moore, Toney Marsh and a score of other regular attendants were out." Arthur Dixwell sat in the bleachers, to get some sun, rather than in his usual seat in the grandstand.[25]

Lovell, who was a partner in the sporting goods firm Lovell Arms Company, exemplified the perilous nature of the business-owner fan for ballclub owners in the 1890s. When Lovell died two years later in 1899 at the age of 51, the firm's creditors forced the dissolution of the company, as the *Globe* reported that "it will prove to be one of the most tangled up messes in a business way which has occurred in Boston for many years." In March 1900, the Iver-Johnson Company acquired what was left of the stock of the Lovell Arms Company, which the *Globe* remarked would make it "one of the largest exclusive sporting goods concerns in the country." The Iver-Johnson brand of guns would remain a mainstay of the gun industry into the 1990s.[26]

In September 1897, the *Globe* reported on the departure of "125 local and suburban 'rooters' that left the Park Square station at 6:45 last night" on a train to Baltimore to see the Boston club battle the Baltimore Orioles. The traveling party included "many businessmen, a clergyman, physicians, seven women, and several others who daily occupy seats on the bleachers back of third base." The *Globe* listed all 125 members of the traveling party. The key phrase here is "bleachers" instead of "grandstand," in which the *Globe* tacitly recognized a changing mix of spectators from the "old standbys" at Opening Day.[27]

The lowercase "rooters" soon became the proper name "Royal Rooters." The group was closely identified with Mike "Nuf Ced" McGreevey, who owned the Third Base Saloon located near the South End Grounds and was listed as one of the 125 travelers to Baltimore. McGreevey, of Irish decent, was one of the new breed of small-business owners who wasn't quite of the same ilk as wealthy long-time Boston fans like Thomas Lawson or Arthur Dixwell. McGreevey has been characterized as "perhaps the most influential baseball fan of all time." Other, more middle class, members of the Rooters included Charlie Lavis, who owned a bowling alley; Charley Young, who was an accountant; C.W. Smith, who was a druggist; and Charles Green, who owned a wholesale grocer. McGreevey was a prominent member of the Royal Rooters for two decades (including several World Series victories), until Prohibition usurped his ability to make a living as a saloonkeeper. When he died in 1943, there was barely any recollection of his role in fostering a change in the spectator composition at the ballpark.[28]

Another subtle indication of the changing nature of the ballpark spectator is that several major-league ball clubs charged a standard admission of 25 cents in the mid–1890s, in contravention of the league's standard 50-cent fare. For example, both the Philadelphia and Baltimore ballclubs charged 25 cents for general admission, which enabled a fan to sit in the bleachers; patrons needed to pay an additional 25 cents to sit in a seat in the grandstand. As part of the *Boston Globe*'s coverage of the Royal Rooters trip to Baltimore in 1897, the newspaper casually noted that "as general admission in Baltimore is 25 cents," spectators needed to pay extra for grandstand and reserved seats. The low prices for bleacher seats at the ballpark were not a highly publicized event, but a perusal of newspaper advertisements does reveal that there was some effort to attract spectators from other than the upper strata of society.[29]

Clubs in the Sunday-playing cities of the National League—St. Louis, Louisville, Cincinnati, and Chicago (beginning in 1893)—could take the greatest advantage of the larger, but less prosperous, pool of spectators for ballgames. But for the most part, many ballclub owners of the 1890s were just too slow to either recognize, or desire to target, the lower middle-class patron. Doubleheaders were one technique owners used to try to hang on to the traditional small-business owner as spectator.

The changing nature of the spectator base at the ball grounds may also have helped to bring about the term "doubleheader," which, as discussed in Chapter One, was not popularized in a baseball context until 1896 when William Jennings Bryan ran for president on the Democratic ticket. The concept of two games for a single admission fee was usually awkwardly referred to as a regularly scheduled game that was preceded by a postponed game. For example, the opening of one 1892 newspaper account reported: "The New Yorks scored two victories over the Washingtons today. The first one was a postponed game at Washington."[30]

It didn't take long for baseball writers to fashion a shorthand expression for the doubleheader. In the mid–1890s, the term "double bill" meant the opportunity to watch two stage plays for the price of one ticket price at a local theater. For example, under the headline "A Double Bill at the Opera," the *New York Times* reported that "there was a new combination on the programme at the Metropolitan Opera House last night. It consisted of Donizetti's 'Lucia,' ending after the mad scene, and the terse and vigorous 'Cavalleria Rusticana' of Mascagni." In 1897, baseball writers started to characterize a doubleheader as a "double bill." For example, under the headline "New Yorks Broke Even in a Double Header with the Pittsburgs," the *New York Times* reported that "the double bill between the New Yorks and the Pittsburgs did not result in a double victory as most rooters expected." By the end of 1896, the term "doubleheader" was in constant use to describe two ballgames on one day for a single admission, and by 1899 newspapers across the country were also using "double bill" to describe a baseball doubleheader as well as two theater performances.[31]

The doubleheader gained more prominence during the 1898 season, when the National League expanded its playing schedule to 154 games, an increase of 22 games from the 132-game slate that the league had used during the previous five years. The league also extended the playing season by about three weeks to accommodate the additional games, beginning the 1898 season on April 15 (a week earlier than the April 22 start in 1897) and ending it on October 15 (nearly two weeks later than the October 3 conclusion in 1897).

A major reason for the expanded schedule in 1898 was that the Cleveland franchise expected to play home games on Sunday, making it a fifth league city where Sunday baseball could be enjoyed. When the Pittsburgh and New York clubs agreed to lift their ban on participating in Sunday games on the road, the league was able to schedule five games each Sunday in 1898 when the eastern teams were making their western road trips. Cleveland expected to have home games on Sunday in 1898 after its temporary success in 1897, when the club played six Sunday games at League Park after winning a legal ruling that overturned an earlier verdict that upheld the city's enforcement of a state law prohibiting Sunday baseball.

On Sunday, May 16, 1897, the Washington–Cleveland game at League Park was stopped in the first inning when all 18 players on the field were arrested by the Cleveland police. Of all the 18 arrested players, Jack Powell would obtain immortality in legal circles for having played one inning for Cleveland that day. "Arrangement has been made with the authorities whereby only one man will of necessity appear. This one will be Powell, who was put in the game yesterday and assigned to first base," the *Cleveland Plain Dealer* reported about the first-year pitcher on the Cleveland ballclub. "It will be a test case. Powell will know a whole lot about the baseball law when it is finished."[32]

After Powell sat through a trial in police court and was found guilty, his verdict was overturned on July 9 when Judge Walter Ong concurred with the Cleveland club's argument that the Sunday law violated Powell's constitutional rights to personal liberty and also compelled a religious observance. The prosecutor appealed to the Ohio Supreme Court, which issued its decision in *State v. Powell* on April 19, 1898, to uphold the state law prohibiting Sunday baseball. The timing couldn't have been worse, as it was the eve of the adjournment of the Ohio legislature, making it impossible for a bill to be passed in 1898 to legalize Sunday baseball. The National League schedule for 1898, released on March 2, was now in shambles.[33]

In anticipation of increased revenue from Sunday baseball in 1898, the ballclub owners had amended the league constitution to make doubleheaders easier to implement. As *The Sporting News* put it, "double-headers were legalized." Section 45 of the constitution was amended to eliminate the necessity to seek an open date to reschedule a postponed game. "This makes it possible for more 'double-headers' to be played off than heretofore," *Sporting Life* summarized the league's action.[34]

The 1898 schedule included the first doubleheader to be carded on the National League's initial schedule, because the 154-game season forced the schedule-makers to double up games on certain dates. These prescheduled doubleheaders could be construed as early Level 2 doubleheaders, since they most assuredly were not natural consequences of postponed games during the playing season and thus classified as a Level 1 variety. On Thursday, July 21, the 1898 National League schedule called for all 12 teams to play in a doubleheader, since Friday was a getaway day for the western clubs to head home. In particular, St. Louis and Louisville had to leave Boston and Brooklyn, respectively, to get back home for their Sunday games on July 24 (both forsaking a Saturday game for the revenue from a Sunday one). Scheduled doubleheaders were also slated in 1898 for August 15 at Baltimore and October 5 at St. Louis.

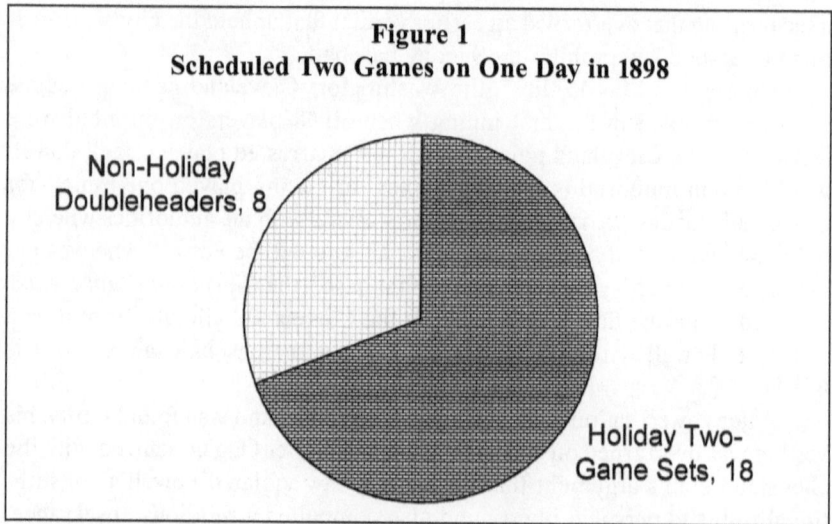

**Figure 1
Scheduled Two Games on One Day in 1898**

The first doubleheaders on an initial season schedule occurred in 1898 when the National League expanded to a 154-game schedule, so that all games could be fit into the allotted number of weeks in the playing season. (Source: Retrosheet database.)

The National League got more than it expected in 1898 from its authorization of and anticipation for more doubleheaders. The bad weather came early and often in the spring of 1898. After four games were postponed on April 28, including the Boston–Philadelphia game that was canceled by snow, a *Boston Globe* headline read: "More Rain; Only One League Game on That Account; Double Headers Will Come Often Later in the Season."[35]

There were an enormous number of doubleheaders played in 1898 due to a plethora of postponed contests (in addition to the eight scheduled doubleheaders), nearly twice the number played two years earlier in 1896. Baltimore, the second-place finisher, participated in 23 doubleheaders in 1898, including back-to-back twin bills with Brooklyn on September 30 and October 1 and New York on October 11 and 12. St. Louis, the league's doormat in 1898 as the team compiled a 39–111 record, also played in 23 doubleheaders. After the club's games with Cincinnati were rained out on May 4 and 5, Cincinnati needed to make a special one-day trip to St. Louis to make up the two games in a doubleheader on June 28. Then as the season wound down in October, St. Louis and Cincinnati played three consecutive twin bills on October 1, 2, and 3 (Cincinnati won five of six games). St. Louis concluded its nightmare season with three more doubleheaders on October 6, 7, and 9.

After the experience of 1898, the 1899 National League schedule was replete with doubleheaders, 27 in all. Louisville, under new owner Barney

Dreyfuss, was scheduled for seven doubleheaders at home (including a Sunday one on May 21) and seven more on the road. No other team was scheduled for more than two doubleheaders at home. Louisville played in 16 doubleheaders during the 1899 season and participated in nine more three-club doubleheaders. Cleveland, abandoned by owner Frank Robison who bought the St. Louis club and transferred his best ballplayers there, was the doormat of the league in 1899 with a 20–134 record. Cleveland played in 27 doubleheaders in 1899 and participated in eight more three-club doubleheaders. Few clubs wanted to play single games with Cleveland, which were likely to command a meager attendance. Louisville's ballpark burned down in mid–August, so Dreyfuss lined up three-team doubleheaders to try to generate some additional revenue.

The three-club doubleheader was a novel arrangement, but because it smacked of overt promotion and was of questionable integrity (nearly all the matches involved the teams owned by Dreyfuss and Robison), it was rarely used after the 1899 season. The three-club twin bill typically involved the home team playing two games for a single admission, the first game against one opponent and the second match against another opponent. The initial such affair occurred on June 11 at Cincinnati, with Louisville the opponent in the first contest and Cleveland the opponent in the second. Louisville and Cleveland were also the opposition at St. Louis on July 9, at Chicago on August 20, at Cincinnati on September 3 and 10, and at Chicago on October 10. Another variation was used on September 24 at St. Louis, where Louisville played two games, the first against St. Louis and the second against Cleveland.

At the dawn of the twentieth century, the economics of major-league ballclubs depended on attendance on holidays, Saturdays, and Sundays. The weekday was a drag on profits. The doubleheader had changed the nature of attendance on weekdays. Soon it would also affect attendance—and thus ballclub economics—on holidays, Saturdays, and Sundays.

5

Early Holiday Doubleheaders

LABOR DAY USHERED IN the inaugural incarnation of a doubleheader played on a holiday, as it was the first of the three national holidays celebrated during the baseball season to convert to doubleheader status, i.e., a single admission for two games rather than separate admissions for a two-game set. This transformation occurred in the late 1880s and early 1890s when Labor Day was still a state holiday celebrated primarily in eastern states such as Massachusetts and New York.

The Labor Day holiday originated in New York City, where the first parade, or "labor demonstration, as the parade was spoken of," was staged by 10,000 marchers, largely union members, on September 5, 1882. "The parade of the working men yesterday was conducted in an orderly and pleasant manner," the *New York Times* reported. "Nearly all were well clothed, and some wore attire of fashionable cut." In 1884 the Knights of Labor, led by Peter McGuire, established the first Monday in September as Labor Day. "I suggested the first Monday in September of every year for such a holiday," McGuire related years later, "as it would come at the most pleasant season of the year, nearly midway between the Fourth of July and Thanksgiving, and would fill a wide gap in the chronology of legal holidays." After New York and Massachusetts established Labor Day as a state holiday in 1887, other states soon followed with similar actions. In 1894, Labor Day was established as a federal holiday.[1]

During the first year of the new state holiday in Massachusetts, the Boston club in the National League jumped on the opportunity to conduct a holiday event since Labor Day coincided with its scheduled game with Philadelphia. At the September 5, 1887, game the *Boston Globe* reported, "It is safe to say without exaggeration, 14,000 people gave up 50 cents to see the Phillies open their series in Boston. As 2,000 persons paid 50 cents extra to enter the grand stand, the total receipts were swelled to something over

$8,000." However, a battle erupted between the two ballclubs over the division of the receipts. If the game were considered to be a holiday, then the clubs would evenly split the money; otherwise, the Philadelphia club would simply get the usual, and smaller, visitor's share of the gate. The Boston owners "refused to divide on the ground that at the time the holiday division of receipts rule was made an understanding was had as to what days were meant," the *Globe* explained. "Since Sept. 5 was made a holiday after the rule was passed," the Boston owners considered that "it does not come under its provision."[2]

In 1888, two teams played the first holiday two-game sets on Labor Day, when they combined a scheduled single game on that date with a postponed game. Boston once again seized the moment. "The click, click of the turnstile at the South End Grounds was like the soft, sweet music of the rustling of an angel's wing" to the ears of the owners of the Boston and Washington clubs, the *Boston Globe* reported on the 3,021 spectators at the morning game, who "were well dressed and looked prosperous," and the nearly quadruple number at the afternoon game when, reportedly, "11,474 was the turnstile count."[3]

Brooklyn in the American Association also played a two-game set on Labor Day in 1888. The opponent was St. Louis, whose owner was Chris Von der Ahe. "I knew nothing about this being a holiday in Brooklyn when I was asked to play two games here to-day — one of them you know is a postponed game," Von der Ahe told reporters on the day of the two-game set. He had agreed to a small increase in the usual guarantee for the postponed game, but said "I get half of the receipts at the afternoon game only," since Brooklyn had designated the two contests as "postponed" and "holiday" games.[4]

The *Brooklyn Eagle* recognized a change occurring in the nature of crowds at holiday events. "The racing and base ball events of Labor Day made Brooklyn and its environs the resort of many thousand people," the newspaper reported on the 30,000 who attended the Futurity Stakes horse race and another 20,000 at both ballgames. "That such multitudes gathered to view the races and the struggles for supremacy on the diamond bears ample testimony to the growing popular interest in outdoor sports ... altogether the sporting events of Labor Day emphasized anew that while the pastimes of the people are numerous and varied, racing and base ball remain the favorite means of diversion for the masses."[5]

The target for holiday ballgames was quickly converting from the "well dressed and prosperous" to "the masses." As Foster Rhea Dulles related in *A History of Recreation*, at this time in the late nineteenth century, "despite long hours of work and the economic precariousness of their lives, or all the more because of such conditions, these wage-earners were eager for amusement of any kind." Vaudeville theatres were popular, as were entertainments venues such as "dime museums, dance-halls, shooting galleries, beer-gardens, bowling-alleys, billiard-parlors, saloons, and other more questionable resorts." Baseball, however, was more popular. "Baseball had come a long way from those early beginnings traced in mid-century," Dulles wrote. "It was far and away the leading spectator sport, a boon to bank clerk and factory-worker, shopkeeper and mechanic" and not just "the business executive."[6]

In 1889, the National League began to recognize the Labor Day holiday in its preseason schedule (the American Association did not), when the Boston and New York teams were slated to host two games on Labor Day. "We have Chicago for two games on Memorial Day; Washington June 17, and Indianapolis on Labor Day, the same holiday attractions as last year but in different succession," the *Boston Globe* noted about the 1889 schedule. "The triumvirs' men play in Cleveland on July 4." There was some wrangling among the ballclub owners to play the Fourth of July games in Pittsburgh, since that city was "a better ball town than Chicago on Independence Day, as the morning game draws as well there as in the afternoon." John Day's New York ballclub copped the Fourth of July date in Pittsburgh that year.[7]

When the Pennsylvania legislature approved Labor Day as a new state holiday commencing in September 1889, the Philadelphia franchises in both the National League and the American Association also decided to host two contests on the new holiday. "Four games—two on each ground—to-day, Labor Day, indeed," the *Philadelphia Inquirer* wrote in a snickering line about the competing holiday matches conducted by the city's two major-league ballclubs. Because both teams were making up postponed games, and perhaps escalated by the intracity competition, each club used a single-admission policy for its Labor Day games in 1889. Advertisements for both matches in the *Philadelphia Inquirer* clearly noted "two championship games for one admission," which was 25 cents at both ballparks. At the Philadelphia Baseball Grounds, home of the city's National League club, "the largest attendance of the season, numbering over 14,000, witnessed the two games." Less than half that number, about 7,000, attended the doubleheader staged by the Athletic club of the American Association club at the Jefferson Street Grounds. Labor Day doubleheaders in Philadelphia would become a staple in the 1890s, as other ballclubs clung to the tradition of the holiday two-game set for the third holiday of the baseball season.[8]

Competition in 1890, sparked by the establishment of the Players League as a third major league, led to further advances in multigame events on Labor Day. At the Polo Grounds, the New York club in the National League staged a single-admission doubleheader against Cleveland, in a quest to entice spectators and deter them from attending the separate-admission two-game set conducted by the New York club in the Players League. In Brooklyn, now a member of the National League after transferring from the American Association after the 1889 season, the ballclub proceeded with the usual morning and afternoon contests slated for the holiday, but then added a third game in the afternoon session, to encourage spectators to see its afternoon match rather than that of the Brooklyn club in the Players League. This was the first of a few three-games-in-one-day events in major-league history (another so-called tripleheader was staged in Baltimore on Labor Day in 1896). When the Players League folded after just one season and the American Association merged into the National League (transferring four franchises and dropping four others), the National League settled into a monopoly major-league status once again in 1892. But this didn't alleviate the holiday scheduling politics.

With the introduction of Labor Day as a third national holiday during the baseball season, National League ballclub owners had to deal with an uneven division of holiday dates among its members. From 1889 to 1891, they grappled with the consequences of dividing up 12 holiday dates among eight clubs, and from 1892 to 1899, they struggled with allocating 18 holiday dates among 12 clubs. Due to Labor Day's distinct concentration in the eastern states—much like the initial days of the Decoration Day holiday—the National League allocated home dates on Labor Day exclusively to ballclubs located in the eastern states from 1889 to 1893. While seeming patently unfair, for several reasons this approach to the Labor Day holiday did not cause a huge uproar among the ballclubs.

From an economic perspective, Labor Day had much less of an impact on ballclubs than did the Decoration Day and Independence Day holidays. Decoration Day occurred within the first few weeks of the season, thus giving ballclubs an immediate financial boost, since all the teams were still viable contenders for the pennant at the time. Independence Day, exactly five weeks later than Decoration Day (the holidays interestingly always fell on the same day of the week), had a somewhat similar impact. However, Labor Day occurred eight weeks after Independence Day. By then, many, if not most, of the teams were effectively eliminated from the pennant race and thus the holiday games generated far less interest among spectators than did the earlier holidays. For clubs still contending for first place, Labor Day could be a good draw for attendance; for others, it was more like just another day near the end of the season.

For example, in 1894, Pittsburgh was assigned a home date for Labor Day with Washington as its opponent. Because Washington usually had an unattractive won–lost record, and indeed was near the bottom of the standings by that September, Pittsburgh declined to schedule two games for the holiday and decided to simply play one game. It was a sound decision, as only about 500 people attended that Labor Day match to see the home team thrash

Washington, 22–1. Similarly, Brooklyn had a Labor Day home date in 1894 with Louisville, where the club had scheduled two contests. When Labor Day arrived, since Louisville was in last place in the standings, Brooklyn decided to nix staging morning and afternoon games and opted instead to have a doubleheader in the afternoon.[9]

Playing two games on Labor Day in separate-admission morning and afternoon sessions was also problematical for many ballclubs because early September was right in the heart of natural doubleheader territory, when clubs were furiously trying to make up as many postponed games as possible via twin bills. This was especially a concern if there were numerous doubleheaders to be played that resulted from a rainy spring. The Labor Day games in Pittsburgh and Brooklyn in 1894 also suffered from this affliction. Both clubs had to play doubleheaders on the preceding Saturday with the same opposing clubs, thus significantly diminishing the value of two separate games on the holiday (or even one, in the case of Pittsburgh). The use of a single admission for two games on the holiday was a defensive measure, when there was a doubleheader being played just before, or after, with the same visiting team. Why would people attend the morning game on the holiday if they could attend two games for the same price on the preceding Saturday?

A third factor that weighed against Labor Day being an economic engine for ballclubs similar to the Decoration Day and Independence Day holidays was that Labor Day always fell on a Monday. Sunday baseball was now a facet of the National League, since the league had dropped its prohibition on such activity for the 1892 season, following its merger with the American Association. For ballclubs located in western cities that could legally play Sunday baseball, this made Labor Day a much less attractive proposition than the other two holidays. In 1893, four of the 12 National League teams regularly conducted games on Sunday — Chicago, Cincinnati, Louisville, and St. Louis. The other ballclubs were not required to play Sunday baseball when visiting these cities, but could elect to do so. Baltimore, Brooklyn, Cleveland, and Washington were Sunday-playing road teams. The ability to derive substantial revenue from Sunday baseball, either as a home club or a visiting one, made the lack of Labor Day dates more tolerable for these eight franchises.

The remaining four ballclubs — Boston, New York, Philadelphia, and Pittsburgh — at the time were legally prohibited from playing Sunday games at their home grounds and abstained from playing road games on Sunday until 1898 (when New York and Pittsburgh commenced the practice) and 1903 (when Boston and Philadelphia finally caved in). The Boston, New York, and Philadelphia franchises thus were accorded preferential treatment in the scheduling of holiday dates during the 1890s. Each of these three Sabbath-observing clubs had at least two holiday home dates each year between 1892 and 1899, and sometimes all three.[10]

5. Early Holiday Doubleheaders 59

Boston, of course, also had Bunker Hill Day on June 17 as a third holiday on its schedule each year, in addition to its annual Decoration Day and Labor Day dates. In 1894, Boston gained a fourth holiday when the Massachusetts legislature converted Fast Day from a floating holiday in early April to be Patriots Day celebrated on April 19. Because it now had three holiday dates within a span of seven weeks, the Boston club elected to have two games only on Decoration Day and play single games on the two Boston-specific holidays. Boston's first home game of the season was typically slated for April 19, which was enough of a spectator-generator itself that the team could forego playing two games on that holiday date.[11]

For the first three years of the National League's 12-club existence, 1892 to 1894, the league generally followed its conventional premerger pattern of allocating Decoration Day and Labor Day dates to eastern clubs and Independence Day dates to western clubs (the only exception being dates granted to Pittsburgh, the easternmost western club, at the expense of Baltimore or Washington). By 1894, though, scheduling politics started to emerge from their hidden venue in the back room of league meetings into the public spotlight. "My holiday attraction, my Fourth of July game, will not attract a corporal's guard," St. Louis owner Chris von de Ahe said after the National League schedule was released in February 1894. "The Washingtons are last now, and will be last all season, yet I am expected to play them on my only holiday at home." Von de Ahe later softened his remarks, in recognition of the tradeoff between holiday dates and Sunday games. "Taking it all in all, we were well treated. It looked like old times to see us scheduled at home for twelve or thirteen Sundays. There's no better city in America for Sunday ball than St. Louis," von de Ahe said. "We got great holiday dates away from home, the Decoration Day assignment at Brooklyn and the Labor Day game at Philadelphia. There's no club that got a better deal than this."[12]

Driving von de Ahe's outburst on holiday scheduling were the huge crowds that were now attending holiday games on Decoration Day and Independence Day. By 1892, the afternoon segment of a holiday two-game set could attract more than 10,000 people, an unobtainable upper bound of holiday crowds in the mid–1880s; total attendance for both the morning and afternoon sessions in 1892 could approach 20,000.

In 1894, both these standards were eclipsed at the Decoration Day match between New York and Cleveland, when 24,500 reportedly squeezed into the Polo Grounds for the afternoon contest and attendance topped 30,000 for both ballgames. "The afternoon attendance broke the record for the Polo Grounds, the official estimate being that 24,000 persons had witnessed the game," the *New York Times* reported in an understated fashion. "The crowd filled every inch of the stands, and later was massed on the field and the embankments." The *Philadelphia Inquirer* was a bit more descriptive about

In the 19th century, holiday two-game sets, which involved separate admission charges for each end of a morning-afternoon doubleheader, often attracted overflow crowds. Ballclub owners, not wishing to turn away paying customers, allowed spectators to stand on the playing field after all seats were filled, such as at this 1887 Decoration Day afternoon game at Washington Park in Brooklyn. (National Baseball Hall of Fame Library, Cooperstown, New York)

the large crowd at the Phillies' Decoration Day match that year: "Just imagine 16,000 people massed upon a ball field, the stands and bleachers packed with humanity as tightly as sardines in a box, and a living wall extending all around the outfield, the players completely encircled by people who formed the sides and ends of this big amphitheatre and you have a picture of the scene at Philadelphia Ball Park yesterday afternoon when the Phillies and the Chicagos came upon the field to play."[13]

The advent of the electric trolley helped to spur the growth of holiday crowds and continue the change in the crowd's makeup. On Labor Day in 1894, "for the first time since Manager Hanlon took charge of the Baltimore Club there will be two games for one admission at Union Park," the *Baltimore Sun* reported. "It being Labor Day two games were scheduled to be played in each of the Eastern cities—one in the morning and one in the afternoon. The Baltimore management decided, however, to play both contests in the afternoon." The result of the doubleheader was that "in human cataracts the people came pouring out of the [trolley] cars, which arrived in rapid succession from every part of the city and adjoining towns." It was not only volume—the reported attendance for the doubleheader was 24,450—but people from many different walks of life. "All classes and conditions of man and womanhood were represented in the vast assemblage," the *Sun* reported. "Merchants, doctors, lawyers, ministers, mechanics, small boys and ladies, the rich and the poor, and low, good, bad and indifferent, met together in one mighty throng of enthusiasts."[14]

In 1895, the National League took action to leverage the huge attendance figures generated in the larger eastern cities for Decoration Day games, as well as more fully integrate Sunday baseball into its holiday scheduling. The league modified its conventional approach to holiday scheduling by allocating Independence Day games to Brooklyn, New York, and Philadelphia, as part of a strategy to have all three clubs host all three holidays in 1895. As a result, Cincinnati, Cleveland, and Louisville had no holiday dates that year. Because ballclubs split the holiday gate, there was little complaining as the larger crowds at these road games were economically beneficial to these clubs.

Holiday attendance in 1895 was spectacular. "Decoration Day is always a good one for baseball, but it was better this year than ever before, as the attendance figures show," the *Philadelphia Inquirer* reported in an account of games across the country. "Last year 74,046 people witnessed the National League games. Yesterday the figures ran up to 94,581, an increase of 20,535. Philadelphia had a banner crowd this year, 26,930 paid admissions being recorded by the turnstiles, an increase of 12,263 over last year." In Philadelphia, "at 7 o'clock last night, 19,000 people wet with perspiration and hoarse from shouting their enthusiasm hurried from the exits, and loading themselves on the steam cars, trolley lines, omnibuses and coupes hurried home to supper well satisfied with the way they had put in the afternoon."[15]

On Independence Day, the *Boston Globe* reported that nearly 23,000 jammed West Side Park in Chicago for the afternoon game against Cincinnati, after 13,000 packed the grounds for the morning game of the two-game set, while more than 30,000 watched two games in Pittsburgh. The size of holiday crowds in many cities clearly affected the game on the field. In Chicago, "the crowd was packed up to the bases lines, and once or twice threatened to stop the game by completely filling the field," the *Boston Globe* reported. "Eighty extra police were called to keep the crowd back. The delays were so many that only seven innings were played before darkness set in."[16]

By arranging intrasectional games on Independence Day—where clubs from the same region met each other rather than the traditional east-west matchups—the league found a winning strategy with its holiday allocation formula in 1895, albeit one that discriminated against several western teams. The only change for 1896 was to deny an Independence Day date for St. Louis and give one to Cleveland. "I have framed the schedule on the same general lines as that of last year, changing the holiday dates so as to give the clubs that had poor attendance last year the strongest clubs to play this year," National League president Nick Young said after the release of the 1896 schedule in February that year. "In other words, I have tried to distribute the 'good things' in the schedule so that every club will receive its share of the sweet as well as the bitter." One of those "bitter" things was a rebuke of von der Ahe, whose St. Louis ballclub suffered without a home holiday dates for three years, 1896 to 1898.[17]

Young further tinkered with the holiday schedule for the 1897 season by deviating from the traditional geographic allocation of Decoration Day dates, scheduling Chicago and Cincinnati for May 30 games as well as games on the Fourth of July. The fallout from this scheduling was that the eastern clubs had to complete a western road trip on the Saturday prior to the Monday holiday that spring, making for tight connections to travel by train on Saturday night and Sunday to get back home for the two-game sets on Monday. Boston, New York, and Brooklyn all canceled their morning games on the holiday, and just played the afternoon contests (which all attracted huge crowds).

Philadelphia, which had played Saturday in Chicago and didn't return home until Sunday evening, maintained its two games with Louisville on the holiday. However, the ballclub converted the scheduled morning and afternoon games into an afternoon doubleheader, the first-ever single-admission doubleheader on Decoration Day. "They will arrive home this evening and to-morrow afternoon they will begin the local campaign against the Westerners, playing two games with Louisville for the one price of admission," the *Inquirer* reported. Besides the players getting some additional sleep on the morning of the holiday, the box office was probably helped out as well since Louisville was in last place in the National League standings. The club even sprang for a newspaper advertisement to entice spectators to watch the two ballgames:

BASE BALL
Philadelphia Ball Park
To-morrow (Monday) May 31
(DECORATION DAY)
Two Games for One Admission, 25c
PHILADELPHIA vs. LOUISVILLE
First Game Begins at 2 P.M.[18]

In 1898 and 1899, Chicago and Cincinnati had Labor Day dates in addition to their Independence Day games. Both teams opted to play their two games on Labor Day in 1899 as a single-admission doubleheader, as did St. Louis with its holiday match. Labor Day was clearly losing its luster as a holiday draw as the nineteenth century came to a close. Among the three Labor Day matches played in the eastern cities in 1899, only the games in

Philadelphia were a conventional morning and afternoon affair. Boston opted to play a single game with Baltimore. In New York, the Brooklyn and New York ballclubs played a home-and-home series, with the morning contest at Washington Park in Brooklyn and the afternoon game at the Polo Grounds in Manhattan.[19]

When the National League shrank back to eight teams for the 1900 season by jettisoning the Baltimore, Cleveland, Louisville, and Washington franchises, the league also reverted back to its pre–1895 standard approach to allocating holidays dates where the four eastern clubs hosted two games on Decoration Day and Labor Day while the four western clubs hosted two games on Independence Day.

In its fifth year of general use as a baseball term in 1900, "doubleheader" was often used interchangeably by baseball writers at this time to signify either a morning and afternoon two-game set (with separate admissions) or two afternoon ballgames for a single admission. For example, in reporting on the Labor Day games in Boston in 1900, the *Boston Globe* published the headline "Pittsburg Wins the Doubleheader" followed by an account of the two games that began, "The Boston team got a bad setback yesterday when Pittsburg defeated them in both morning and afternoon games." Today, this description appears contradictory under our modern-day understanding of the definition of a doubleheader being two games staged for a single admission fee.[20]

The emergence of the American League in 1901 as a competing major-league entity to the National League had an enormous impact on holiday scheduling dynamics, which eventually culminated in the complete conversion of the separate-admission two-game set on all three national holidays during the baseball season to single-admission doubleheader status by the early 1930s.

6

First Sunday Doubleheaders

THE FIRST MAJOR-LEAGUE doubleheader conducted on a Sunday occurred in Brooklyn on September 9, 1888, when the Louisville and Brooklyn clubs of the American Association seized the opportunity to make up a postponed game (a rainout on Saturday, September 8) before Brooklyn headed off for a long road trip. In an account that seemingly found nothing unusual about the occurrence of two ballgames on a Sunday, the *Brooklyn Eagle* blandly reported that "the Brooklyn team played two games at Ridgewood in a drizzling rain yesterday," as the bad weather lingered another day over the Long Island peninsula.[1]

The *Brooklyn Eagle* was so nonchalant about the Sunday event on September 9, 1888, because Sunday baseball at Ridgewood Park was, at the time, so commonplace for the Brooklyn ballclub and its followers. Brooklyn—which had found a haven to play Sunday games at Ridgewood, located in Queens, to circumvent the Sunday laws in the city of Brooklyn—was scheduled for 19 Sunday playing dates on the 1888 American Association schedule as the only Sunday-playing club in the East. Sunday ball was slated every Sunday at Ridgewood Park except when Brooklyn was traveling in the West. When Brooklyn played road games in the East, the ballclub arranged for one-game homestands back in Brooklyn in the midst of those road trips to get in Sunday games at Ridgewood Park.

Ridgewood Park was located in Queens County, just over the border from Kings County where the city of Brooklyn was. In 1888, this was an isolated rural area of Long Island comprised of small villages, one of which was Ridgewood, which was not all that easy or pleasurable to reach. One writer described two ways to travel to Ridgewood. The first was to "get on a horse car and when I was nearly starved to death to get off, and after walking several miles across the country, I would hear some yells. Follow the yells as the crow flies and I would soon be at Ridgewood Park." The other route was "getting a hack and riding over the cobble stones that pave the streets one will pass over on the way to Ridgewood," which the writer called a "gastronomic event" with his "insides shaken into a condensed vacuum after that ride." Despite the difficult trip to Ridgewood, thousands of baseball fans made their way to the Sunday ballgames conducted there.[2]

Kings Country at this time was a mostly rural area, as the city of Brooklyn then consisted of just the territory near where the Brooklyn Bridge connected Long Island to lower Manhattan Island. Ridgewood was five miles to the east of Brooklyn in 1888, as Williamsburg, Flatbush, and Bushwick were then independent entities within Kings County. Brooklyn annexed these towns over the next several years, before Brooklyn itself was annexed by New York in 1898. While on today's map Ridgewood is right on the Brooklyn border, in 1888 the two places were not remotely adjacent to each other. Because of its positioning in a Sabbatarian region, Ridgewood, like many Sunday havens of its kind, was "a tiny island of illicit professional baseball on Sunday" located within an "ocean of strict Puritan observance of a Sunday day of rest." The climate of the Sunday games of the Brooklyn ballclub was distinctly different from the Sunday games staged in St. Louis or Louisville where Sunday baseball occurred openly on the regular ball grounds used for games the rest of the week.[3]

While the two Sunday games in Brooklyn in early September 1888 comprised a single-admission event, it wasn't the first time that two games had been played on a Sunday by major-league ballclubs. On Sunday, April 18, 1886, the St. Louis club of the American Association played morning and afternoon games against Pittsburgh. St. Louis used the morning game to make up the postponed contest of the previous day, which was to be Opening Day of the 1886 season for St. Louis. The regularly scheduled Sunday game in the afternoon drew 12,000 spectators, about four times the size of the crowd at the morning match. The unusual two-game set so close to the beginning of the season was designed to preserve, in the Sunday morning game, some of the cachet of the rained-out Opening Day contest, which would have been lost, due to the Sunday afternoon game, had St. Louis rescheduled the postponed game to be part of a doubleheader in its Monday and Tuesday matches with Pittsburgh (or waited until later in the season to play off the postponed game).[4]

To comprehend the development of the Sunday doubleheader into a Level 3 doubleheader that significantly affected the history of major-league baseball, one needs an understanding that the concept of Sunday baseball in the late nineteenth and early twentieth centuries was an issue that evoked as much emotion as abortion does today. "Sunday baseball" long ago evaporated as a term in our sports vocabulary. During the period 1876–1934, though, the term had a very real context in then-current sports lexicon.

Sunday baseball described the once unusual phenomenon of men playing baseball on a day many considered sacred in the belief that the Lord had set it aside as a "day of rest" to observe the Sabbath. Men playing baseball on Sunday—a once peculiar, and often illegal, event—has been transformed into such a common occurrence today that a specific phrase to describe the activity is no longer necessary. At the end of the nineteenth century and in the early twentieth century, though, Sunday baseball was a polarizing expression.

People take for granted today that major-league baseball can be played on Sunday without interference by the government. The right to play baseball on Sunday, though, was not so easily ordained as an inalienable right among the populace. Groups on both sides of the issue, to play or not to play sports on Sunday, harbored strong opinions about the justification of their positions. Slowly, Sunday changed from a day of rest to a day of leisure and ultimately to a day of recreation.

The issue was fought both figuratively in court and literally on the baseball field. A few players—such as 1897 Cleveland pitcher Jack Powell—gained ever-lasting legal fame when court cases were pursued up to the state Supreme Court or became legal precedents. On-field confrontations between Sabbatarians and baseball spectators were more common and could be contentious. In the third inning of the July 20, 1890, American Association game outside of Rochester, New York, a justice of the peace accompanied by several constables and members of the local Law and Order Society marched onto the baseball diamond and ordered the players to stop the game. The officials underestimated the intensity of the ballclub's followers, though. "As the players came in ... spectators began to pour out upon the diamond and shout derisively at the officers," the *Rochester Herald* described the scene. "Here and there a cushion seat went flying through the air and the crowd surged thicker and thicker." When it appeared that a fight would ensue, Rochester manager Pat Powers stepped in and convinced the constabulary that if they'd let the game continue, then the players would report the next day to the justice's office. The justice, "deeming discretion the better part of valor, accepted the terms and departed."[5]

The Puritan settlers on the shores of this country were the impetus for various state laws banning not only professional baseball on Sunday but also most recreational activities. The motivation of our country's forefathers was the Fourth Commandment of the Bible, which states: "Keep the Sabbath day to sanctify it, as the Lord thy God hath commanded thee. Six days shalt thou labor and do thy work. But the seventh day is the Sabbath of the Lord thy God." Thus, to the Puritans, Sunday was the Lord's Day, a day free from labor, or more simply, a day of rest.

Puritan opposition to sporting activities, not just on Sunday but during any day of the week, became part of the American ethos. It wasn't as simple as the Puritans merely disliking amusements; they had their reasons. Being among the first settlers, the harsh conditions required the Puritans to continually work. "Merely to keep alive in a land which to their inexperience was cruel and inhospitable demanded all their energy," Foster Rhea Dulles wrote in *A History of Recreation*. Starvation, disease, and attacks by the natives among other dangers were constant perils. There was no time for amusements since there was one basic fact in the colonies—"if the settlers did not direct all their energy to their work, they could not hope to survive." This Puritan attitude toward sport gave rise to the oft-repeated contention that "Puritans forbade bear-baiting, not because of the pain it caused the bear, but because of the pleasure it afforded the spectators."[6]

However, the Puritans denounced sports and other amusements such as dancing not so much to suppress merriment but rather because they considered them to be frivolous and unproductive, and distracted from a common mission. "Puritan life was to be a totality, a society with no seams," Bruce Daniels concluded in his book *Puritans at Play: Leisure and Recreation in Colonial New England,* which turned out to be the dark side of the Puritan restraint on sports. "Leisure and recreation posed a special threat to the ideal of a unity of experience. Play suspended the normal rules of life and substituted its own rules, which allowed violence, deception, destructive competition, even outright lying. Play mocked the community and its moral standards. And, most horrifying of all, formal play had its own rituals, which competed with social rituals for loyalty and time."[7]

Initially, the New England colonies didn't pass laws governing ballgames and blood sports, since public distaste for them served to limit the activities. As more non–Puritans arrived as settlers, though, laws became necessary to restrict sports and amusements on the one day of the week that people might find the time to participate in them—Sunday. "Along with many other long-lived customs, the Puritans brought a strict form of Sunday observance to the New World that influenced how other British North American colonies developed their own blend of Sunday regulations," Alexis McCrossen wrote in *Holy Day, Holiday: The American Sunday*. "Sunday laws—known as "blue laws" because of the supposed color of paper on which they were published in colonial Connecticut—emerged out of widely shared respect for Sunday. Both law and custom set the day apart from the rest of the week." Over time, as immigrants of more diverse backgrounds arrived, the hard line of the Puritan Sunday faded, although the Sunday laws didn't disappear. Instead, they were adopted in most of the colonies and also in the new territories as settlers moved west.[8]

Sunday laws were accepted, or at least tolerated, as long as the United States had an agrarian economy, where there was a clear line between six days of work and one day of rest, and residents were mostly of English ancestry. That began to change in the mid–nineteenth century with the rise of the Industrial Revolution and the arrival of immigrants from other European countries to work in the new factories and mills. The Industrial Revolution immutably changed life. Urban areas replaced rural ones as centers of influence and immigrant workers dominated city dwellings, bringing with them a different perspective on Sunday, known as the Continental Sabbath. "In an industrializing society still dependent on armies of agricultural laborers, Sunday stood in opposition to relentless work for the majority of nineteenth century Americans," McCrossen wrote in *Holy Day, Holiday: The American Sunday*. "The six working days blended into one unit—the workweek—in contrast to Sunday, the day of rest." The average workweek at the turn of the century was typically at least six days of ten-hour workdays.[9]

While Sunday was deemed to be a day of rest for working people, just how "rest" was best utilized, however, differed between locales in the East and the West. By the 1870s, many cities west of the Allegheny Mountains, especially those dominated by immigrants from Germany and other European countries, observed a Continental Sabbath where people participated in festivities and sporting events. Thus, St. Louis, Cincinnati, and Louisville were the initial major-league cities where Sunday baseball was played. Conversely, in cities on the eastern seaboard, Sunday was a day of piety and quiet solitude.

In the late nineteenth and early twentieth centuries, laws in many states continued to prohibit most labor as well as numerous other activities on Sundays. These Sunday laws were justified by the state's alleged interest in regulating the health and welfare of its citizens through a weekly "day of rest." Convoluted legal rationales were often employed to explain the "coincidence" that Sunday, the religious day of rest, was also designated as the state-mandated day of rest. The Sunday laws posed a huge problem for many people who desired to view a match of the increasingly popular game of professional baseball. Because they worked six days a week for ten hours a day, workers in the burgeoning industries of America generally were excluded from the opportunity to observe a ballgame. Sunday doubleheaders were thus highly popular among working class people, who were a new group of potential spectators that ballclub owners could tap for revenue.

The first Sunday doubleheaders were all conducted in the American Association, since the National League—with ballclubs located in Sabbatarian strongholds such as Boston, New York, and Philadelphia—prohibited Sunday baseball before the 1892 season. These early Sunday doubleheaders in 1888 were Level 1 doubleheaders, with the second game serving to make up an earlier postponed game between the two teams.

Two weeks after the initial Sunday doubleheader in Brooklyn, Billy

Barnie and Billy Sharsig—the early two-for-one innovators—helped to engineer twin bills on Sunday, September 23, when their Baltimore and Athletic ballclubs were in Kansas City and Louisville, respectively. Rain had prevented the Baltimore–Kansas City game on Friday, September 21, but rather than play a doubleheader on Saturday, the two clubs instead agreed to make up the postponed game as part of a doubleheader on Sunday. In Louisville, a tie game on Saturday with the Athletic ballclub was replayed as the second game of a twin bill on Sunday. Kansas City, which was in last place in the American Association in 1888, was also involved in Sunday doubleheaders at St. Louis on October 7 and at Louisville on October 14, after games on the preceding Saturday were washed out by rain.

Barnie and Sharsig were also involved in the next wave of Sunday doubleheaders in 1890, which were clearly of the Level 2 variety. On Sunday, September 28, 1890, the Baltimore and Athletic teams played twin bills at St. Louis and Toledo, respectively, in which the second game represented the moving up of the scheduled contests on Monday, September 29. The reason was an expected very small attendance on Monday, since the ballclubs had experienced meager attendance at their games on Saturday, September 27. "The day was too cold to play ball, and 100 spectators kicked themselves to keep warm and also for turning out on such a day," the *Philadelphia Inquirer* reported on the Saturday game in Toledo with the last-place Athletic club. In St. Louis, "owing to the cold weather the attendance was only 200" for the Saturday game with Baltimore. These two Level 2 doubleheaders set the stage for the expansion of the Sunday doubleheader concept during the 1890s.[10]

The farewell doubleheader debuted at the end of the 1891 American Association season, when Milwaukee advertised two games to be played on October 4, the last day of the season. The idea was to elevate spectator interest to carry over to the next season. However, as cold weather set in during early autumn, Milwaukee drew just 400 people to its season finale. "It would have been difficult to have picked out a more miserable day for the closing of the baseball season that was yesterday," the *Milwaukee Sentinel* reported. "The rain of the night previous had left the grounds in a condition of muddiness rivaling the bogs of the Dismal Swamp and it was almost worth a man's life to attempt to run between the bases." For example, in the first inning, George Shoch hit the ball to right field and "ploughed through the mud to second base." When the next batter hit the ball to center, "the ball got stuck in the mud and while Easton was excavating it, Shoch scored." While spectators had been promised two games as a farewell performance, "[they] were amply satisfied with one game, as they would have frozen to death sitting through another one" in the wintry weather.[11]

As the American Association was clearly on its last legs during the 1891 season, the Sunday-playing league merged with the Sabbatarian-oriented National League, with the senior circuit absorbing four of the Association's eight clubs to create a 12-team field for the 1892 season. In reality, though, only four of the dozen franchises in the merged league had National League origins: Boston, Chicago, New York, and Philadelphia. In addition to the four clubs taken in directly as a result of the merger (Baltimore, Louisville, St. Louis, and Washington), another four clubs had recently transferred from the American Association to the National League (Pittsburgh in 1887, Cleveland in 1889, Brooklyn in 1890 and Cincinnati in 1890; the latter three due to legal problems with staging Sunday baseball). So it was only natural that a condition of the merger be that ballclubs could opt to play Sunday baseball.

Since St. Louis and Louisville had been conducting Sunday baseball at the major-league level since 1882, and Cincinnati had from 1884 to 1889, while in the American Association, all three ballclubs staged Sunday games in the inaugural year of Sunday baseball in the National League in 1892. It was not surprising that soon thereafter all three clubs began to experiment with Level 2 doubleheaders on Sunday. For the most part, these Level 2 Sunday doubleheaders during the 1890s occurred under one of three conditions: (1) late in the season during September and October, (2) against inferior competition, or (3) before a club left for a lengthy road trip. In 1893, Chicago joined the other three ballclubs as a Sunday-playing city and by mid-decade was hosting a few Sunday doubleheaders itself under similar circumstances. Sunday was still a big enough draw by itself to warrant just a single game on that day, as evidenced by the record crowds in Cincinnati on July 19, 1896, and in Chicago on April 30, 1899. Therefore, the Level 3 doubleheader to optimize attendance on Sunday throughout the season was not yet needed.[12]

The Cincinnati ballclub organized a Level 2 doubleheader late in the 1892 season when it moved its scheduled single game with St. Louis on Monday, October 3, to be part of a twin bill on Sunday, October 2. "The regular game scheduled for Monday was played on this date [October 2], crowding two games into one afternoon," *Sporting Life* reported. "The reason for it was that this was the last base ball [on] Sunday [that] Cincinnati would have this season." Because attendance at Monday games was usually fairly light, Monday games became a popular choice to reschedule as the second game of a Sunday doubleheader.[13]

For Sunday doubleheaders against inferior competition, the Washington ballclub was a popular candidate in the early 1890s, since the club consistently finished among the bottom three spots in the league standings. Because of its poor won-lost record, the Washington team was not a good attraction for attendance, so its games typically drew a small crowd. For example, the Washington–St. Louis match on Friday, September 15, 1893, at St. Louis drew just 150 customers; a Sunday doubleheader two days later on September 17 attracted 5,500 people.[14]

One of the earlier-season Sunday doubleheaders during the 1890s was held on July 29, 1894, at St. Louis. The rationale was that this was a getaway day before the ballclub departed for a road trip to visit the eastern clubs in the league.

The Sunday doubleheader became a larger feature of the regular season in 1898, since the schedule had been expanded to 154 games. More than a dozen Sunday doubleheaders were staged in 1898 at the four Sunday-playing cities in the National League, with St. Louis being a popular choice late in the season for a Sunday doubleheader opponent because it was inferior competition. The St. Louis ballclub of 1898 was one of the worst all-time in major-league history, finishing with a 39–111 record. St. Louis played in four Sunday doubleheaders in September and October out of the available six Sunday dates in the league schedule (St. Louis lost all eight games in those doubleheaders).

Sunday baseball reached its nineteenth century zenith on April 30, 1899, in Chicago when 27,489 persons crowded into the West Side Grounds to see Chicago play St. Louis. "The huge bleachers were piled full of joyous but uncomfortable spectators and around the field crowding in almost to the diamond was a circular mass of people," the *Chicago Tribune* described the throng at the game. "At times the field crowd would stampede and, sweeping away all the police, would bear down upon the players as if to break up the game, while the masses in the stands would rise as one man and cheer while the police in cordons drove back the encroaching mob." However, before the 1899 season concluded, Chicago was engaging in Sunday doubleheaders.[15]

Finances were the problem. "Twelve clubs have stayed through the season by dint of switching dates, violating the schedule, and resorting to every possible means to help the financial end of the game, to the detriment of the sport," the *Chicago Tribune* reported in early October, two weeks before the 1899 season concluded. Doubleheaders were one technique used to try to stem the red ink. In 1899, the first scheduled Sunday doubleheader appeared on the National League schedule, slated for May 21 at Louisville. However, the weather was dreadful so only one game was played that day, as the second game was cancelled. The doubleheader hit another road bump in 1899, when many three-club doubleheaders—branded as more low-brow P.T. Barnum than respectable National League—were conducted on Sundays. Louisville, under new owner Barney Dreyfuss, participated in nine three-club Sunday twin bills. In just a few years, though, Dreyfuss, then owner of the Pittsburgh ballclub, would be a decided opponent of the doubleheader.

Dreyfuss was willing to go to great lengths to engage in a Sunday doubleheader in 1899, because Eclipse Park in Louisville had burned down with two months left in the season. Dreyfuss tried to continue games by using temporary stands for spectators, but attendance soon dwindled. Things looked dreary for Louisville as "some people profess to believe that it is the last League game that Louisville patrons will ever see." In early September Dreyfuss rescheduled the club's remaining 14 home games as Louisville converted into an orphan team for the final six weeks of the National League season. Every weekend for the rest of the season, the wandering Louisville team used Sundays at the other three Sunday-playing cities to play in a three-club doubleheader, where the home team played two games for a single admission, the first game against one club and the second game against a different club.[16]

The logistics of arranging the three-club doubleheader were not always convenient, but a good attendance could be assured if the weather cooperated. For the September 10 twin bill, Cincinnati had to train in from St. Louis to be the host club, while Cleveland traveled from Chicago and Louisville from Pittsburgh. The first game with Cleveland was cut short at seven innings to allow the Cleveland team to catch a train to Philadelphia. After the second contest with Louisville went its full nine innings, the Cincinnati club hopped on a train to go to Washington while Louisville traveled to Baltimore. Attendance was reported to be 7,135 people, which provided a decent cut for all three clubs.[17]

Another twist on the three-club doubleheader was used on Sunday, September 24. Rather than host St. Louis playing two games that day, Louisville, the visiting club, played both ends of the doubleheader against different opponents. Louisville defeated St. Louis in the first game and on an essentially neutral site defeated Cleveland in the second.

Louisville played the final three Sundays of the season at Chicago, although the ballclub could squeeze in just two games. On October 1, the weather was so bad that Louisville opted to not play the second part of its twin bill with Chicago, as "a drizzling rain filtered down upon the 700 who came out to see the advertised doubleheader and delayed the start by almost an hour." The following Sunday, October 8, Louisville did play Chicago in the second game of the doubleheader. And on October 15, Louisville played its last National League contest in the second game of the doubleheader at Chicago, a victory in an eight-inning game called by darkness.[18]

Clearly, the 12-club National League was too unwieldy a number, with spectator interest waning in many cities early in the season when it became apparent those ballclubs had no chance to win the pennant. Adding further embarrassment, syndicate baseball had decimated the clubs in Cleveland and Baltimore, while Louisville had become an orphan team late in the season. These three teams, along with Washington, were dropped from the

National League after the 1899 season ended, cutting the league back to its eight-club structure prior to the merger with the American Association for the 1892 season. With only three Sunday-playing cities in the National League—St. Louis, Chicago, and Cincinnati—the Sunday doubleheader took on a greater importance as the twentieth century dawned.

7

Tinkering with Doubleheaders

IN 1901 ALL THE SPADE WORK done over the previous decade and a half by ballclub owners in the American Association and the National League to popularize the doubleheader accelerated forward when the American League emerged as a competing major-league entity to the National League.

Since the National League had released its 1901 schedule first, at the end of February, the American League had the opportunity to avoid or arrange scheduling conflicts in the three cities that had franchises in both leagues (Boston, Chicago, and Philadelphia). The American League chose conflict creation. When the AL released its 140-game schedule three weeks later, its Boston club had 25 conflicts with the city's National League ballclub; the Chicago and Philadelphia ballclubs had similar conflicts of 21 and 10, respectively.[1]

The scheduling conflicts were certainly intentional. In Boston, 19 of the 25 conflicting dates were during May and June, right at the beginning of the season. Particularly interesting was the selection of Saturday, September 14, to go head-to-head in Boston and Philadelphia, with a scheduled doubleheader in both American League ballparks to compete with single games in the cross-town National League parks where those clubs would play their last home games of the season. The American League also scheduled four doubleheaders for Saturday, September 28.

These prearranged doubleheaders on the 1901 American League schedule were an early application of the Level 3 doubleheader concept, to try to optimize attendance on a ballclub's best attendance day of the week. Because Sunday baseball was still legally prohibited in Boston and Philadelphia in 1901, Saturday was the best attendance day of the week for those two clubs. A half-holiday in effect at many businesses allowed many more people to go to a Saturday afternoon ballgame than could get to a game during the workweek.

7. Tinkering with Doubleheaders

In 1902, after the American League released its schedule first, which had no doubleheaders, the National League retaliated. The National League schedule contained not only a number of conflicting dates in the four cities that now had franchises in both leagues (St. Louis was the addition), but it also had scheduled doubleheaders for five dates in August. The last of the five scheduled twin bills in 1902 was on Sunday, August 24, when Brooklyn visited Chicago. This Sunday doubleheader helped to ignite a great expansion of the two-for-one concept during the first decade of the twentieth century. With Chicago and St. Louis being two-league cities that allowed Sunday baseball, ballclubs in both leagues elevated the Sunday doubleheader idea.[2]

The August 24 doubleheader in Chicago drew 11,000 people, but more importantly it showed that a one-game road trip for a Sunday match could be quite beneficial. Brooklyn traveled from Pittsburgh, where it had played on Saturday, to play two games in Chicago, before returning to Pittsburgh for another game on Monday. If there was any doubt that this strategy made good economic sense, the August 24 doubleheader in Cincinnati clinched agreement. The two contests with Pittsburgh attracted a reported audience of 24,597, the "largest crowd that ever attended a ball game in Cincinnati," before Pittsburgh grabbed a train to return home to play Brooklyn on Monday.[3]

In September the St. Louis Browns hastily scheduled a doubleheader at Sportsman's Park for September 14, which played opposite a single game that the National League Cardinals had scheduled for that day. But to play it, St. Louis had to travel overnight after participating in a doubleheader on Saturday in Cleveland. The following weekend, the Browns were scheduled to be in St. Louis, and had booked a twin bill with Cleveland for Sunday, while the Cardinals were on the road. However, the Cardinals arranged to play a doubleheader on Sunday, September 21, as the Monday game with Cincinnati "was moved forward to make yesterday's double header as a counter attraction to the Sportsman's Park affair."[4]

In 1903, the two major leagues agreed to coordinate their schedules to minimize conflicting dates and doubleheaders. But this further elevated the Sunday doubleheader situation. While there were fewer conflicting Sunday doubleheaders in Chicago and St. Louis, the two ballclubs in each city established a pattern of playing alternately throughout August and September, with a smattering in May and June, so that baseball fans in the two cities had a steady dose of Sunday doubleheaders to sample. The two clubs in St. Louis conducted nearly a dozen Sunday doubleheaders in 1903, beyond the usual menu of a few during the season to make up postponed games.

The quintessential evidence that the doubleheader was proliferating in the first decade of the twentieth century was the remarkable record set in 1903 by New York Giants pitcher Joe McGinnity, who pitched and won three doubleheaders not only over the course of that one season but also within the span of one month. In August 1903, the New York Giants played 11 doubleheaders and just nine single games, due to the excessive number of postponed games that John McGraw's squad needed to make up. McGinnity's record accomplishment in August 1903 wasn't a stunt; he needed to pitch. McGraw used a three-man pitching staff for the most part that season, with McGinnity, Christy Mathewson, and Dummy Taylor doing the bulk of the pitching for the Giants.[5]

McGinnity, a 32-year-old right-hander who won 31 games for the Giants in 1903, started 12 of the 31 Giants games that August, winning seven and losing five. Six of those wins came in the three doubleheaders he pitched. McGinnity's twin-victory doubleheader performances came on August 1 in Boston, August 8 against Brooklyn at the Polo Grounds, and August 31 against Philadelphia in New York.

After the first doubleheader victory in Boston on August 1, the headline "Pitches 18 Innings; McGinnity, 'The Iron Man,' Wins Both Games" graced the top of the sports page in the *Boston Globe*. "It was bad enough to lose both games to New York at the South End Grounds yesterday by scores of 4 to 1 and 5 to 2, but it was 'kinder rubbin' it in' to have McGinnity of the Giants pitch both games and win them," the *Globe* reported. "Thirteen hits, seven in one game and six in the other, were all that the Boston team got during the 18 innings that the 'iron man' was in the box."[6]

While it's often thought that McGinnity gained his "Iron Man" nickname by having pitched and won those three doubleheaders in 1903, as demonstrated by the *Boston Globe* coverage, McGinnity had actually acquired the sobriquet long before that time. "The nickname came from his off-season work in his wife's family business, an iron foundry in McAlester, Oklahoma," as one biographer concisely recounted. McGinnity could just as well have acquired the nickname at the end of his baseball career. "He was also an 'Iron Man' in terms of longevity: he pitched professionally until age 54, racking up 246 wins in the major leagues and another 240 in the minors, a combined total topped only by Cy Young." McGinnity had longevity, both to pitch a doubleheader in one day and to pitch more than 30 years, because he threw with an easy-going motion, owing "his durability to a style of delivery that saw him alternate between overhand, sidearm, and a wicked underhanded curve that he called 'Old Sal.'"[7]

The second doubleheader victory, against Brooklyn at the Polo Grounds on August 8, came with a lot more difficulty. While McGinnity defeated Brooklyn, 6–1, in the first game, the Giants trailed, 3–2, going into the bottom of the ninth inning of the second one. However, the Giants rallied to tie the score against Brooklyn pitcher Oscar Jones. Then with runners on first and third bases with McGinnity due up, George Van Haltren pinch-hit for the pitcher and singled home the winning run to give McGinnity his second doubleheader win of the month.

Although he didn't bat in the ninth, McGinnity had a role in helping his team to victory that inning. He had scored the Giants' first run of the game in the third inning when he stole home, which caused some consternation among the Brooklyn players. Umpire Tim Hurst had sent McGinnity to third base after he had ruled that he had been interfered with when he stole second base. "McGinnity stood on third base rubbing a supposed bruised leg while the [Brooklyn] players argued with the umpire. They were so absorbed in the dispute that Schmidt, the pitcher, walked away from his box and left the ball lying in the middle of the diamond," the *New York Times* reported. "McGinnity, cleverly coached by McGraw, took advantage of this opportunity and stole home. The Brooklyn played looked sheepishly at each other and then protested more vigorously while the crowd cheered derisively." Hurst ejected Schmidt from the game, which caused Brooklyn to send Jones, who had pitched the first game, back to the mound for the duration of the second game. In the ninth inning, with 15 innings pitched under his belt for the day, Jones apparently ran out of gas as the Giants rallied for the victory.[8]

The third doubleheader victory came easily on August 31 against Philadelphia, as McGinnity defeated the Phillies, 4–1 and 9–2, in two games that had a total elapsed time of three hours and three minutes. "At the end McGinnity showed no sign of fatigue—in fact, he seemed fresh enough to tackle the visitors for a third contest if that were necessary," the *Times* reported.[9]

McGinnity also pitched both ends of two other doubleheaders during his major-league career. In September of 1901 while pitching for Baltimore in the American League, he had a split decision in both a September 3 doubleheader against Milwaukee and a September 12 twin bill against Philadelphia. He nearly had a fourth career doubleheader victory in the September 12 match, when he won the first game but lost the second game when he gave up the winning run in the ninth inning.

An enduring symbol of the doubleheader that is second only to Ernie Banks of "Let's play two!" fame, McGinnity begrudgingly gained everlasting fame not only in doubleheader circles but also in general baseball legend and lore. "Most of Joe's other records are forgotten and there is a tendency to regard him as something of a freak, as though those three double victories in one month were his sole contribution to baseball history," Tom Meany wrote in the 1950s, ten years after McGinnity had entered the Baseball Hall of Fame. "Actually, Joe holds several major league marks, all of which are tributes to his great stamina." The best known record is the 434 innings that McGinnity pitched during the 1903 season, which still stands as a modern-day National League record and probably will never be eclipsed.[10]

One hundred years after McGinnity's doubleheader feat, the *New York*

Times evoked his name in the headline of an editorial—"Where Is Iron Man McGinnity?"—as the newspaper commented on the work habits of modern-day ballplayers. "Curt Schilling's gutsy performance in winning two post-season games while pitching with a bloody ankle has given us the heroic image we cherish in our sports figures," the *Times* noted. "But even Schilling's feats cannot obscure the fact that today's pitchers, who don't seem to be able to throw complete games, are softies compared with the stars of yesteryear ... [who] grew up in an agrarian, self-reliant culture in which people finished their own chores." The legend of Joe "Iron Man" McGinnity lives on.[11]

Ballclub owners tended to focus on the success of doubleheaders at the box office and overlook, for the most part, a number of negative concerns associated with the two-for-one concept. These concerns could have compromised the integrity of the game if the games were more about attendance than the championship. As *The Sporting News* once editorialized, "There is not a sound argument for a double-header, except to swell the gate receipts of a ball club, and when men arrange baseball games to swell receipts and not to play them for a championship, they hippodrome the sport."[12]

Physical condition of the ballplayers was one concern. The results of the second game could be unduly influenced by the stamina, rather than the skill, of the ballplayers. "Double-headers in semi-tropical weather are the bane of a ballplayer's existence, and he would rather waive his day's salary than labor from shortly after noon til dusk," the *New York Evening Journal* reported in 1898. "But, dual combats will attract the bargain-seeking throng, and so long as the ducats roll in what do the magnates care?" In addition, not all starting players, notably catchers, would appear in both games of a doubleheader.[13]

Playing conditions at the ball park were another concern. Overflow crowds on the outfield in small ballparks could change the outcome of the game due to "ground rules" related to balls hit into the spectators. Second games were often curtailed before nine innings were played, due to darkness or otherwise, which precluded the opportunity for a comeback victory that might occur if the game extended its full nine-inning length.

There were also moral considerations in the nature of the rationales used to postpone a game and reschedule it as the second contest of a double-header. There were instances where slightly inclement weather was used as an excuse to postpone a game rather than stage a game in front of a small crowd. "The postponement of the encounter for use as a curtain raiser this afternoon will attract several thousand fans" compared to the 600 at the Cincinnati ballpark when the rain came down, the *New York Evening Journal* reported such a situation in 1898. "The wisdom of the 154-game schedule is now being proved," the *Washington Post* reported late in the 1904 season. "National League teams remain idle one day and play double-headers the next in order to draw a crowd." An even more flagrant excuse used by some ballclubs was to avoid a twin bill due to injuries to key players. Then there was the growing sentiment that the home team had an advantage in a doubleheader against a stronger club, as expressed in "it is seldom that a visiting team captures both sections of a double-header."[14]

Owners recognized that doubleheaders might detract from single-game attendance, as fans waited for a two-for-one date to get more for their money, so both leagues prohibited doubleheaders during the first series with each club. While this practice avoided competition during the first half of the season between single games and twin bills, the result was a proliferation of doubleheaders in the second half of the season. This result was deemed tolerable, since the better-performing clubs would still draw well, one game or two, and the two-for-one concept would likely improve overall attendance for below-.500 clubs. Pittsburgh owner Barney Dreyfuss was a leading opponent of the use of doubleheaders in the National League. "I have only the welfare of the game at heart when I object to its being placed on the bargain counter — two games for one price of admission in order to have a few hundred more people come into the grounds," Dreyfuss said in 1904. "The only reasons I have for trying to have them eliminated from the National League is that they cheapen the game, make the players dissatisfied and tire the spectators."[15]

Doubleheaders became a larger part of the playing season in 1904 when both leagues expanded to a 154-game schedule. Although there was a limited number of scheduled doubleheaders (including, infamously, an October 10 doubleheader between Boston and New York in the American League), the 1904 schedule created a surge in the number of Level 1 doubleheaders that needed to be squeezed in before the regular season concluded. The same thing had happened with the previous experiments with 154-game schedules in the National League in 1892 and 1898–1899. With the exception of four days (two of which were Sundays) there was a doubleheader played every day during September and October of the 1904 season. Boston and New York, the two best clubs in the American League in 1904, each played 12 doubleheaders during the September/October period, including five with each other, as the two clubs battled for the American League pennant.

The fifth and final doubleheader between Boston and New York on October 10, which decided the 1904 American League pennant on the last day of the season, became one of the first legendary twin bills to be remembered for decades. That doubleheader also became the cornerstone for the storied rivalry between the Red Sox and Yankee ballclubs, which was still heatedly contested one hundred years later. In 1904, though, the doubleheader was simply an exciting conclusion to a tight pennant race between the Boston Americans and the New York Highlanders.

Originally, the American League schedule called for four games to be played in New York during the final series of the season between Boston and New York, including an innovative season-ending doubleheader on Monday, October 10. With a postponed game added into the mix, the final series expanded to five games, with a single game on Friday, October 7, and doubleheaders on Saturday, October 8, and Monday, October 10 (with Sunday as a day of rest, due to the Sunday law in New York that prohibited professional baseball on that day). The five-game, season-ending series in New York certainly looked to be an advantage for the Highlanders, who by midseason were competing with Boston in a neck-and-neck race for the American League pennant.

However, the owners of the New York ballclub apparently had little faith in their own team, as they reached an agreement during the summer to rent out American League Park (commonly called Hilltop Park) for college football games in September, October, and November. In mid–July, Columbia University announced that it would play its football games at American League Park rather than at the Polo Grounds, where the school had played the last several years. Five games were slated for late September and early October when the Highlanders would be on an extended road trip, and several more games were scheduled after the conclusion of the baseball season. There was just one minor problem. "There will be a conflict in the early part of October," the *New York Times* reported. "On Oct. 8, the day on which Columbia is due to play Williams, the baseball team has a game at home with the champion Bostons. This will probably be shifted to some other city." The lure of a few dollars of rental income from college football had obliterated the Highlanders' scheduling advantage.[16]

Perhaps the New York owners believed the Highlanders would clinch the pennant before the final series with Boston. But the upshot was that the Saturday doubleheader was transferred to Boston. It was a decision that would haunt the ballclub for years. Instead of five games in New York, the Highlanders played a Friday afternoon game in New York, jumped on a train to Boston for two games on Saturday, and returned to New York for two games on Monday. All this after the team had spent the previous two weeks traveling through the Midwest on trains. As writer Ed Linn noted in his book *The Great Rivalry: The Yankees and the Red Sox, 1901–1990*, the season-ending series was eventually defined as "the pennant that was lost on Jack Chesbro's wild pitch," but it could be more aptly labeled as "the pennant that was lost through the stupidity of the Yankee front office." The lure of rental income was too much to resist for the ballclub owners, who gave away a date on which the team could possibly clinch the pennant in order to host a college football game.[17]

Jack Chesbro, New York's star pitcher and a future Hall of Famer, turned out to be the goat rather than the hero of the final series, as Boston captured the American League pennant in the decisive doubleheader on Monday, October 10. Chesbro pitched and won the opening game of the five-game series on Friday, defeating Boston, 3–2, on a chewed-up playing surface for his 41st victory of the season. Columbia had defeated Tufts in a football game at Hilltop Park just two days earlier, in the last of five football games played there during the Highlanders two-week road trip. The victory vaulted New York into first place, a half game ahead of Boston. Chesbro only faltered from there.

Chesbro, a spitball pitcher, claimed that throwing the pitch put less pressure on his arm than a fastball, so that he could pitch with less rest than other pitchers. Manager Clark Griffith used Chesbro frequently in 1904, starting him in one-third of the ballclub's games that year. Chesbro completed 48 of his 51 starts in 1904, pitching 454 innings. However, Chesbro pushed himself beyond his limits in the final series. Standing on the train platform at New York's Grand Central Station, he reportedly talked Griffith into allowing him to pitch on Saturday, with no days rest. "But you worked today. You can't pitch them all," Griffith is said to have replied to Chesbro's request. "You want to win the pennant, don't you? I'll pitch and I'll win," Chesbro is said to have countered. In an ill-advised move, Griffith started Chesbro in the first game on Saturday.[18]

Before a crowd of 30,000 people that jammed into Boston's Huntington Avenue Grounds, Chesbro lasted just three innings in the first game on Saturday, as he was knocked out of the box in the fourth inning when Boston scored six runs. It was just the third time all season that Chesbro had failed to complete a game that he started. Boston clobbered New York, 13–2, in the first game and then took the second game, 1–0, behind the shutout pitching of Cy Young, which put the team in first place by one and a half games; New York needed to sweep the doubleheader on Monday to win the pennant. Back at Hilltop Park that day, Columbia defeated Williams, 11–0, in a football game played before a crowd of 3,000. That was about 25,000 shy of the anticipated attendance for a pennant-deciding baseball doubleheader that day.

Chesbro was back pitching in the first game on Monday, making his third start in four days. The match was tied 2–2 when Boston mounted a rally in the top of the ninth inning. Lou Criger, Boston's weak-hitting, slow-footed catcher, stroked a single to lead off the ninth. He advanced to second base on a sacrifice and to third base on a ground out. With Fred Parent at bat with two outs and Criger on third base, Chesbro cemented his future legacy when his spitball sailed several feet over the head of catcher Red Kleinow to the backstop, which allowed Criger to score the go-ahead run. Boston won the first game, 3–2, to capture the pennant when pitcher Bill Dineen shut down a New York rally in the bottom of the ninth by striking out Pat Dougherty for the final out. The second game of the doubleheader, now meaningless to the standings, was rapidly completed in one hour and ten minutes, with New York eking out a 1–0 win.

"Chesbro would forever be remembered as the man who lost the pennant on a wild pitch," one writer summarized the pitcher's role in the fateful doubleheader on October 10. "No banner season has ever ended on a more sour note, and some commentators even traced the pitcher's subsequent decline to his costly mistake." Nominally, Chesbro had a fabulous season, with a 41–12 record and a 1.82 earned run average. But the decision to start Chesbro in a game on each of the last three days of the season had contributed substantially to New York losing two of its last four games in the twin season-ending doubleheaders. Because Chesbro was out of baseball by 1910, and Griffith went on to become the owner of the Washington Senators ballclub, Chesbro has been cast as the demon who lost the pennant for New York. Virtually no one now blames infielder Jimmy Williams, whose throwing error in the seventh inning in the first contest on Monday allowed two Boston runs to score and tie the game that New York had once led, 2–0. That was the conclusion of one newspaper via the headline: "New Yorks Lose by the Errors of Williams and Chesbro." Williams first to blame, Chesbro second; no mention of the role of Griffith.[19]

The October 10 doubleheader became legendary partially because of its impact on the 1904 pennant race, but more importantly because it was an initial confrontation in the storied, longstanding rivalry between the American League ballclubs in Boston and New York. "There is no rivalry on the face of the earth that can compare with the Yankees vs. Red Sox," Linn wrote. "It's everything a rivalry ought to be. Us Against Them. It's not only New York against Boston. It's New York against New England. The canyons of Wall Street and the caverns of Madison Avenue vs. the White Hills of New Hampshire and the Green Mountains of Vermont. We the People vs. the Barons of Entrenched Priviledge. The spacious expanse of Yankee Stadium against the looming monster of Fenway Park."[20]

The sale of Babe Ruth by the Red Sox to the Yankees in 1920, following Boston's winning of five World Series titles in two decades, triggered a cataclysmic turn of events in the rivalry. New York went on to win 26 World Series championships before Boston finally eluded "The Curse of the Bambino" to win another World Series title in 2004. During the intervening years, there was plenty of excitement, and heartbreak for Boston fans, during the era of Ted Williams/Joe DiMaggio, Mickey Mantle, and Carl Yastrzemski/ Reggie Jackson. There were several last-day-of-the-season showdowns, highlighted by Bucky Dent's home run in the 1978 playoff game and Aaron Boone's walkoff home run in the 2003 American League Championship

Series. It all started with Jack Chesbro's wild pitch in a doubleheader on the last day of the 1904 season.

Another ramification of the 154-game schedule in 1904 was the informal policy adopted by clubs in both leagues of playing only seven innings in the second game of some doubleheaders. Completing all nine innings of the second game of a twin bill before darkness had always been a concern since the advent of the doubleheader in the 1880s, especially late in the season during September and October. But the two-for-one doubleheader in 1904 started to deviate toward being a one-and-three-quarters-to-one deal for the spectator.

Most shortened second games of a twin bill were justified by train schedules to travel to the next destination on the baseball schedule. "Five innings constituted the second game, as the visitors were obliged to catch the 6 o'clock train for New York," the *Boston Globe* reported in September 1904 when Boston's Saturday doubleheader with Brooklyn to make up a rainout on Friday had to be cut short. Many newspaper reports used the euphemism "called by agreement" when describing such a situation, as in "the second game was called in the seventh inning by agreement," such as occurred in the Boston–Philadelphia and Cincinnati–St. Louis doubleheaders played on October 8 in the National League.[21]

Although the majority of shortened-by-agreement games occurred in the National League, there were also a few in the American League. For example, the second game of the October 5, 1904, doubleheader between Washington and Detroit was shortened by agreement to five innings due to cold weather. The first game began "before a shivering crowd, variously estimated at from 85 to 100 persons." After the conclusion of the first game, "with a grain of mercy in his voice, the umpire announced before the second game that the captains had agreed to play only five innings, owing to the general frigidity of the occasion."[22]

A shortened doubleheader was still shortened, which didn't set well with many observers. "We have observed that in both major and minor leagues a great many games have been shortened by mutual agreement to seven innings on days when double-headers were to be played," *Sporting Life* editorialized late in the 1904 season. The publication thought the shortened games were clearly a violation of league rules that required nine innings to be played unless the umpire ended the game under the drawn and called game rules. Therefore, the shortened games were illegal and shouldn't be counted in the standings. "Double-headers are bad enough without affording excuse for laxity of discipline or violation of rules that may lead to other abuses. We believe that double-headers should be expressly prohibited." While the seven-inning second game was generally abhorred by many, there were two sound reasons for employing this technique.[23]

First, there was an inequity in the likelihood of completing nine innings in the second game of the doubleheader, because the probability depended upon the location of the match. In the pre-artificial-light era, completion of the second game depended on the timing of sunset, which varied among the ten cities that hosted major-league ballclubs in 1903 (and for the next several decades through 1952). While clock time is consistent among cities located in a particular time zone, the timing of sunset depends on a city's longitude. Thus, sunset occurs earlier in cities in the eastern portion of a time zone than it does in cities located in the western portion of a time zone. For instance, in the Eastern Time Zone, sunset in Boston, located at 71 degrees longitude, occurs roughly 20 minutes earlier than it does in Washington, D.C., located further west at 77 degrees longitude.

The timing of sunset was not a huge concern between the months of May and August, the heart of the baseball season. During those four months, sunset occurred after the 6:00 P.M. dinner hour in all major-league cities, thus reasonably allowing time for both games of a doubleheader to be completed before the sun went down. However, in those pre-daylight-saving-time days, sunset times after Labor Day created a dicey situation for two games of a doubleheader to be completed in September and early October. For example, the 20-minute time differential between sunsets in Boston and Washington could allow for the playing of two additional innings in Washington before a game was ended by darkness. That could mean the difference between the second game of a doubleheader being stopped by darkness after seven innings or going the full nine innings.

Second, a fixed end date of the second game accommodated the changing nature of the spectator who could attend a game during the workweek. Seven innings or any quasi-specific end point to the second game that roughly coincided with the 6:00 P.M. dinner time appealed to many spectators who couldn't remain at the ballpark until a second game concluded possibly around 7:00 P.M. This approach especially appealed to those businessmen who now lived in the suburbs. It also appealed to employees who toiled for the newfangled corporations and who couldn't get away from their jobs to see a game that began at 2:30 P.M., but could get to the ballpark at 4:30 to see at least one of the two games of the doubleheader. Again, many of these spectators would be inclined to leave the ballpark by dinner time.

Spectators were also traveling longer distances to see ballgames because of advances in commuter railroads with connecting trolley lines, as well as the introduction of the automobile. In 1903 there were no doubt a few "horseless carriages" that transported spectators to the ballpark to supplement the coterie of horse-drawn carriages and legions of fans that arrived via electric trolley cars. Although the automobile would more dramatically affect ballpark attendance later in the decade, the advent of the interurban trolley had a more immediate impact on the number and variety of ballpark patrons early in the first decade of the twentieth century. While the electric streetcar tied city center with the new suburbs five miles outside the city, the interurban trolley connected outlying towns with the city center, and smaller cities among each other. As one commentator has noted, "In the early years of the twentieth century it was possible to travel from Maine to New York City using only the electric trolley." The interurban trolley permitted a whole new segment of society—businessmen in outlying towns and burgs—to more easily attend a weekday ballgame. A doubleheader was an even better deal.[24]

But the interurban trolley did more than help to shape the landscape of cities. "In creating new suburbs, the interurbans helped to foster an upwardly mobile class of Americans that would soon demand private transportation as a proper adjunct to house ownership." However, the prime era of the interurban was very fleeting. Between 1900 and 1910, the number of cars manufactured increased from 4,000 per year to nearly 200,000 annually. In 1908 Henry Ford introduced the Model T—"a motorcar for the multitudes"— which propelled the interurban into oblivion. "It will be large enough for the family but small enough for the individual to run and care for," Ford said of the Model T. "It will be so low in price that no man making a good salary will be unable to own one."[25]

Indeed, the automobile was transforming, as it "opened up a whole new world to a large segment of the population," changing aspects of education, medical services, and types of food to eat. "Culturally, the automobile was also a boost," wrote Frank Coffey and Joseph Layden in their book *America on Wheels: The First 100 Years*. "Civic and artistic functions—museums, galleries, theater performances—were suddenly accessible to people who lived in rural areas." Equally accessible were the ballparks where professional baseball was played.[26]

By 1906, shortened second games by agreement in the National League were fairly common, whether for transportation or other reasons. But they were starting to be perceived more negatively than positively. "By agreement of the two teams, on account of the dark day and the late start, the second contest was cut down to five innings," the *New York Times* reported after the Giants defeated Pittsburgh 10–4 in the first game. "The 8,000 spectators could well have dispensed with some of the first to have had more of the second game."[27]

Three no-hitters occurred in shortened second games of doubleheaders in 1906, demonstrating another downside to the informal policy, as the three pitchers were denied an opportunity to finish out nine innings to pursue a "real" no-hitter. Jack Weimer, Stoney McGlynn, and Lefty Leifield were all denied a chance at baseball immortality, and have been relegated to footnote status in the record books.[28]

The concern with shortened second contests came to a head in 1907. There were dozens of shortened games "by agreement" in the National League, occurring in June, July, and August, and not just in September and October when the onset of darkness was a real concern. For example, the Pittsburgh and Cincinnati clubs left Pittsburgh after their June 22 game to travel to Cincinnati for a Sunday doubleheader on June 23. The second game was abridged to seven innings to allow both clubs to catch a train back to Pittsburgh for their game there on Monday.

Perhaps more flagrant were the two perfect games that ended prematurely, as both pitchers were precluded from attempting to accomplish the feat over a full nine innings. Rube Vickers pitched a five-inning perfect game on October 5, which ended naturally by darkness after the first game of the doubleheader lasted 15 innings. The other shortened perfect game was an even more egregious situation.

Ed Karger, a left-hander for the St. Louis Cardinals, pitched a seven-inning perfect game against Boston in the second half of a doubleheader on Sunday, August 11. In mid-August in St. Louis, this game ended by agreement in sunshine, as both ballclubs sought to catch a train to travel east to their next scheduled contests on Tuesday, August 13. The 24-year-old Karger easily retired 21 consecutive Boston batters. "With the approach of the fifth inning it was realized that there was the possibility of a no-hit game and the crowd reminded him to pitch his best," the *St. Louis Post-Dispatch* reported. "He did pitch his best and the support was perfect. Not one man came near enough to reach the initial bag to make even one decision close." The wire service report of Karger's accomplishment, carried in numerous newspapers across the country, unabashedly said: "Not one Boston player reached first off Karger, who pitched the second game, limited to seven innings by agreement." Karger may well have handled six more Boston batters if he had been given the opportunity, to be included in the exclusive contingent of pitchers who have hurled nine-inning perfect games.[29]

Karger has, for the most part, been excluded from that select circle of pitchers who are recognized as throwing a perfect game. After Charlie Robertson pitched his perfect game for the Chicago White Sox in 1922, the *New York Times* reported that "in the long history of major league baseball since 1875 but five other perfectly pitched games in which no batter reached first base safely have been turned in." Karger's effort 15 years earlier was not listed among those five perfect games. Karger was long forgotten when Don Larsen pitched his perfect game in the 1956 World Series, as the newspapers noted that Larsen was the seventh pitcher in baseball history to pitch a perfect game.[30]

Over the years, Karger has occasionally been included on lists of perfect games, such a filler item in agate type in the *New York Times* on April 23,

1984. But even those occasional references were expunged in 1991 when the major leagues' committee for statistical accuracy redefined a no-hitter as "one in which a pitcher or pitchers complete a game of nine innings or more without allowing a hit." The baseball establishment officially recognized Karger for a "notable achievement," but not a no-hitter.[31]

The *Complete Baseball Record Book* published by The Sporting News identifies Karger (and Vickers) under the heading "Perfect Games of Less than Nine Innings." But few other publications provide similar recognition. The book *Perfect: The Inside Story of Baseball's Sixteen Perfect Games* never mentions Karger, even in its appendix of nearly perfect games. The book *27 Men Out: Baseball's Perfect Games* also never mentions Karger, even though it contains an extensive appendix of "Perfect-Game Curios" that focused on the anomalies of Harvey Haddix and a five-inning perfecto by Dean Chance.[32]

Karger has not been completely forgotten. The Associated Press issues a "This Date in Baseball" listing that many newspapers carry when they have space to fill in the sports section. Karger's accomplishment is often noted there: "1907—In the second game of a doubleheader, shortened by agreement, Ed Karger of the St. Louis Cardinals pitched a seven-inning perfect game." If only that train had left an hour later in 1907 and the game not shortened by agreement, Karger might be recognized alongside Cy Young, Addie Joss, and Charlie Robertson as the earliest modern pitchers to hurl a perfect game.[33]

St. Louis Cardinal pitcher Ed Karger was victimized in 1907 by the prevailing practice of shortening the second game of a doubleheader to seven innings "by agreement" of the two ballclubs. When Karger pitched seven perfect innings on August 11, he never had the opportunity to try to hurl two more perfect innings to achieve pitching immortality with a nine-inning perfect game. (National Baseball Hall of Fame Library, Cooperstown, New York)

Doubleheaders attracted a lot of adverse publicity after the conclusion of the 1907 season. "Calling games by mutual consent before the expiration of nine innings is a dangerous practice and should be discouraged," the

Philadelphia Inquirer commented. "The practice of arranging double-headers on the slightest pretext, merely to bring a few more admissions to the ground, regardless of the prior arrangements of the schedule, went to such extremes last fall that it was adversely commented upon throughout the Untied States." National League president Harry Pulliam even weighed in on the subject. "Temporarily there may been a slight gain, but the game was done no good by making it cheap and common," Pulliam remarked. "The patrons of a club think no more of the management in the long run because a few contests happen to be slipped in at cut rates, and it is probable that some admissions are actually lost because some spectators hold back, hoping that a team will play doubleheaders." While Pulliam hoped to have new rules promulgated to stop the doubleheader abuses, the ballclub owners didn't back him on that stance. However, Pulliam did sway the owners indirectly to curtail the practices. With the shortened second game "by agreement" disavowed in 1908, the doubleheader settled into being a full-fledged two-for-one value.[34]

On September 26, 1908, in the middle of a heated pennant race, Ed Reulbach of the Chicago Cubs pitched both games of a doubleheader against Brooklyn and not only won both of them, a la Joe McGinnity, but also pitched a shutout in both of them. The double shutout was a feat never accomplished before that date, and one that hasn't been duplicated since. Chicago won the first game, 5–0, as Reulbach yielded just five hits. In the second contest, Reulbach was even better, giving up only three hits as Chicago blanked Brooklyn, 3–0. "Reulbach performed the powerful feat of shutting out the Superbas twice this afternoon to the music of fife and drum," the *Chicago Tribune* reported. "The grace, style, endurance, and speed of Mr. Reulbach fits into this remarkable baseball race. He put the locals away so easily in the curtain raiser that [Manager Frank] Chance granted his request to go in and bring them again."[35]

The double shutout on September 26 was all the more remarkable because the two whitewashings were sandwiched around two more shutouts by Reulbach on September 19, when he pitched ten scoreless innings in a 0–0 tie at Philadelphia, and on October 1 when he hurled a two-hitter at Cincinnati in a 6–0 victory. At the time, Reulbach established a National League record of 44 consecutive scoreless innings as the Cubs went on to claim the National League pennant in 1908 following the one-game playoff after the regular season ended to replay the infamous "Merkle boner" game. As Emil Rothe wrote in a 1973 *Baseball Digest* article on Reulbach's accomplishment, "With the Giants and Cubs destined to finish the season in a tie and Pittsburgh only a half game behind, Reulbach's unique double shutout must certainly be credited as a significant contribution to the Chicago cause."[36]

7. Tinkering with Doubleheaders

When frequent rains postponed so many ballgames in 1909 that nearly 200 doubleheaders were played, by far the most in major-league history at the time, baseball writers came up with new nicknames to substitute for the term that had been in general baseball usage for less than 15 years. "Bargain bill" was the first nickname to gain widespread use as a replacement for doubleheader. "The bargain bill of two games for one fee brought out a big Monday crowd of ardent spirits who fall for that sort of thing," the *Chicago Tribune* reported on September 22, 1908. "Twin bill" was another expression that gained traction in the press around this time. "In spite of the chilly wind which blew through the stands a crowd which numbered close to 8,000 saw the twin bill," the *New York Times* reported on October 8, 1910, about a season-ending doubleheader.[37]

Both new terms for a doubleheader reflected the promotional aspect of the concept, which would haunt ballclub owners for the next two decades. Attendance at weekday games started to founder around 1910, as spectators held back on attending single games during the week to wait for the "bargain" day when two games could be seen for the price of one admission. "Twin bill" was an adaptation of the theater term "double bill," which had been in widespread use for decades to describe two shows for the price of one admission. However, theaters that advertised the availability of a double bill were considered to be less respectable entities, something that ballclub owners desperately wanted to avoid as the doubleheader entered its maturity phase during the 1910s.

8

Expansion of the Holiday Doubleheader

WHEN THE AMERICAN LEAGUE used scheduling conflicts in 1901 to challenge the National League's monopoly on major-league status, it opted to completely avoid any holiday conflicts that season. While the National League continued with its alternating east-west-east approach for the three holiday dates, the American League adopted a nearly opposite west-mixed-west approach.

However, in 1902, the American League successfully battled the National League head-on with conflicting games on Decoration Day in Boston and Philadelphia and on Independence Day in Chicago. As a result, the two leagues agreed to integrate their playing schedules as part of their general peace agreement in 1903. "The first 'harmony' meeting between representatives of the big baseball leagues began today," the *Boston Globe* reported in February 1903. "The object of the meeting is to smooth out conflicting rules and to adopt nonconflicting schedules."[1]

Schedule-makers adopted a holiday scheduling strategy where home dates in each league were allocated half to eastern clubs and half to western clubs for all three national holidays. For example, in the American League in 1904, eastern ballclubs New York and Boston hosted two-game sets on Decoration Day in addition to western ballclubs Cleveland and Detroit. On Independence Day in 1904, Philadelphia and Washington were the eastern holiday hosts, while Chicago and Cleveland were the western ones. The Labor Day lineup mirrored the Decoration Day one. This approach to holiday scheduling served as the foundation for allocating holiday home dates for several decades.

One by-product of this holiday strategy was that same-city conflicts between the two leagues could easily be minimized. For instance, the Boston and Philadelphia ballclubs never had conflicting home dates on holidays, and they often alternated holiday dates each year. A prime example of this practice occurred in 1904 when the Boston club of the American League had home dates for Decoration Day and Labor Day, while the Boston club of the National League was home on Independence Day. In 1905, the opposite occurred, with the Boston Americans home on Independence Day, while the Boston Nationals had home dates on Decoration Day and Labor Day. The overarching concept was that the cities of Boston and Philadelphia would host games on all three holidays each year, with a club in one league having one holiday date and the club in the other league having two.

A similar concept was used for the three franchises located in New York City. The Brooklyn and New York clubs in the National League alternated Decoration Day and Independence Day dates each year, though there might be coinciding games at home on Labor Day. The two Manhattan franchises, the New York club in the American League and the New York club in the National League, also alternated Decoration Day and Independence Day dates each year, and beginning in 1908, they also began to alternate all three holidays like Boston and Philadelphia so that there were no conflicting home dates.

Boston and New York, in both leagues, were scheduling partners for the one-half eastern segment of a Decoration Day or Independence Day holiday slate. For example, in 1904 when Boston and New York in the American League both had home dates on Decoration Day, they were the visiting clubs for the Independence Day games staged in the eastern cities. In 1905, the opposite was the case. Philadelphia and Washington were also scheduling partners for the eastern segments in the American League, while Brooklyn and Philadelphia were scheduling partners in the National League.

This was the first series of holiday scheduling that achieved a level of symmetry and relative equity (i.e., eliminating the political factor) among the eight ballclubs in each league. Because by this time holiday gate receipts for general admission were typically split between the two ballclubs on a holiday date, this method of holiday scheduling was more acceptable than it would have been in the 1880s and 1890s. However, for another three decades, holiday scheduling continued to be intertwined with Sunday baseball availability.

Cleveland had an overallocation of holiday dates in the American League until the Ohio legislature changed the law to allow Sunday baseball beginning with the 1911 season. For the eight years from 1904 to 1911, Cleveland had home dates for every Decoration Day and Independence Day and most of the time on Labor Day. Detroit always had two holiday home dates from 1904 to 1908 for the same reason; when Sunday baseball was legalized for the 1908 season, Detroit's holiday allocation was reduced.

Pittsburgh owner Barney Dreyfuss used the Sunday-law prohibition in Pennsylvania to gain an excess of holiday dates for three decades, as he was able to convince the other National League owners that his Sunday home-game preclusion was such a large financial detriment that it warranted Pittsburgh getting home dates for all three national holidays. Until Pennsylvania law was changed to permit Sunday games in the 1934 season, Pittsburgh was a host team for all three holiday dates every year from 1903 to 1933.

Two elements worked in Pittsburgh's favor to gain this overallocation of holiday dates. Dreyfuss was in charge of making the schedule for the National League, at the time a very detailed and unenviable task, which gave him significant influence with the other ballclub owners. Also, attendance at the morning game of a two-game set in Pittsburgh was usually much better than in other cities, providing for a combined draw that had a favorable financial attribute for the visiting ballclub. For instance, the morning crowd in Pittsburgh for Independence Day in 1908 was reported to be 14,585, slightly larger than the 14,493 reported at the afternoon game.[2]

The additional holiday dates for Cleveland, Detroit, and Pittsburgh before these ballclubs could play Sunday baseball at home came at the expense of Chicago, Cincinnati, and St. Louis, which were veteran hosts of Sunday baseball. Accordingly, there was no attempt to alternate holiday schedules of the two teams located in both Chicago and St. Louis, just simply to avoid have conflicting home dates on any holiday. Cincinnati ever had more than one holiday date each season, and in many years the Reds had none.

During this period, two-game sets on Patriots Day and Bunker Hill Day became a staple of the holiday schedule in Boston, alter-

Pittsburgh Pirate owner Barney Dreyfuss, an avowed hater of the two-for-one doubleheader, loved the separate-admission morning-and-afternoon holiday twin bill. From 1903 until he died in 1932, Dreyfuss secured home dates for his Pittsburgh ballclub for all three national holidays each season. (National Baseball Hall of Fame Library, Cooperstown, New York)

nating each year between the two Boston ballclubs. For instance, in 1903, the National League club hosted Patriots Day and the American League club hosted Bunker Hill Day; in 1904, the Americans had the Patriots Day games and the Nationals had the Bunker Hill Day games.

Decoration Day, or Memorial Day as the holiday was increasingly called, was the flagship date among the three national holidays celebrated during the baseball season. Total attendance on Memorial Day typically exceeded the attendance levels on each of the other two holidays. For example, in a *Boston Globe* analysis of attendance during the 1906 season, Memorial Day attendance totaled 85,362 for the ballgames in the American League, higher than both the 77,991 level on Independence Day and 56,411 on Labor Day. In the National League, attendance on Memorial Day was 75, 538, topping 70,840 on Independence Day and 40,033 on Labor Day.[3]

Coming as it does first chronologically on the calendar, Memorial Day generated a certain degree of enthusiasm among baseball fans since the season was just a few weeks old and all ballclubs still had a chance to contend for the pennant. Ballclub owners also loved Memorial Day, since they could capitalize on that fan enthusiasm from a business perspective. Although general admission fees were split equally between the two contending teams on a holiday date, the host club fully captured the additional fees from grandstand and preferred seating as well as other ancillary revenue such as scorecards and concession purchases.

While Memorial Day was the plum holiday, Independence Day was a close runner-up in popularity. As seen in the 1906 attendance statistics noted above, the number of spectators at Independence Day ballgames was just a few thousand lower than those on Memorial Day. Labor Day was clearly the laggard among the three holiday dates on the baseball calendar. In 1906, attendance at Labor Day games was substantially lower than either of the other two holidays.

There was a brief attempt to add a fourth general holiday to the major-league baseball schedule—Columbus Day, on October 12. After the New York legislature established Columbus Day as a legal holiday in that state in 1909, Brooklyn president Charlie Ebbets lobbied hard to convince the other National League owners to extend the playing season into mid–October to take advantage of a fourth holiday. "A baseball day can be made of Columbus Day because the public wants some form of amusement on a holiday," Ebbets said. "It is up to the clubs to play morning and afternoon or doubleheaders in the afternoon on Columbus Day." Ebbets succeeded in getting the 1910 schedule extended to October 12, but only for a single game not a traditional holiday two-game set.[4]

Although two games were not scheduled on October 12, 1910, the makeup of a postponed game did permit a doubleheader to occur in Brooklyn, as "the

Dodgers and the [Boston] Doves celebrated Columbus Day by going through with a double-header at Washington Park." Attendance was fairly tepid by baseball's holiday standards, at just 5,000 for the last-day-of-the-season, two-for-one affair. Not only were spectators generally more interested in football by mid–October, but ballclubs could also be disinterested in regular-season games by this time. Over in Manhattan in 1910, the New York Giants closed out their regular season on October 11, seemingly unimpressed with the opportunity to play on Columbus Day. The Giants were more interested in getting ready for their post-season exhibition series slated to begin on October 13 with their cross-island foe, the Yankees of the American League.[5]

In 1911 Ebbets tried once more to create interest in a Columbus Day set of baseball games, this time arranging for the Dodgers to play the Giants on the holiday. While attendance increased slightly to 8,000, the attitude of the Giants showed little change from the previous year. Having clinched the 1911 National League pennant, the Giants were more concerned with preparing to battle the Philadelphia Athletics in the World Series. So, the Giants sleepwalked their way through two games, which were easily won by the Dodgers. The *New York Times* humorously considered the doubleheader sweep to be unusual since "Brooklyn doesn't take a doubleheader from the Giants any oftener than Columbus discovered America." In 1912, the National League moved to conclude the season earlier, on October 6, and thus ended Ebbets' experiment to play baseball on the Columbus Day holiday.[6]

Given its late-season appearance on the calendar and lower attendance dynamics than the other two holidays, Labor Day was the first of the three holidays where ballclubs made a concerted effort to convert from separate-admission morning and afternoon games to a single-admission doubleheader in the afternoon. The competition for spectator dollars in the cities that hosted franchises in both the National and American Leagues helped to fuel the conversion of Labor Day games to doubleheader status. In 1902, when the two leagues were feuding, the Chicago White Sox of the American League and the Philadelphia Phillies of the National League both staged single-admission doubleheaders on Labor Day. The following year there were two more Labor Day doubleheaders hosted by Cincinnati and the St. Louis Browns.

On Labor Day in 1903 there was also a rekindling of the home-and-home holiday series that clubs had tried in the 1880s. "The Brooklyn and New York National League teams played two games yesterday," the *New York Tribune* reported the day after the holiday. "The first game was played in the morning at Washington Park, Brooklyn, and was won by the Giants by a score of 6 to 4. The second game took place at the Polo Grounds...." The morning match in Brooklyn attracted a decent crowd (9,300) while 23,623 people attended the afternoon contest on the Giants home turf. The two clubs had hoped to derail the efforts of the New York Highlanders in the American

League to stage morning and afternoon games at Hilltop Park on the holiday. The two Manhattan-based ballclubs directly arm-wrestled for spectators on Labor Day in 1905 and 1906, each staging single-admission matches on the holiday before reverting in 1907 to the traditional morning and afternoon games.[7]

The St. Louis Cardinals established more of a long-term trend in Labor Day scheduling by hosting single-admission doubleheaders in 1905 and 1907. Frank Robison, one of the St. Louis ballclub owners, was an avowed advocate of doubleheaders "to increase the popularity of baseball." The prevalence of Sunday doubleheaders in St. Louis stemmed from Robison's beliefs. "I am in favor of playing doubleheaders on every Saturday afternoon and doubleheaders on Sunday as well where Sunday baseball is allowed," Robison said in 1907. "When a man goes to a ball game he wants to get there early. He doesn't want to be sitting around and watching the players practice. He wants base ball." From that perspective, it was a natural extension to play a doubleheader on a holiday.[8]

The Cardinals were one of the first ballclubs to target a working-class audience, rather than middle-class businessmen that dominated the spectator strategy of most other ballclubs at the time. The "man" that Robison referred to in his statements above was the average worker, which the *St. Louis Post-Dispatch* profiled in a 1902 article entitled "Bleacherite Is the Critic." The writer, who sat in the bleacher section at a game, described the spectator as "sunburnt, back-bent, squint-eyed, neck-strained, harsh-voiced" who wore an open shirt (and never a coat) with a straw hat on his head and handkerchief around his neck to stay cool. "The food of the Bleacherite is peanuts, his drink is beer—in bottles, his amusement is roasting Jesse Burkett or some other leftfielder," the writer described the spectator's sustenance. "He is THE critic. It is up to him to see that there is fair play, that his pitcher gets encouragement, that the opposing players hear his opinions of them," the writer continued. "Baseball, the greatest of games in the greatest of countries, and its future is in the hands of the Bleacherite, and he is equal to the task."[9]

The conversion of holiday ballgames in St. Louis to single-admission status from two separate contests was driven by consumer conditioning. The prevalence of Level 1 doubleheaders to make up postponed games and Level 2 doubleheaders to increase attendance on Sundays gave the St. Louis baseball spectator ample opportunity to see two games for the price of one. And the Cardinals were a lousy team back then—usually finishing in last or next-to-last place in the standings—so the ballclub owners needed to work at attracting fans to the ballgames since the team's winning ways couldn't be used. Two separate-admission games on a holiday—a perfect day to appeal to average workers—could no longer be tolerated from a marketing perspective. The St. Louis experience set the foundation for all holiday ballgames to eventually be played as single-admission doubleheaders.

St. Louis was the first ballclub to break the separate-admission mold for contests played on Independence Day, when the Cardinals hosted a single-admission doubleheader with Cincinnati on July 4, 1908. The Cardinals played nine other doubleheaders at home during the 1908 season—five Sunday ones, two on Saturday, and two during the workweek—so the pattern from a spectator perspective was clear. One of those Sunday doubleheaders occurred on July 5, the day after the holiday, so it was even clearer that a separate-admission two-game set on July 4 would be perceived unfavorably compared to the two-for-one offer the next day. This was especially the case given the competition on July 5, since the league-leading St. Louis Browns played a one-game homestand that Sunday. If Robison hadn't died in September 1908, the trend of single-admission doubleheaders on the Fourth of July might have expanded faster than it did among major-league ballclubs.[10]

The Cardinals resumed Independence Day doubleheaders in 1912, but other ballclubs didn't emulate them until 1913, when the Chicago Cubs and St. Louis Browns duplicated the Cardinals' holiday-scheduling strategy. Rather than play morning and afternoon games, the *Chicago Tribune* reported that "the Cubs and Reds will telescope their holiday bill into a doubleheader in the afternoon beginning at 1:30 o'clock." By 1913, Sunday doubleheaders were an ordinary aspect of the baseball spectator's life in both Chicago and St. Louis (nearly a dozen staged in 1912), making the holiday two-game set with separate admissions standout as an antiquated anomaly.[11]

In 1914, the Chicago Cubs and St. Louis Browns were the first ballclubs in the National and American Leagues in the twentieth century to play a single-admission doubleheader on Memorial Day, the flagship holiday on the major-league baseball calendar. Part of the reasoning was competition from the Federal League, a third major league that had begun operating that year, which had placed ballclubs in several cities to compete directly with the two established major leagues. Chicago was one of those cities. "Instead of the morning and afternoon games arranged by the schedule makers, the Cubs and Cardinals will clash in a double header on the west side this afternoon," the *Chicago Tribune* reported. "The bargain entertainment is carded as a counter attraction to the twin bill booked by the Chifeds" at the new Weeghman Park on the city's north side.[12]

The Federal League helped to accelerate the movement to single-admission status for the two games played on a holiday. At least one-half of the four holiday matches played by the eight ballclubs in the Federal League during its two-year tenure 1914–1915 were conducted on a single-admission basis. On Memorial Day in 1914, the Chicago and St. Louis clubs in the Federal League announced that they would play single-admission doubleheaders on the holiday, forcing the Cubs and Browns to do likewise to attract spectators. All four holiday matches on Independence Day in 1914 in the Federal League were doubleheaders, as were three-fourths of the Labor Day matches.

The competition from the Federal League spawned a plethora of Labor Day doubleheaders in the National and American Leagues in 1914, as the Cubs and four other ballclubs carded them, including Cleveland and Detroit in the American League. Single-admission holiday doubleheaders exploded in 1915, as six such events were staged in the National League and four in the American League. Five of them were conducted on Independence Day, as the established two leagues fought to stave off the Federal League. Brooklyn joined the fray by arranging for a single-admission event at two-year-old Ebbets Field, in the face of competition from a home-and-home holiday card between the Brooklyn and Newark, New Jersey, ballclubs in the Federal League on all three holidays that year.[13]

For ballclubs in eastern cities that couldn't play Sunday games, it was hard to ignore the economic merits of separate-admission games on a holiday. For example, when the Boston Braves were charging toward the National League pennant in 1914, a Labor Day doubleheader in Boston drew 35,000 for the morning game and 38,000 for the afternoon game, for an enormous 70,000+ attendance for the two holiday ballgames. The Braves borrowed Fenway Park from the Red Sox, since it was impossible for such a large crowd to fit into the tiny South End Grounds facility.[14]

But that was also the problem. The new ballparks built during the 1909–1915 period were designed to accommodate large, but infrequent, crowds during the season. Ballclubs played for the two or three huge attendance dates. There was a new economic model for ballclub owners: (1) bulk up on Opening Day and holidays; (2) feast on Sunday games (if legally permitted), Saturdays, and doubleheaders; and (3) try to weather single games played Monday through Friday.

Large attendance figures were usually associated with winning teams. For example, in the 1906 attendance analysis noted earlier, the Chicago Cubs and the Chicago White Sox were the top-drawing teams in each league—and the only ones to top 500,000 in home attendance—and not coincidentally were the pennant-winners in each league that year. The next largest component of attendance was holidays. In 1906 holiday games represented about eight percent of league-wide attendance. In the American League, total attendance for the three holidays was 219,764; for the entire year, clubs drew 2,787,404. In the National League, total attendance for the three holidays was 180,413; for the entire year, clubs drew 2,631,808. Holidays were even more significant at the individual club level. For example, in 1906, the Boston Red Sox drew 25,242 on Decoration Day and 14,525 on Labor Day; the combined total represented more than 10 percent of the club's total attendance of 413,298 for the season. Add in Opening Day, at 17,697, and the combination of holidays and Opening Day nearly equaled 15 percent of the season's total attendance. Add in the crowd from the Patriots Day holiday (12,125 at the morning game and 27,287 in the afternoon) and the proportion jumped to nearly 25 percent. The other 70 of the club's 77 home games comprised the remaining 75 percent.[15]

Several new ballparks were constructed during the 1909–1913 period, which offered more safety for spectators (they were steel and concrete rather than wooden) and more seating capacity. These new, bigger ballparks were designed not so much to accommodate the working man, but rather to handle multiple levels of seat pricing levels for various types of middle-class businessman and more prosperous spectators. Most of the new ballparks were located on trolley lines, but on the outskirts of the central business district and thus more convenient for businessmen than the average worker.

It was not by strategic planning, and only by accident, that this crop of larger ballparks contributed to future attendance growth through spectators of modest means. "A characteristic of the generation of owners that built or rebuilt early twentieth-century ballparks was that none was a member of an established late nineteenth-century upper-class family," Edward White wrote in *Creating the National Pastime*. "They were not interested in owning a baseball club in order to demonstrate that they were members of the idle rich. On the contrary, they were interested in owning a ball club in order that they might someday become members of the idle rich, and social lions in the process." Instead of actually working at being progressive and targeting the spectators of modest means, the ballclub owners for the most part chose deception.[16]

Owners and executives of ballclubs crafted an image of being philanthropists whose main concern was that baseball be "the embodiment of the values that make America great." However, behind the scenes, they "positioned themselves as the gatekeepers of the American way of life" by conniving with the media to highlight the so-called baseball creed. As Mitchell Nathanson described in his essay "Gatekeepers of Americana," baseball was good for America because the game "intermingled people from all walks of life" and its underlying virtues "could be used to instill the proper values in America's children as well as educate immigrants to the American way of life." The ballclub owners were much like John D. Rockefeller, the classic robber-baron-turned-philanthropist, in that they were far more akin to a ruthless businessman than social activist. They hoped to get rich as the former and be remembered as the latter. The big problem was that most baseball owners and executives in that era were not very good at forecasting needs for the future.[17]

Shibe Park in Philadelphia, the first of the new ballparks, opened in the spring of 1909, and could seat 23,000. "The lower stands held fifty-five hundred steel folding chairs, the upper forty-five hundred," Bruce Kuklick described the facility in his book *To Everything a Season: Shibe Park and Urban Philadelphia*. "In right and left field astride the foul lines two bleacher sections had rows of wooden benches embedded in the reinforced concrete. The twenty-five-cent bleachers held thirteen thousand." While Kuklick quoted Philadelphia Athletics owner Ben Shibe as believing that those "who live by the sweat of their brow should have as good a chance of seeing the game as the man who never had to roll up his sleeves to earn a dollar," Shibe seemingly thought they would be part of the 7,000 in the standing-room section at the back of the bleachers or among the 10,000 that could stand on an embankment in the outfield as part of an overflow crowd.[18]

Forbes Field in Pittsburgh was the next new ballpark to open, in the summer of 1909. In addition to an expansive two-tier grandstand and nominal bleacher sections, Forbes Field also touted the availability of box seats for more prosperous spectators. There were 263 boxes, each with eight seats, which were placed on the roof tier and lined the main and balcony tiers of the grandstand.[19]

When Comiskey Park in Chicago opened in the summer of 1910, it had four types of seating—boxes, grandstand, pavilion, and bleachers—which set the pace for the other new ballparks to follow, such as Fenway Park in Boston (1912), Navin Field in Detroit (1912), the refurbished Polo Grounds in New York (1911), and Ebbets Field in Brooklyn (1913). Of the 35,000 seats at Comiskey Park, 6,400 were in the boxes, where Chicago's commercial and political elite paid a dollar, or more, for each seat. The grandstand contained 12,600 seats (at 75 cents), the pavilion had 9,000 seats (at 50 cents), and the bleachers could hold 7,000 (at 25 cents). As Robin Faith Bachin related in her book *Building the South Side*, "This pricing policy effectively confined the working-class fans to the bleachers, reserving the grandstand and pavilion for white-collar and middle-class spectators."[20]

Attendance at major-league ballgames had doubled during the first decade of the twentieth century—if the newspaper reports can be believed—shooting up from 3.6 million spectators in 1901 to 7.2 million in 1909. Ballclub owners apparently believed that their targeting of white-collar businessmen as spectators would continue to increase attendance, and thus built their new ballparks to accommodate that growth. "The game was growing up, and patrons were no longer willing to put up with nineteenth century conditions," Barney Dreyfuss, owner of the Pittsburgh ballclub, explained why he built Forbes Field. "Besides, the park was located in a poor neighborhood, and many of the better class of citizens, especially when accompanied by their womenfolk, were loath to go there." There was a flaw, however, in the strategy.[21]

As David Nasaw noted in his book *Going Out: The Rise and Fall of Public Amusement*, by 1908 attendance "was not only higher than ever before but as a percentage of the population of the area served by big-league clubs higher than it would ever be in the future." And the owners were raising ticket prices, not lowering them. "At a time when other commercial amusement centers were beginning to eliminate distinctions between customers (heading to a one-price movie-theater policy), the baseball club owners were emphasizing them by segregating the cheap from expensive seats." The ballclub owners seemed to be more concerned with minimizing the corrosive effects of the ballgames played during the workweek than maximizing the positive impact of huge crowds on the few dates each year that filled the new ballparks. Nasaw summarized the tenuous economic position that the ballclub owners had created for themselves, when he wrote, "Though the baseball clubs could have boosted admissions and profits as the vaudeville halls had by increasing the number of cheap seats, they did not."[22]

With the collapse of the Federal League after the 1915 season, most ballclub owners canned the single-admission doubleheader for holiday games in 1916 and reverted back to the morning-and-afternoon approach. However, the entry of the United States into World War I sparked a retreat to single-admission doubleheader status for holiday dates during the 1917 and 1918 seasons. Soon thereafter, though, the separate-admission holiday two-game set was inexorably transformed into an endangered species by 1926 and ultimately was defunct by 1935.

9

Maturity of Doubleheaders

By 1909, THE DOUBLEHEADER was a central part of the major-league playing season, with nearly one-third of all ballgames conducted in a two-per-day format, up from one-quarter of all ballgames ten years earlier (see Appendix C for details). Not that the initial schedule of either league in 1909 was replete with two-games-on-one-day festivities. Contests on the three national holidays (plus the two Boston-specific holidays), usually staged as separate-admission events, represented only four percent of the scheduled games. There were also 13 non-holiday twosomes on the initial schedule, usually staged as single-admission events, which comprised another two percent of the schedule.

Most of the non-holiday scheduled doubleheaders were included to compensate for the lack of Sunday baseball in the eastern cities of both leagues. For example, when Pittsburgh visited St. Louis, Chicago, or Cincinnati, the ballclubs could schedule four games over four days, with the series finale on a Sunday, since Sunday baseball was legal in those three western cities. However, when Pittsburgh visited Philadelphia, New York, or Boston, four games would have to be squeezed into three days before the series ended on Saturday, since Sunday baseball was not yet legal in these eastern cities. Thus, Pittsburgh had doubleheaders on the schedule for Friday, July 9, in New York and on Saturday, July 24, in Boston. There were a few Saturday twin bills, slated by eastern clubs, and one Sunday doubleheader on the 1909 schedule, slated for August 15 when Brooklyn visited St. Louis. This scheduled Sunday doubleheader seemingly was an experiment in regard to a proposal that was floated in 1910 to expand the length of the season.

The majority of two-games-on-one-day activity in 1909 resulted from the ad hoc scheduling of doubleheaders to make up postponed and tied games. These Level 1 doubleheaders clogged up the playing calendar during the months of August and September, since frequent rains earlier in the season had created numerous postponements. "Bad weather has so far played havoc with the schedules of the two leagues, no less than 30 games having been postponed because of rain or cold," the *Boston Globe* reported less than three weeks into the 1909 season. "This means a lot of double-headers for the leaders when they get going well" later in the season. The Washington ballclub wound up playing eight consecutive doubleheaders from July 27 through August 5, to set an American League record.[1]

There were also a few Level 2 doubleheaders in 1909, as ballclubs sought to take advantage of Sunday baseball whenever possible. Pittsburgh arranged for several one-day road trips on the National League schedule to play Sunday games in Chicago and Cincinnati between its matches in Pittsburgh on Saturday and Monday. Some of these one-game stands turned into two-game stands, such as the May 2 and May 30 doubleheaders in Chicago, by advancing other games slated for later in the season. A more obvious example of finagling with the schedule was Cleveland's May 9 Sunday doubleheader in Chicago, between Cleveland's home matches on Saturday and Monday; neither ballclub had been scheduled for even one game on that Sunday.

Given the significant number of ballgames played during the season as single-admission doubleheaders at the dawn of the 1910s, it became increasingly challenging for ballclubs to justify conducting separate admissions for two games on a holiday. Several teams already conducted Labor Day games on a single-admission basis, such as the New York Giants who played their Labor Day twosome in 1909 on a two-for-one basis. The St. Louis Cardinals had broken the mold on Independence Day in 1908; the Chicago Cubs would do so on Memorial Day in 1914.

Attendance at major-league baseball games reached an all-time high of 7.2 million in 1909, which was double the volume of spectators who had attended ballgames just eight years earlier in 1901. However, combined attendance at National and American League games would not exceed that 1909 figure for another decade, until a pudgy pitcher-turned-outfielder named Babe Ruth donned a Yankee uniform in 1920 and began swinging for the fences at the Polo Grounds in the second year of legal Sunday baseball in New York City. Sunday baseball was a huge driver of overall attendance figures in the western cities of the two leagues. However, without the ability to legally stage Sunday games in eastern cities, ballclubs often resorted to doubleheaders to attract spectators to the ballpark. As legal Sunday baseball slowly crept eastward during the 1910s and 1920s, the separate-admission morning game on a holiday decreased in economic value as multiple Sunday dates during a season supplanted one or two holiday dates as the primary generator of overall attendance.[2]

In 1910, the doubleheader was nearly institutionalized into the major-league schedule, when Brooklyn club president Charlie Ebbets proposed that the National League expand the playing season from 154 games to 168. Ebbets' plan to handle the majority of the additional 14 games was to schedule doubleheaders on Sunday in the western cities and on Saturday in the eastern cities where Sunday baseball was still prohibited by law. This would have created a fixed number of ten or so doubleheaders for each ballclub. A big concern was how the new doubleheaders would integrate with existing circumstances. "The long schedule would give us double headers about half the season," Pittsburgh president Barney Dreyfuss remarked at the time, "considering the number of games we would have to double up on as the result of wet weather." What Dreyfuss was really saying was that he didn't want the appeal of his new Forbes Field ballpark to be its cheaper seats. Dreyfuss didn't see the demand for doubleheaders from the core of his wealthier fans.[3]

Ebbets had a different perspective on attendance. "Mr. Ebbets admits the great number of double headers, but defends his position by saying the public favors these bargain day entertainments," the *New York Times* reported on Ebbets' proposal before the National League meeting in New York in February 1910. However, only the owners of a few ballclubs were willing to use the doubleheader as a promotional tactic to encourage more fans to attend ballgames in the inexpensive seats at the ballpark rather than continue to focus primarily on more prosperous fans. Siding with Ebbets were the owners of the Chicago and St. Louis ballclubs, which already played a number of Sunday doubleheaders each season, along with the ownership of the Philadelphia Phillies.[4]

Discussions about a possible 168-game schedule caused a delay in the adoption of the National League schedule for 1910. After the owners remained deadlocked on the proposed lengthening of the schedule, they agreed to continue the existing 154-game schedule but extended the schedule to mid–October so that the new Columbus Day holiday could be accommodated. "It would be a great mistake to fill up the season with too many doubleheaders," *Sporting Life* editorialized. "If this idea is carried too far, it may be so, by and by, that the big crowd will only go when doubleheaders are being played and will not feel that they are getting enough for their money if there is only one game in the afternoon." That concern would be put to the test in the next few years.[5]

A turning point in the history of the doubleheader came in May 1914 when the city of Cleveland changed from the Central Time Zone to the Eastern Time Zone. The extra hour of evening daylight in Cleveland ensured that nearly all doubleheaders at League Park would result in two complete games. The additional hour of daylight also reduced the number of tie games in Cleveland, which would need to be replayed as the second contest of a doubleheader. In 1915, the city of Detroit also switched from the Central Time

Zone to the Eastern Time Zone, with similar benefits to matches played at Navin Field. These de facto efforts to replicate what we now know as daylight saving time created the impetus for ballclub owners to support the nascent daylight saving movement in this country. As Michael O'Malley noted in his book *Keeping Watch: A History of American Time*, "businesses involved in recreation, like baseball leagues, for example, stood to gain dramatically from extended daylight." If ballclubs could start their games at 4:30 P.M. rather than 3:30 P.M., they would attract more office workers as spectators, and thus increase attendance and profits, which O'Malley termed "a perfect example of the charms of saving daylight, especially for the wallets of baseball leagues and team owners."[6]

Combined with a change in Ohio law in 1911 that finally permitted Sunday baseball within the city of Cleveland, the time-zone switch helped to increase the popularity not only of doubleheaders during the workweek but also on Sunday. The extra daylight in Cleveland late in the season on September 27, 1914, ensured that both ends of a Sunday doubleheader at League Park against the New York Yankees could be completed in their entirety—and that Nap Lajoie could collect his 3000th lifetime base hit that day. Before 1914, there was a fair chance that the second contest might have been curtailed by darkness before nine innings could be played.[7]

The emergence of the Federal League in 1914 as a third major league also changed the character of the doubleheader. The Federal League substantially modified the cost aspect of the basic economic model of the established major leagues. "The Federals offered [players] an avenue of escape from the hated reserve clause and resulted in significantly higher salaries all around the league," Marc Okkonen wrote in his history of the Federal League. "Owners were forced to tear up existing contracts and raise the stakes to avert defection by star players." With higher expenses, the ballclub owners needed greater revenues to make money.[8]

However, the Federal League used the doubleheader concept to help attract spectators to its ballgames so that it could solidify its position as a major league. Franchises in the Federal League had a greater propensity to stage single-admission doubleheaders on the holidays, as discussed in Chapter Eight. This action forced ballclubs in the National and American Leagues where there were competing Federal League clubs to convert their separate-admission events to single-admission status in order to remain competitive. The Federal League also liberally used scheduled Saturday doubleheaders and ad hoc Sunday twin bills to bolster the league's attendance prospects.

Until 1914, the scheduled Saturday doubleheader had been a technique used only by eastern ballclubs, particularly in Boston, to compensate for the lack of legal Sunday baseball in their cities. The Federal League scheduled

Saturday doubleheaders in western cities such as Chicago, St. Louis, and Kansas City to extend this concept beyond the eastern seaboard. On Saturday, August 21, 1915, the league went so far as to schedule three Saturday twin bills.

The Sunday doubleheader in the East was one of the Federal League's lasting legacies following its demise after the 1915 season. By placing a franchise in Newark, New Jersey, for the 1915 season, the Federal League brought Sunday baseball on a legal basis at the major-league level to within a short train ride from New York City. It was the farthest east that continuous Sunday baseball had been played in 25 years, since Brooklyn last played Sunday games at Ridgewood Park in Queens during 1889 in its final year in the American Association. To accomplish this feat, the Federal League orchestrated the move of the 1914-pennant-winning, but deeply indebted, Indianapolis club to Newark. The new club was christened the Newark Peppers and played its games in a new 21,000-seat stadium a short distance from downtown Newark in adjoining Harrison.

Schedulers accommodated the Newark club by providing for 17 Sunday dates within the 26-week schedule; many of the Sunday dates consisted of a one-game series to optimize the attendance prospects from the massive population of the nearby New York City metropolis. Baltimore traveled by train into Newark four times for one-game stands, while the Buffalo club did likewise twice. However, spectators did not flock to the Peppers' Sunday games due to the perceived difficulty of getting to Harrison, New Jersey. So, to attract more spectators, the Peppers began to play doubleheaders on Sunday. The first Sunday doubleheader was on June 13, and the Peppers played nine Sunday twin bills in all.[9]

The other Federal League clubs that could play legal Sunday baseball emulated the efforts of the Peppers to play Sunday doubleheaders; it wasn't unusual to have two or three doubleheaders on the Federal League Sunday card in 1915. Due to this Sunday activity, along with a proliferation of postponed games, the three major leagues in 1915 played 33 percent of their games via a two-games-on-one-day format, the highest percentage since the first doubleheader was played in 1882. This magnitude of doubleheaders wouldn't be topped until the Great Depression.

While the Federal League was trying to draw crowds with Sunday doubleheaders, legal fees associated with the Federal League's anti-trust lawsuit against the National and American Leagues, along with other legal actions against individual clubs, pushed Federal League franchises to the brink of bankruptcy. The Federal League settled the lawsuits in December 1915 and then went out of existence. As part of the legal settlement, the ballparks owned by the Federal League clubs become the property of Organized Baseball. Today, the most famous remnant of the Federal League is Weeghman Park, which eventually became Wrigley Field after the Chicago Cubs began to play its home games there in 1916.

Competition from the Federal League was not the only competition faced by major-league ball clubs on holidays and Sundays, as other entertainment activities started to play a more prominent part of the life of many potential ballpark spectators. By 1915, not only had the Federal League caused consternation with the two older major leagues by its scheduling of doubleheaders, the motion-picture theater emerged as a legitimate entertainment option for many of spectators that usually attended afternoon ballgames.

Two decades after the invention of the Vitascope by Thomas Edison in 1896, the movie venue had graduated from its lowbrow nickelodeon roots into an opulent edifice dubbed a movie palace, with sophisticated-sounding names such as Bijou, Majestic, and Grand. The movie palaces were built only to show movies, and they created the atmosphere for movie-goers that "when you enter these portals you stray magically from the dull world of confusion and cares into a fairy palace whose presiding genius entertains you royally." The first movie palaces were the Regent and the Strand, which opened in New York City in 1913 and 1914, respectively. The movie palaces "started a new style in motion picture theaters: comfortable seats, thick rugs, elegant lounges, velvet draperies, gilt-and-marble ornamentation—all the trappings of wealth that had previously belonged to a select few in the orchestra of a legitimate theater—and all for twenty-five cents." The success of the Regent and the Strand was largely due to their manager, Samuel Roxy, who would go on to become a movie theater mogul. Baseball now had serious competition for the entertainment dollar.[10]

Expansion of the movie palace concept accelerated in 1915 when the full-length silent epic *Birth of a Nation* thrilled movie-goers nationwide. Air-conditioned theaters emerged in 1916 (in Chicago, borrowed from the refrigeration experiments at the Chicago meat markets), which allowed patrons to escape the summer heat. Why sit in an uncomfortable wooden seat at the ballpark and swelter in the sun when you could sit in a plush seat in an air-conditioned movie theater? It was a question some baseball fans began to ask. For two games of a doubleheader, fans would perhaps swelter in a wooden seat; they were less inclined to do so for a single ballgame.

World War I was the next big influence on the expansion of the doubleheader concept. As a wartime measure, the United States adopted daylight saving time in March 1918, after several years of lobbying for the time change by various organizations. National League president John Tener spoke in favor of daylight saving time in early 1917 when he said, "I am one of those who believe that recreation, either the participation in it actively, or in witnessing some form of sport, is an absolute essential to life." Daylight saving time in all major-league cities (except Detroit, which had recently changed time zones to increase daylight year-round) led to fewer tie games caused by darkness that needed to be replayed as doubleheaders and fewer doubleheaders shortened by darkness. After the war ended, although Congress abolished national daylight saving time in August 1919, several states—notably Massachusetts and New York—retained daylight saving time on a local basis.[11]

After a reversion to separate-admission holiday two-game sets in 1916 following the demise of the Federal League, single-admission holiday doubleheaders regained popularity during the war years of 1917 and 1918 as ballclubs sought to attract spectators to empty ballparks. Cincinnati hosted a Memorial Day doubleheader in 1917, the club's first holiday home game in five years. There were Independence Day doubleheaders in St. Louis in 1917 and 1918, staged by the Browns and Cardinals, respectively. On Labor Day 1918—the last day of the regular season due to a premature wartime ending—five of the eight holiday matches were conducted as single-admission doubleheaders. This was a distinct turning point in the admission status of holiday ballgames, for after World War I ended, some eastern ballclubs began to regularly schedule single-admission doubleheaders on holidays, while other clubs continued with the traditional structure of morning and afternoon games.

A primary reason for the change to single-admission holiday doubleheaders after World War I was that legal Sunday baseball arrived on the East Coast. With legal blessing for Sunday baseball in Washington, D.C., in 1918 and New York in 1919, there was far less financial importance attached to the morning contest of a separate-admission two-game set on a holiday.

Sunday baseball became legal in Washington, D.C., in 1918 when the Board of Commissioners of the District of Columbia rescinded its regulations prohibiting Sunday games on May 14. The Board cited as its reasons for permitting Sunday baseball the large increase in the population of the district since the war started and the need to provide recreation and amusement to this larger population. "Soldiers in and around Washington will benefit by the new regulations," the *Washington Post* noted. "Two thousand of them will be admitted free every Sunday and arrangements are being made to set aside a certain space for them which will enable them to see the games without even paying a war tax." On May 19 the Washington Senators hosted their first Sunday game.[12]

The war also spurred the legality of Sunday baseball in New York. In 1917, the three New York City ballclubs played benefit matches for war-relief organizations, seeking special dispensation to schedule the games on Sunday in order to maximize contributions. Charlie Ebbets was arrested at Brooklyn's benefit game on July 1 and was subjected to a trial for his alleged misdeeds in hosting such a game. At the New York Giants' benefit game on August 19, Giants managers John McGraw and Cincinnati Reds manager Christy Mathewson were summoned to appear in court for violating the

Sunday law. The judge "not only exonerated McGraw and Mathewson of any guilt in playing on Sunday, but commended the managers for lending their services to such a patriotic cause." Because the arrest of Mathewson—a former star pitcher for the Giants, hero to many New Yorkers, and avowed abstainer from playing baseball on Sunday when he was a ballplayer—was considered an action way over the top, the movement to legalize Sunday baseball in New York soon bore fruit.[13]

Legalized Sunday baseball took two years to materialize in New York before Governor Al Smith signed the Sunday baseball law on April 19, 1919. "I realize that a very substantial portion of our people most conscientiously oppose permission to indulge in recreation or sports of any kind on Sunday," Smith said in a statement at the time of the signing. "I respect their opinions and I believe that in those opinions they are entirely conscientious." However, Smith went on to say, "I believe that before any class of our citizens should be given the right to impose their views upon this question, on which people so widely and conscientiously differ, upon those who disagree with them, they should, at least, represent the sentiment of the majority in their respective communities."[14]

To ameliorate the conservatives on the Sunday baseball issue, the New York law contained a "local option" provision, which allowed any city or town to prohibit Sunday baseball within its borders; the law also required cities and towns to affirmatively approve the playing of Sunday baseball. The Board of Alderman in New York City passed an ordinance on April 29 to permit Sunday baseball, as required by the new law. The vote was 64–0. Mayor John Hylan quickly signed the ordinance and on May 4, 1919, Sunday baseball at the major-league level finally occurred in New York.[15]

The Giants and Dodgers played the first legal major-league Sunday games in New York, before the largest crowds ever to witness games in either ballpark (outside of a World Series game)—35,000 at the Polo Grounds and 22,000 at Ebbets Field. "The two record crowds of yesterday formed the baseball public's verdict on a campaign for Sunday outdoor pastimes which has been going on for many years. Yesterday was the first time since Rip Van Winkle butted into the bowling party that folks have been able to see professional baseball without danger of being called before His Honor in the morning," the *New York Times* commented. "Those who have been skeptical about just how Sunday games would be received here were surprised that such a vast throng could come to the Polo Grounds on a Sunday afternoon, sit through two hours of baseball, and leave without any disorder or rowdyism."[16]

The two Boston franchises led the way among eastern clubs toward full adoption of the single-admission holiday doubleheader. After the Braves hosted a single-admission twin bill on Labor Day in 1918, the Red Sox did likewise in 1919. "Today's double-header will be something out of the ordinary," the *Boston Globe* reported. "Two games for the price of one admission on a holiday is something the [Red Sox] fans have not been treated to heretofore, and no doubt a big crowd will be out for the bargain day attraction." Although the single-admission event was staged out of necessity, because the Red Sox had traveled to Washington for a Sunday game the day before and didn't arrive back in Boston until Monday morning, the fans became accustomed to it. In 1921 the Braves and Red Sox began to conduct all their holiday events on a single-admission basis.[17]

The Bunker Hill Day holiday, celebrated on June 17 in Boston, was the first holiday to completely convert to single-admission status. After two decades of conducting two games on a separate-admission basis, the Bunker Hill Day games in 1921 were staged as a single-admission doubleheader. "Upwards of 25,000 enthusiastic fans saw the Red Sox win both games of the doubleheader with the Tigers yesterday afternoon," the *Boston Globe* reported on the first doubleheader of the season at Fenway Park. Part of the reason to switch the Bunker Hill Day games to a single-admission basis was competition from local baseball games, since there was an extensive schedule of high school and college matches on the holiday. The ballgame between Holy Cross and Boston College was slated for the late afternoon in 1921, while many high school contests, like the Somerville–Medford game, were played in the morning.[18]

The Patriots Day holiday celebrated in Boston was an exception to the secular trend of holiday scheduling, because there was an excellent reason to have a break between the two separate-admission games. Besides baseball, Patriots Day also featured the running of the Boston Marathon, whose route passed close to Fenway Park and Braves Field. The *Boston Globe* described the rationale for the scheduling of the two ballgames: "The morning one will start at 10:30 and the afternoon game at 3:30, the half hour delay being made to allow ball fans who wish to see the finish of the Marathon run a chance to see the road racers and then get to the ball park in time to see the beginning of the afternoon game." The intertwining of two baseball games with the Boston Marathon on Patriots Day kept the separate-admission holiday two-game set viable into the 1950s, long after its utility had been expunged for the three national holidays celebrated during the baseball season.[19]

The only tripleheader in major-league history—three games for the price of one admission—was played on October 2, 1920, when a three-game series between the Cincinnati Reds and Pittsburgh Pirates at Forbes Field was crammed into one day. In the previous two instances when three games had been played on one day (in 1890 and 1896), separate admissions were charged for a single game in the morning and a doubleheader in the afternoon.[20]

The 1920 tripleheader was originally slated to be a single game on Friday,

October 1, and a doubleheader on October 2, as a prelude to the Reds heading back to Cincinnati and the Pirates to Chicago to play Sunday games to finish the season. With the Reds in third place, three and a half games ahead of the fourth-place Pirates, Pittsburgh had faint hopes of finishing in third place if they could win their final four games and the Reds lost their last four. Finishing in third place was important, because the third-place club shared in the World Series pool, while the fourth-place club did not.

When the Friday game was rained out, Pittsburgh owner Barney Dreyfuss petitioned National League president John Heydler to play three games on Saturday. In an ironic twist, Dreyfuss, who was constitutionally averse to artificial doubleheaders, wanted to contrive a tripleheader. But since the motive of Dreyfuss in the situation seemed to be clearly oriented to competition and not attendance, Heydler authorized the unusual configuration of games.[21]

In the first game of the tripleheader, which started at noon, the Reds blasted the Pirates, 13–4, to quickly clinch third place and render the remaining two games moot as far as the final standings were concerned. Reds manager Pat Moran rested his regular players in the second and third games, by inserting a combination of reserves and pitchers into his lineup. Moran used three pitchers in the field in the second game: Dutch Ruether at first base, Fritz Coumbe in center field, and Rube Bressler in right field. For the record, the Reds won the second game while the Pirates won the third game.

A pivotal event in the history of the holiday doubleheader took place on July 4, 1923, when the New York Yankees staged a single-admission doubleheader on the Independence Day holiday at their three-month-old, 60,000-seat ballpark, Yankee Stadium. The grandiosely named ballpark—stadium was then a term reserved for unique, majestic playing grounds such as those built for the Olympics or a national exposition (and the football arena at Harvard)—was designed to allow more spectators in the cheap seats than did its predecessors like Shibe Park and Ebbets Field that needed to be expanded following their initial construction. Yankee Stadium had three tiers, with the first tier seating 25,000 people, the mezzanine tier 10,000, and the third tier another 10,000. The bleachers were advertised to seat 25,000. These figures from the spring of 1923 add up to 70,000, which turned out to be a bit higher than the actual number of available seats in the Bronx coliseum, which was closer to 60,000. Still, Yankee Stadium, with its triple decks that "majestically rise from the banks of the Harlem," could hold, by far, the largest crowd of any baseball arena in the country.[22]

Departing from the recent New York City tradition for holiday contests where separate-admission morning and afternoon games were conducted, the Yankees opted for a single-admission doubleheader, hoping to fill the stadium to capacity. The crowd gradually swept into Yankee Stadium for that Fourth of July doubleheader, as "what looked like a 25,000 throng at 1:30

was a full-fledged gathering of 45,000 by 3:30." A goodly portion of the holiday crowd sat in the least expensive sections of the ballpark. "It was noticeable that the bleacher attendance was the heaviest of the season except for that of the game which opened the big arena," the *New York Times* reported. "The first and second tiers were well congested, and the third tier held a good-sized audience." The Yankees had firmly established that the Boston way of conducting holiday games was definitely the new trend in holiday scheduling.[23]

The last traditional morning-afternoon ballgames on a holiday in New York City were staged on Memorial Day in 1923, when the New York Giants attracted 12,000 to their morning game and a reported 45,000 to the afternoon game. For their Labor Day games, the Yankees' intracity rivals, the New York Giants and Brooklyn Dodgers, both staged a single-admission doubleheader. In Manhattan, 40,000 people jammed into the expanded Polo Grounds to watch the Giants, while over in Brooklyn "more than 13,000 persons came out to see the holiday bargain bill." All five holiday twin bills in 1924 among the Yankees, Giants, and Dodgers were contested as single-admission doubleheaders.[24]

One driver of the conversion to single-admission status on the holidays was the logistics of emptying a decent-sized crowd from the ballpark after a morning game and preparing for a large crowd to re-enter for the afternoon contest. With many patrons using public transportation to get to Yankee Stadium, there was certain to

```
BASEBALL
```

YESTERDAY'S RESULTS.

NATIONAL LEAGUE.
Philadelphia 7, New York 4.
(First game.)
New York 14, Philadelphia 5.
(Second game.)
Brooklyn 8, Boston 3.
(First game.)
Boston 5, Brooklyn 1.
(Second game.)
Pittsburgh 4, St. Louis 1.
(Morning game.)
Pittsburgh 15, St. Louis 5.
(Afternoon game.)
Cincinnati 7, Chicago 1.
(First game.)
Cincinnati 4, Chicago 2.
(Second game.)

AMERICAN LEAGUE.
Philadelphia 9, New York 7.
(Morning game.)
Philadelphia 6, New York 5.
(Afternoon game ; 14 innings.)
Boston 9, Washington 4.
(Morning game.)
Washington 5, Boston 2.
(Afternoon game.)
Detroit 12, Cleveland 7.
(Morning game.)
Detroit 10, Cleveland 2.
(Afternoon game.)
Chicago 5, St. Louis 2.
(First game.)
Chicago 4, St. Louis 2.
(Second game.)

This score report of Memorial Day ballgames in 1925 from the *New York Times* illustrates the changing nature of holiday two-game sets in the major leagues in the 1920s. In 1925, half of the holiday twin bills were conducted as single-admission doubleheaders (first game/second game notations) while the other half were staged as traditional separate-admission matches (morning game/afternoon game notations).

be logjams on the train lines. A more significant driver of the single-admission holiday doubleheader at Yankee Stadium was the Yankees' profitability. Even before the ballclub moved into its own ballpark in 1923, the Yankees were a highly profitable organization due to the huge crowds at Sunday games at the Polo Grounds to see Babe Ruth. As Kenneth Winter and Michael Haupert wrote in their article "Yankees Profit and Promise," "Through the first five years of their ownership, Huston and Ruppert lost a total of $30,000. This was more than made up for in 1920, when the team turned a profit of more than $370,000." The turnaround was due to 1920 being the first year of legal Sunday baseball in New York City. The Yankees' profits reached nearly $500,000 in 1923, their first year in Yankee Stadium as crowds exceeding 50,000 attended the Sunday games at the new ballpark during the first three months of the season. The club also generated additional revenue from renting out the stadium for boxing matches and college football games. The Yankees didn't need two ballgames with separate admissions on a holiday to be immensely successful on the business side.[25]

Sunday games now usurped holiday contests as the more significant business driver of nearly all major-league ballclubs. Eleven of 16 teams could now play Sunday home games, and the other five (the Boston Braves and Red Sox, the Philadelphia Athletics and Phillies, and the Pittsburgh Pirates) had fairly lucrative Sundays through their one-game road trips to nearby Sunday-playing cities. The Braves and Phillies regularly played on Sunday in Brooklyn, the Athletics in Washington, and the Pirates in Cincinnati. With the western ballclubs now regularly playing holiday twin bills as a single-admission doubleheader, and the New York and Boston clubs as well in the East, the separate-admission holiday two-game set was on course for extinction. The three Pennsylvania-based franchises were the last holdouts for the single-admission holiday doubleheader, since Sunday baseball was prohibited in Pennsylvania before the 1934 season; the Phillies converted in 1930 while the Athletics and Pirates held out until 1935.

The Yankees set the standard for large crowds in the 1920s. At the Independence Day doubleheader in 1927, "the biggest crowd in history, more than 74,000 persons, stampeded into the Yankee Stadium yesterday afternoon to watch the Yanks inflict a fearful beating on the Senators in both sections of the holiday doubleheader." The *New York Times* went on to report, "There never was a World Series crowd that approached this record breaking assemblage, for the reason that in the World Series the management did not dare to pack the cash customers in as solidly as they were packed yesterday." And it wasn't just Babe Ruth and Lou Gehrig that attracted spectators. The stadium's location, on subway lines that connected to populous Manhattan and adjacent to the growing Bronx neighborhoods where middle-class residents fled the gritty urban areas of the city, contributed to the ability of the "skyscraper among baseball parks" to attract huge throngs of people.²⁶

While the Yankees attracted large crowds for their holiday doubleheaders and single Sunday games at Yankee Stadium, the occasional Level 1 Sunday doubleheader could result in an enormous crowd. The September 9, 1928, doubleheader with the Philadelphia Athletics set an attendance mark that wasn't topped for more than two decades. The headline on the *Times* sports page was "Crowd of 85,265, Baseball Record, Sees Yanks Win Two," which adorned the game account about how the Yankees had defeated the league-leading Athletics and left 100,000 more on the streets outside the stadium seeking admission. The Yankees went on that month to capture their third straight American League pennant, and sixth within the past eight years. "Jake Ruppert's team had staked a position in the baseball business that almost no other franchise could hope to challenge," Neil Sullivan wrote in his book, *The Diamond in the Bronx*. "The commercial significance of Yankee Stadium was evident from day one. Even the accurate count of 60,000 in attendance was far greater than any other ballpark for Opening Day in 1923 ... the first game at Yankee Stadium was roughly equivalent to all the other Opening Day crowds in the rest of the American League together." The doubleheader was just one beneficiary of that success.²⁷

Fueling the expansive crowds at the ballpark were shorter workweeks for the middle class and working class people—generally reduced to 45 hours in the 1920s from 60 hours in the 1890s—which "provided ordinary Americans with both more leisure time and more disposable income to spend on an ever-expanding variety of recreational activities." Given the breadth of entertainment options that were available as emerging competition to baseball, the crowds at doubleheaders were all the more astounding. Amusement parks such as those on Coney Island in Brooklyn and the trolley parks located outside of other cities had flourished over the previous decades. Beaches beckoned potential bleacher spectators with their cool breezes in the comparison to the often stifling conditions in the crowded ballparks during midsummer. Professional boxing, especially the popularity of Jack Dempsey, and the rise of college football competed for the dollars spent at the ballpark. And there was also the movie theater.²⁸

The golden age of the movie palace hit its zenith in 1927 when two events occurred. In March the 6,200-seat Roxy Theater opened at 50th Street and 7th Avenue in New York City. This movie palace, the size of an average ballpark just 25 years earlier, signified the height of the theater-building trend that saw the country "dotted with a thousand Xanadus decreed by some local (or chain-owning) Kubla Khan, [whose] pleasure domes gave expression to the most secret and polychrome dreams" of their owners. There were movie palaces in all the major-league cities, such as the Albee in Cincinnati, the Fox in Detroit, and the Capital in Chicago. In October the *Jazz Singer* premiered as the first "talkie" movie, with its pictures coordinated with a sound track, which exponentially increased demand among movie-goers. The movie-going public could partake of these pleasures from late morning to midnight, at their pleasure, unlike the ballpark where the game was constrained to two hours in the late afternoon.[29]

In one way, the movie palaces spurred greater interest in attending ballgames through the newsreel, which boomed in 1919 when *Fox Movietone News* revolutionized the fledging technology. With the growing popularity of Babe Ruth, sports coverage represented the single largest category of film news, representing about one-quarter of all newsreel footage. "Americans could thus see the Babe in action almost as often as they went to a movie theater."[30]

While the Yankees were experiencing doubleheader success in September 1928, the Boston Braves were achieving historical futility with doubleheaders. Between September 4 and 16, the Braves set major-league records by playing in nine consecutive doubleheaders and losing five consecutive ones during that period.[31]

The Braves' bad luck began when the club's Labor Day doubleheader with Brooklyn on September 3 was rained out. "Thus the bad weather, which has vexed the Boston club all season, was consistent and persistent to the end," the *Boston Globe* commented on the holiday postponement. "Vexed" would turn out to be an appropriate term for the club's streak of twin bills. In the first of nine consecutive doubleheaders, the Braves lost both games to Brooklyn at Braves Field on September 4 before sweeping both games the following day. The Braves then moved on to Philadelphia for a previously scheduled doubleheader on September 6. However, rain canceled both games that day, necessitating twin bills on both September 7 and 8. After splitting the first doubleheader with the Phillies and losing both games in the second one, the Braves headed back to Boston.[32]

To make matters worse, the Braves were already slated to play four consecutive doubleheaders with the New York Giants, to make up postponed games from earlier in the season. "Doubleheaders are on the card for each day," the *Globe* reported. "Baseball fans should get their fill of bargain bills before the series comes to a close Thursday night." The Giants won all eight games among the four doubleheaders, in a series that extended to Friday because the Wednesday doubleheader was washed out. To get in the fourth doubleheader with the Giants, the Braves secured the agreement of the Chicago Cubs to cancel its scheduled Friday game with the Braves and combine it with Saturday's contest to create a ninth straight doubleheader. The Braves and Cubs split the Saturday twin bill, to end the Braves' five-doubleheader losing streak.[33]

A new term entered the doubleheader lexicon in the mid–1920s when "nightcap" was increasingly used to describe the second game of a doubleheader. While the traditional meaning of the term "nightcap" was a cloth cap worn to stay warm while sleeping, the term was also used to describe an alcoholic drink imbibed near the end of the day before going to sleep. Much like the original transformation of the term "doubleheader," it's not entirely clear how "nightcap" obtained its place in baseball terminology.

Baseball writers seeking a creative way to describe a game account sometimes used the alcoholic-drink connotation. "The Doves took the eye-opener, 4 to 3, and the Trolley Dodgers the nightcap, 6 to 0," the *Boston Globe* reported on a doubleheader in 1908. While the term was sporadically used in conjunction with baseball through the 1910s, "nightcap" was used more often beginning in 1920. This timing coincided with the effective date of the 18th Amendment to the United States Constitution, which outlawed the manufacture and distribution of alcoholic beverages. The timing also coincided with the national publicity given to Babe Ruth and his home-run–hitting prowess with the New York Yankees. Since there was widespread noncompliance with the 18th Amendment, and Ruth was reputedly a frequent non-compliant, the timing of the newspaper use of "nightcap" in the baseball sense was probably not coincidental. By 1926, newspapers across the country routinely described the second game of a doubleheader as a nightcap.[34]

Cleveland pitcher Dutch Levsen achieved ever-lasting fame in a nightcap at League Park on August 28, 1926, when he defeated the Red Sox, 4–3, in both games of a doubleheader. Levsen was the last man to pitch two complete-game victories in one day. With the Indians chasing the Yankees for the pennant, Levsen volunteered to work the second contest, informing manager Tris Speaker that his arm felt fine. In the 1920s it was still not unusual for a pitcher to work both games of a doubleheader; just two years earlier in 1924, both Herman Bell of the Cardinals and Urban Shocker of the Browns had pitched and won two games in one day. But Levsen turned out to be the last pitcher to accomplish that feat, yielding just four hits in each game against the Red Sox to cop two of his 16 victories that year.[35]

The *Boston Globe* heralded Levsen's performance with the headline "Indians Take Double-Header, Using Only One Pitcher" with a subhead "Levsen Humbles Sox Twice in an Afternoon." The *Globe*'s account indicated that Levsen didn't tire very much over the course of hurling 18 innings and surrendered just eight hits. "Levsen went through both games as if he were simply taking a workout," the *Globe* reported. The writer added that at one point during the second game a Cleveland fan shouted at the Boston bat boy, "Get in there and bat—see if you can't make a hit."[36]

Radio was a new technology that came into general use in the 1920s, which in certain major-league cities helped to spark the creation of more doubleheaders. Most ballclub owners thought radio broadcasts of ballgames would decrease the number of spectators in the stands at the ballpark. "They won't come to the park if you give the game away" was the oft-touted lament of the owners. However, a few owners believed that radio broadcasts of home games increased interest in their ballclubs and expanded the market for spectators to view games at the ballpark.

"The first owner to see radio's promise to boost fan interest was Cubs' boss William Wrigley," Paul Adomites wrote in his seminal article "Baseball on the Air." In 1925, Wrigley invited all Chicago radio stations to broadcast the Cubs games for free. Adomites added, "Sam Breadon, the Cardinals' owner, followed suit soon thereafter, in the first two attempts to develop regional followings." Wrigley and Breadon were not so much interested in broadcast rights fees, but rather the free publicity within the broadcasts that would generate additional attendance at the ballpark. Because St. Louis and Chicago were the westernmost ballclubs in the major leagues, they had a potential following not just from fans in the immediate urban area but also from outlying rural areas. Radio broadcasts encouraged fans in Iowa and Wisconsin to travel to Chicago to see the Cubs games; likewise, radio made Cardinals fans and future ballpark patrons out of listeners in Arkansas and Kentucky.[37]

Few other ballclub owners followed the lead of Wrigley and Breadon in embracing radio in the 1920s. "In general, teams in the eastern cities shied away from the radio, while those in the West embraced the new technology," Jules Tygiel wrote in *Past Time: Baseball as History*. "By the end of the decade, St. Louis, Cleveland, Detroit, Cincinnati, Boston, and Chicago all featured regular broadcasts of home games, but none of the New York, Washington, D.C., or Pennsylvania teams followed suit."[38]

Both the Cubs and the Cardinals staged Level 2 doubleheaders to encourage their new fans in outlying areas to attend ballgames. The Cubs focused those efforts on Saturday twin bills, to not dilute their drawing power on Sundays, while the Cardinals escalated their use of Sunday doubleheaders. For example, in 1926, the Cubs arranged a Saturday doubleheader on July 10 against Brooklyn prior to a single game between the two teams on Sunday. The Cardinals, on the other hand, played a single game that Saturday with Boston and then arranged for a doubleheader with the Braves on Sunday.

Breadon had gradually increased the number of Sunday doubleheaders that the Cardinals played each year during the 1920s. While the Cardinals had been playing Sunday doubleheaders on a regular basis since 1902, Breadon had a bigger financial motivation—the Cardinals were now a tenant, playing at Sportsman's Park that was owned by the Browns, and not the owner of a ballpark (their grounds had been sold to pay off ballclub debts).

The Cardinals started playing their games at Sportsman's Park in 1920; after seating in the ballpark was expanded in 1925 (the Browns had pennant hopes back then), Breadon arranged for more Sunday doubleheaders. He elevated his Sunday doubleheaders to Level 3 status in 1930, when every Sunday home game was staged as a doubleheader.

10

Scheduled Sunday Doubleheaders

By 1929 Sunday was the new holiday in baseball economics, because Sunday games increasingly drove both attendance and the bottom line for those franchises located in states that legally permitted Sunday baseball. Holiday games started to take a back seat on the accountant's ledger, as most ballclubs had abandoned the morning game of the traditional separate-admission holiday twin bill in favor of two afternoon games for a single admission.

Sunday began to transform from a single game to twin bill in the western cities where Sunday baseball had been played for four decades or more. In St. Louis, Cardinals owner Sam Breadon enhanced the Sunday doubleheader from Level 2 to Level 3 status in 1930, a strategy that generated future notoriety for St. Louis to be called the birthplace of the Sunday doubleheader. In fact, the Level 2 doubleheader had been around since the last few years of the American Association in the early 1890s, before its debut in the National League in 1892. Although Breadon was often considered to be the father of the Sunday doubleheader, he was more accurately the popularizer of that concept. As *The Sporting News* remarked about Breadon's strategy, "Sam Breadon has been the target for considerable raillery, because of his Sunday doubleheaders, but he knows his St. Louis and he knows its workers do not take afternoons off during the week for amusement."[1]

Breadon grew up in a tough part of New York City, near the docks in Greenwich Village, which led to his street-smart ways in running the Cardinals ballclub. "In the Ninth Ward I learned never to run away from a fight," Breadon told writer Dan Daniel in an interview after he had relinquished ownership of the ballclub in 1947. "I have followed that precept all my life. If there is a scrap in baseball, I don't dodge it." Breadon moved to St. Louis in 1904 to work at the world fair. Afterward, he worked as a car mechanic in the fledgling automobile business and eventually became prosperous by owning his own car dealership. With the Cardinals in a financial crisis after

World War I, Breadon along with other "civic-minded men" bought stock in the club to keep it in St. Louis. In 1920 Breadon, the largest stockholder, was elected president of the Cardinals.[2]

In the mid–1920s, because the Cardinals were a tenant at the Browns-owned Sportsman's Park, Breadon opted to schedule doubleheaders on Sundays with greater frequency than his rivals in either major league. This scheduling policy drew the ire of a number of other ballclub owners, who took to calling these Level 2 doubleheaders by the disparaging term "synthetic doubleheader" under the guise that these doubleheaders were, unlike a Level 1 contest, man-made rather than naturally formed (due to weather postponements). Daniel championed Breadon as the inventor of the synthetic doubleheader, writing in a 1947 article about doubleheaders in the postwar era, "With patronage for single games on Sundays not too opulent, Breadon adopted the stratagem of pulling games up to make double bills when there were no postponements with which to produce them in dear old St. Louis."[3]

Sunday doubleheaders just made good business sense for the Cardinals. "Even when the Cardinals were winning, their clientele was coy. St. Louis fans liked to spend the entire afternoon at the ballpark on a Sunday. Sam got in the habit of moving games forward to create those crowd-catchers," Daniel stated in a 1949 profile of Breadon. "From Boston to the Mississippi, Breadon was excoriated for his strictly financial maneuver. Baseball writers everywhere blasted Sam for his 'phony expedient.' But those synthetic double bills proved highly successful. The Cardinals ditto."[4]

The owners' wrath for Breadon's synthetic doubleheaders related more to his tactics and less about the concept. He'd often cancel a ballgame on questionable weather-related merits to ostensibly produce a Level 1 doubleheader. For example, in May 1928, a writer noted, "You could not have asked for a nicer day [in St. Louis], except that it was a trifle too warmish and rather sticky. A heavy dew fell in the morning and Maestro Breadon seized on this alleged rainfall as an excuse for calling off the ball game" to play a Sunday doubleheader. When the weather didn't cooperate with Breadon's desire to create a Level 1 Sunday doubleheader, he would "cancel Monday games with visiting clubs and set them back as part of Sunday doubleheaders" to create a Level 2 doubleheader. Because Breadon deployed both techniques on a regular basis throughout the season, they became Level 3 Sunday doubleheaders.[5]

Breadon had to resort to these practices because, amazingly, despite their popularity with ballpark spectators and radio listeners, Sunday doubleheaders in the 1930s rarely appeared on the initial season schedule. During the 1920s, there were only two Sunday doubleheaders prescheduled on the initial league calendars: August 15, 1920, in St. Louis and September 15, 1929, in Chicago. During the 1930s there were just sporadic sightings of Sunday doubleheaders on the initial schedules. The St. Louis Cardinals might have one Sunday doubleheader on the preseason schedule, usually one later in the season like the August 30 one with Pittsburgh on the 1931 schedule. It wasn't until 1939 that Sunday doubleheaders began to be incorporated into the official league schedules.

Breadon started the systematic creation of Level 3 Sunday doubleheaders late in the 1929 season, when he arranged for twin bills on the five Sundays (September 8 to October 6) during the Cardinals final homestand. For the 1930 season, Breadon arranged for a doubleheader on every Sunday during a Cardinals homestand. The Braves and the Reds also joined the Cardinals as regular creators of Sunday doubleheaders in 1930. With so many Sunday twin bills being created on an ad hoc basis, in addition to the inevitable weather-related postponements of games in the spring months, the National League periodically announced schedule revisions throughout the season. For example, in July 1930, the National League announced a dozen new doubleheaders, including two Sunday ones for the St. Louis Cardinals. In May 1931, the National League made numerous schedule adjustments, including the creation of three Sunday twin bills for the Boston Braves.[6]

St. Louis Cardinals owner Sam Breadon is considered to be the father of the synthetic doubleheader. Breadon elevated his strategy of occasional doubleheaders on Sunday in the 1920s into an every–Sunday occasion late in the 1929 season and throughout the 1930 season. Part of Breadon's motivation to regularly stage Sunday doubleheaders was that the Cardinals were a tenant at Sportsman's Park in St. Louis, which was owned by the American League's St. Louis Browns. (National Baseball Hall of Fame Library, Cooperstown, New York)

The Boston Braves were late entrants to the Sunday doubleheader sweepstakes. While Breadon began to institutionalize the Sunday doubleheader in the late 1920s, ballclubs located in Massachusetts and Pennsylvania still coped with just being able to play one game on Sunday. Massachusetts and Pennsylvania were the last states that hosted major-league baseball clubs to permit Sunday baseball, with legal prohibitions that weren't lifted until the 1929 and 1934 baseball seasons, respectively. Laws prohibiting Sunday sports went back more than a century in both states.

Sunday laws in Massachusetts were first established in 1650, but a harsher law was passed in 1671 that provided "whoever shall profane the Lord's day, by doing unnecessary servile work, by unnecessary travailing, or by sports and recreations, he or they that so transgress, shall forfeit for every such default forty shillings, or be publicly whipped." More significantly, this law also included the possibility of being put to death for playing a ballgame. "If it clearly appears that the sin was proudly, presumptuously and with a high hand committed, such a person therein despising and reproaching the Lord, shall be put to death or grievously punished at the judgment of the court." The Pennsylvania legislature passed a law in 1794 that provided a four-dollar fine or six-day imprisonment for people that performed "any worldly employment or business whatsoever on the Lord's day, commonly called Sunday, works of necessity and charity only excepted, or shall use or practice any unlawful game, hunting, shooting, sport or diversion whatsoever, on the same day."[7]

These laws persisted through the nineteenth century and remained in place to thwart Sunday baseball in both states throughout the first quarter of the twentieth century. In 1926, with nearly two-thirds of major-league clubs able to host baseball games on Sunday, there were concerted efforts in both Massachusetts and Pennsylvania to challenge the continued appropriateness of the ancient statutes prohibiting Sunday baseball.

In Pennsylvania, the Sesquicentennial Exposition, held in Philadelphia to celebrate the 150th anniversary of the signing of the Declaration of Independence in 1776, was open on Sundays, much to the dismay of Sabbatarian groups that believed the 1794 Sunday law should apply to the event, notwithstanding its national significance. After the Philadelphia Athletics obtained a judge's order to play a Sunday game at Shibe Park on August 22, the Pennsylvania Attorney General charged the Athletics with violating the 1794 Sunday law. The case was argued all the way to the Pennsylvania Supreme Court. On June 25, 1927, in a unanimous 7–0 vote in *Commonwealth v. American Baseball Club of Philadelphia*, the Supreme Court agreed with the Attorney General that baseball was worldly employment and thus the August 22, 1926, test game violated the 1794 Act.[8]

In Massachusetts, New York lawyer Emil Fuchs had purchased the Boston Braves in 1923. Since Fuchs had worked for the New York Giants and saw how successful Sunday baseball was in New York, he went right to work trying to obtain passage of a similar bill in Massachusetts. Rather than go the normal legislative route, which had been a fruitless venture, Fuchs, a capable lawyer, sought another legal route. With enough voter signatures on a petition, Fuchs could get a proposed law on the ballot for consideration by the voters even if the legislature disapproved of the matter. In August 1925, proponents of the ballot question submitted more than three times the number of required signatures to get the question on the November 1926 ballot. A snag, though, derailed that plan. Some of the petitions that voters signed referenced "Sunday baseball," while other petitions referenced "Sunday sports," the latter being the language in the actual ballot question. The Massachusetts Supreme Judicial Court, therefore, considered that there were two separate petitions and thus ordered the ballot question removed from the 1926 ballot.[9]

After the 1926 fiasco, proponents had no trouble obtaining the required number of signatures to put the matter on the 1928 ballot as a voter referendum. Massachusetts voters overwhelmingly approved Sunday sports on November 6, 1928, when Question 2 on Sunday sports garnered 803,281 "yes" votes to 467,550 "no" votes. There were a number of restrictions in the new Sunday sports law: games could be played only between 2:00 and 6:00 P.M., games could not be played within 1000 feet of a church, and under the "local option" provision, individual cities and towns also had to approve the playing of Sunday games.[10]

In the November election, the count of Boston voters was substantially in favor of the Sunday sports initiative by more than three-to-one (172,800 to 54,418). However, after two inexplicable delays by the Boston City Council, allegations surfaced that a city councilor had solicited a bribe from Fuchs in order to approve Sunday baseball. The alleged bribe occurred on November 23, two weeks following voter approval of the ballot referendum, when City Councilor William Lynch on behalf of a group of a dozen city councilors approached Fuchs. A "bribery scandal" erupted, involving numerous public hearings in January 1929 that were captured in great detail by the more than half a dozen daily newspapers then in Boston. After three weeks of public hearings without any definitive conclusions reached, the Boston City Council finally passed the Sunday sports ordinance at its February 11 meeting and the two major leagues could finally issue the official schedules for the 1929 season.[11]

Rain cancelled the first scheduled Sunday game in Boston between the Braves and the Giants on April 21, 1929, giving the Red Sox the honor of playing the first Sunday match on April 28 against the Athletics. However, the game was held at Braves Field, not Fenway Park, because the new law specified that games weren't permitted within 1000 feet of a church, to appease the law's religious opponents. The Church of the Disciples being within 1000 feet of right field in Fenway Park prevented the Red Sox from scheduling Sunday games at their own ballpark until 1932 when the law was changed.[12]

However, even with the newfound right to play Sunday baseball in Boston, the Sunday doubleheader soon made its debut at Braves Field on June 23, 1929. This twin bill immediately illustrated the problem that would periodically surface with Sunday doubleheaders in Boston. With just a four-hour window to play baseball on Sunday under the new Massachusetts law (games could only be conducted between 2:00 and 6:00 P.M.), completing nine innings in the second contest sometimes proved problematical. The second game on June 23 was stopped in the seventh inning with the Braves ahead of the Phillies, 7–5. When the Sunday curfew was executed to end a Sunday doubleheader, the score of the game reverted to the score at the end of the last-completed inning. This principle resulted in much consternation over the years in Boston, and eventually in Philadelphia and Pittsburgh as well, once Sunday baseball was legal in Pennsylvania.

Breadon's extensive use of the Sunday doubleheader in St. Louis helped to save major-league baseball during the 1930s. After the stock market crash in October 1929 ushered in the Great Depression, attendance at major-league ballparks plummeted by 40 percent, from a 1930 peak of ten million to six million for the 1933 season. "The early thirties brought sparse crowds, deficits, a dramatic contraction in minor-league operations, and relentless retrenchment throughout the baseball business," historian Charles Alexander wrote in *Breaking the Slump: Baseball in the Depression Era*. By 1931 "it became impossible to deny that the Great Depression had finally caught up with big-league baseball."[13]

To help stem the decline in attendance, the number of Sunday doubleheaders rose over the next four years in direct correlation with the increase in the unemployment rate. Sunday doubleheaders increased from 27 in 1929 to 69 in 1931, as unemployment rose from 5.5 percent to 16.3 percent over the same period. Two years later in 1933, there were 107 Sunday doubleheaders staged in the major leagues, while the unemployment rate jumped to 25.2 percent. In 1931 half the Sunday schedule was routinely doubleheaders; by 1933 it was not unusual to have six or seven doubleheaders on the Sunday card.[14]

The substantial increase in Sunday doubleheaders during the 1929–1933 period rescued major-league baseball from oblivion. Since fewer people could afford to attend baseball games in the early 1930s due to the tough economic times, Sunday doubleheaders helped to attract spectators on the day that people who did continue to hold jobs could most easily get to the ballpark. Without the 1929–1933 expansion of Sunday doubleheaders, the attendance decline would have been far worse for major-league ballclub owners.

Baseball executives had a simple answer for the lower ballpark attendance. "What is the matter with baseball? I have asked all of the prominent men in the game," sportswriter Fred Lieb wrote in 1933. "They all have the

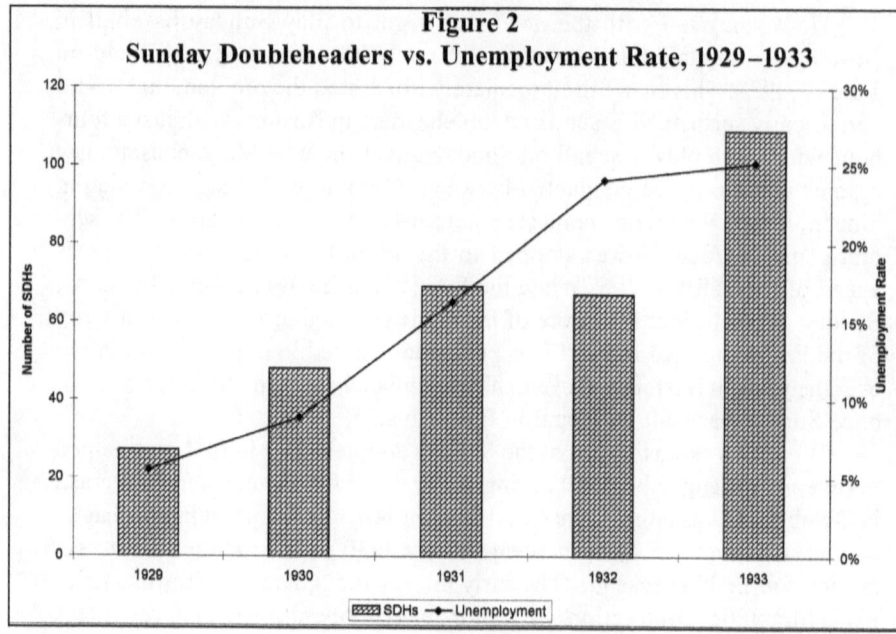

**Figure 2
Sunday Doubleheaders vs. Unemployment Rate, 1929–1933**

The number of Sunday doubleheaders surged dramatically during the Great Depression in direct correlation to the rise in the unemployment rate, as ballclub owners struggled to overcome meager attendance at weekday games. (Sources: Bevis, "Evolution of the Sunday Doubleheader," and Jensen, "The Causes and Cures of Unemployment in the Great Depression.")

same answer: The depression." National League President Heydler told Lieb, "We have been hit pretty hard the last year, but then who hasn't? Show me the man or the business which has gone through the last few years without suffering any loss of income or trimming of expenses." American League President Harridge told Lieb, "There is nothing radically wrong with baseball.... When practically everything in the commercial world, and to some extent in the amusement world, has been greatly affected by the depression baseball has carried on to a surprising degree." Commissioner Landis curtly responded to Lieb in a note: "Dear Mr. Lieb: Acknowledging receipt of your letter, if you will tell me what is the matter with the newspaper business, the banking business, the steel business, the railroad business and every other kind of business, I will tell you what is the matter with baseball. Very truly yours, K.M. Landis." However, while baseball blamed its problems on the economic depression, it was too simplistic an explanation.[15]

If, due to the Great Depression, people didn't have money to spend, why did huge crowds attended Sunday doubleheaders? People flocked to Sunday doubleheaders in 1933, as seen by these *New York Times* headlines from a

Monday edition in August 1933: "60,000 See Indians Divide Twin Bill," "Braves, Reds Split As 40,000 Look On," and "50,000 See Giants Lose, Then Tie." On September 16, 1934, with Dizzy Dean and his brother Paul pitching both ends of a doubleheader for the Cardinals against the New York Giants at the Polo Grounds, the *New York Times* called the crowd of 62,573 "the biggest single-day gathering in the history of the National League." The Cardinals won both games that day, on their way to overtaking the Giants to cop the National League pennant.[16]

High unemployment was part of the reason for declining attendance, but not the sole or even primary reason. "In the Great Depression, prolonged cyclical unemployment turned into irreversible structural unemployment for 10 percent of the labor force," historian Richard Jensen wrote in his article "The Causes and Cures of Unemployment in the Great Depression" in 1989. "Five million previously 'normal' workers suddenly and utterly unexpectedly fell into the hard core trap and could not escape." Jensen contended that "a revolution in labor management took place during the 1920s," in which "American industry shifted from reliance on a vast supply of unskilled workers performing heavy or repetitive tasks, to more skilled workers using more machinery in more complex ways, under the eyes of engineers watching for signs of waste or possibility for improvement." These structurally unemployed workers would have been bleacher-ticket customers at the ballpark, if they ever attended a ballgame at all.[17]

The real problem for baseball was the very meager attendance at ballgames played on weekday afternoons. "Unable to draw paying attendance for games scheduled early in the week, baseball magnates have tried to jack up their receipts by offering the fans two games for the price of one," a *Literary Digest* article concluded. Some owners thought Sunday doubleheaders were detrimental to single-game gates. "If we spoil week-day gates by scheduling synthetic doubleheaders, it will be a bad thing," the article quoted one baseball executive. Others were more realistic, "favor[ing] them as the only solution to books saturated in red ink."[18]

If the primary reason for the weak weekday attendance was the high unemployment rate, then fewer spectators would have sat in the bleachers (those fans for the most part being the workers and laborers impacted by workforce cutbacks by employers) and tickets for box seats would have remained relatively steady (those fans for the most part being businessmen who did the employing of others). An analysis of the visiting share of gate receipts at Yankee Stadium during the 1930s showed the percentage of cheap seats (visiting ballclubs received 20 cents per ticket for bleacher and general admission seats) rose from 24 percent in 1929 to 37 percent in 1933, relative to reserved and box seats that visiting ballclubs were compensated at the rate of 30 cents per ticket. As David Surdam concluded in his analysis of the receipts data, "Fans simply moved around Yankee Stadium, switching to the cheaper general admission and bleacher seats and away from the reserved and box seats."[19]

A larger factor that impacted baseball attendance was a change in the nature of employers that fundamentally reduced the number of people who could attend an afternoon ballgame during the workweek. The rapid expansion of the "chain store" concept, which involved "retailing merchandise through store units owned and controlled by a corporation," forced many independent businessmen to shut down in the 1930s and arguably "produced a nation of clerks as a result of their policy of centralizing control at the home office" as a replacement for local owners. Grocery stores, gas stations, and variety stores were the largest segments of the economy affected by chain stores. "That chain stores in many instances have forced independent retailers out of business cannot be denied," one observer noted in 1929. "To the extent that these retailers are desirable citizens and a valuable part of the social life of the community, the community suffers." Ballclub owners suffered because these independent businessmen had the time flexibility to attend an afternoon ballgame. While the greater mechanization of jobs discussed above mostly affected attendance in cheaper seats on Sundays, the decline in independently-owned businesses significantly impacted attendance in pricier seats during the workweek.[20]

Another element contrary to the ballclub owners' position was the irony that greater leisure hours due to employment in the 1930s actually resulted in increased spending on recreation, not less spending. As Susan Currell wrote in her 2005 book *The March of Spare Time: The Problem and Promise of Leisure in the Great Depression*, "Despite economic hardship, leisure time had continued to grow, and an increasing share of the national income was spent on recreation ... revolutionizing the way Americans spent their nonworking hours." Commercial amusements such as movie theaters, radio, dance halls, and road houses increased their competitive impact to spectator sports such as major-league baseball. Movie going was one of the most popular commercial leisure pursuits of the 1930s, according to Currell, who cited a contemporary survey that "attending the movies was the third most popular leisure activity, only topped by the cheaper pursuits of radio listening and reading newspapers." Movie promoters offered giveaway nights and double features "to lure the Depression-hit public into spending their last few dollars."[21]

Ballclub owners had a love-hate relationship with the Sunday doubleheader. At the December 1931 winter meetings, the owners voted that synthetic doubleheaders violated schedule rules and that "henceforth, no club or clubs can arrange such synthetic doubleheaders without the consent of the presidents of both leagues." For the 1932 season, the owners cut player salaries and reduced roster sizes to pare expenses, rather than reduce admission prices at the box office or plan to use doubleheaders to encourage more spectators to come to the ballpark. *The Sporting News* thought the ending of synthetic doubleheaders was good for baseball. "Double-headers created in major league baseball to upset the dignity of the schedules and the leagues, to play for the immediate gate receipts at possible injustice to six other clubs, to make paramount the issue of commercialism—which is so rife now—have been wiped out of baseball" the baseball weekly editorialized at the time.[22]

The ballclub owners nixed the Level 3 Sunday doubleheader at a time when the policies of the Hoover administration had proved to be an abject failure in restoring confidence in the U.S. economy to end the Great Depression. The 53 percent decline in the Dow Jones Industrial Average during 1931 was the index's worst calendar-year performance since its inception in 1896 (and remained the index's worst-ever return through the first decade of the twenty-first century). That the 1931 stock-market performance was a second consecutive double-digit negative return—the Dow had declined 34 percent in 1930—made the economic situation even more dour as the unemployment rate rose to 16 percent during 1931. While the large number of disgruntled unemployed seemed to edge the nation closer to open rebellion, as evidenced by the shootings at the Ford River Rouge automobile factory outside of Detroit in March 1932, one historian observed that predictions of a revolution "were more common among the potential victims than the putative revolutionaries." Not surprisingly, with continuing poor attendance prospects at the ballpark, the ban on Sunday doubleheaders was abandoned early into the 1932 baseball season.[23]

There were fewer doubleheaders conducted in 1932 than in 1931, which had witnessed the most doubleheaders, as a percentage of total games played, in the history of major-league baseball. However, as the unemployment rate elevated to 24 percent during 1932, meaning that one of every four men was out of work, and the stock market declined for a third straight year, the country, not just major-league baseball, was clearly in serious trouble. Franklin Roosevelt easily defeated Hoover in the presidential election in November 1932, as citizens hoped that Roosevelt's espoused "New Deal" would rid the country of its troubles and restore the good times. However, the four-month period between the election and inauguration in March 1933 (since shortened to two and a half months) plunged the nation into further calamity as many banks closed, virtually shutting down the flow of money. FDR's "bank holiday" in March 1933, just a few weeks before the start of the baseball season, didn't bode well for increased attendance at the ballpark.

Doubleheaders dotted the major-league baseball landscape during the 1933 season, as more than three-eighths of all ballgames were conducted through twin bills, setting a new high in major-league history. When the volume of doubleheaders exploded in 1933 at the depth of the Great Depression, there was an outcry for sanity in scheduling. "If Sunday doubleheaders are to become a regular thing, they should be so incorporated in the schedules," *The Sporting News* editorialized that spring. "We know nothing more meaningless than the present schedules, with games charted for as late as September being moved up at the whim of a club owner to create a Sunday doubleheader in May." As the baseball publication later commented, "As a result, carefully-prepared schedules became mere scraps of paper before the season had gone far, and the fans were lost in a maze of altered dates, which made it impossible for them to tell when games would be played."[24]

Owners were reluctant to put Sunday doubleheaders on the schedule for the same reason owners had opposed them for decades: giving away the game. "Fear is voiced in some quarters that baseball is going to become a weekend sport, instead of a daily affair. Its possibility does counsel serious consideration of the probable effects of the arbitrary shifting around of weekday games to make possible double-headers on Sunday," *The Sporting News* commented. "There is such a thing as carrying the practice so far that the fans through habit will expect double bills as a regular diet ... it's a known fact that some people deliberately stay away form the week-day games where it is a known fact that twin bills will be held on Sunday."[25]

Nonetheless, the times demanded innovation. Many minor-league clubs, attempting to remain financially viable, had been scheduling Sunday doubleheaders and playing night games since 1930. But major-league owners were more resistant to change. "We are not going in for any hippodrome stuff," Clark Griffith, owner of the Washington ballclub, said in regard to a 1933 proposal for interleague play during the hot summer interval from July 5 to mid–August. "The American League is a big league," asserted Griffith. "Our business has held up at least as well as any other. We're going on just the way we are."[26]

The Sunday doubleheader was the owners' idea of a discount promotion during this time, providing a free second game for the price of admission to one game. This helped to optimize attendance on Sundays, but did nothing to rescue the gate at weekday games. Just how poorly attended weekday games were during the Great Depression is hard to determine, since newspapers generally only reported the large crowds on Sunday and assiduously avoided mentioning small crowds on the other days. Owners were reluctant to discount prices for weekday games (generally $2.00 for box seats, $1.50 for reserved seats, $1.00 for general admission, and $0.50 for bleachers). Rather, they seemed to accept that money-cramped spectators would downsize their purchases. "The black shadow of depression which has blighted industry for four years, did not rest upon the professional diamond," *Baseball Magazine* remarked in a 1933 editorial. "But as industry became more and more prostrated and the national income ebbed, there came a lessening attendance, a disposition to seek bleacher rather than grandstand seats."[27]

Ballclub owners were extremely reluctant to use promotions to encourage ballpark attendance. They focused on the diminishing demand of the traditional customer base rather than try to expand demand to reach new customers. This is the only rational explanation for the owners' cutback on Sunday doubleheaders for the 1934 season. After a dismal 1933 season on the financial front, ballclub owners once again voted to curtail Sunday doubleheaders by not permitting them in 1934 before June 15. At the winter meetings in December 1933, owners failed to recognize fan popularity of Sunday twin bills during the 1933 season. Instead, the owners voted to use a uniform baseball in both leagues. "I think the decision to adopt a uniform ball is one of the most constructive moves in baseball history. From now on every major league player will hit and throw the same ball. Finer comparisons can be drawn from batting averages of both leagues," said National League president Heydler. Compared to the Sunday doubleheader, the uniform ball was a minor matter. Yet, rather than directly address economic issues through the Sunday doubleheader, the owners incomprehensibly looked to the uniform ball as a financial panacea.[28]

At least all 16 major-league ballclubs could play Sunday baseball during the 1934 season because the Pennsylvania legislature finally approved a Sunday baseball law in 1933. A local option provision via a state-wide referendum wasn't good enough for Pennsylvania, as it was in Massachusetts; the Quaker State legislators wanted local referendums to assuage their concerns that municipal councils would railroad through a Sunday baseball ordinance where voters would actually disapprove of the notion. In late March, legislators approved these voter referendums, but they wouldn't be conducted until the November 1933 election. When the bill arrived on the desk of Governor Gifford Pinchot for signature, he asked that it be amended to provide that 10 percent of admission prices at Sunday sports events go to unemployment funds. With this amendment, Pinchot resolved two political issues at the same time, funding unemployment relief and legalizing Sunday baseball. Pinchot signed the bill on April 25. "I am emphatically opposed to the commercialization of the Sabbath," Pinchot said in a statement accompanying his signing of the bill. "But in a State which has Sunday trains, Sunday concerts, Sunday golf, Sunday tennis, and a host of Sunday activities of many kinds, the possible addition of baseball and football between the hours of 2 and 6, if the people of any locality vote for it, will not seriously change the present picture." Pinchot went on to conclude, "I have been warned that it will be politically expensive for me to sign this bill. In all probability that is true. But I am not concerned with politics. I am concerned with what I believe to be right—and I believe it is right to sign it." Pennsylvania voters never did elect Pinchot to another political position in the state, though Philadelphia and Pittsburgh voters overwhelmingly approved the Sunday sports referendum on November 7. Philadelphia approved the measure 370,858 to 57,740 as all 50 wards in the city returned favorable majorities. The Phillies, Pirates, and Athletics all sported Sunday home games on the 1934 schedule.[29]

Although Sunday laws had been liberalized in Massachusetts and Pennsylvania to allow ballgames on the Lord's Day, Sunday laws remained a slight thorn in the side of the major-league ballclubs when it came to the increasingly popular Sunday doubleheader. The laws in both Massachusetts and Pennsylvania provided for a 6:00 P.M. stopping time for Sunday games. Indeed, at the first Sunday doubleheader staged in Pennsylvania, on September 9, 1934, between the Phillies and the Cardinals, the second contest was cut short when nine innings couldn't be completed before six o'clock.[30]

The "Sunday curfew" was a vexing problem, since certain game situations presented the opportunity for teams to practice skullduggery. If a team rallied to take the lead in what would be the final inning, if completed, that team was prone to hurry up by intentionally making outs to get the inning completed and on the books to obtain the victory. Conversely, the team that lost the lead in that situation was prone to stall so that the inning would fail to be completed by the curfew. If the stall was successful, the rally would be negated and the team would escape a loss since the score would revert to the tally at the end of the last completed inning.

The first prominent case of stalling for the curfew occurred in a 1930 Sunday doubleheader in Boston. On July 13, the Braves had won the opening game against the Chicago Cubs. Leading 3–0 in the bottom of the eighth inning of the second game, the Braves tried to stall, highlighted by the batting skills of Rabbit Maranville. "The Rabbit had done some stalling by batting off fouls in the eighth," the *Boston Globe* reported, "so as to prevent the game going into the ninth, as the ninth was not going to be started after 5:40." Contemporary newspaper accounts of the game failed to disclose the exact number of foul balls that Maranville poked, but later recollections put the number at 14. The Braves ended the bottom of the eighth inning at 5:38, two minutes short of the informal new-inning cutoff associated with the Sunday curfew.[31]

When Maranville's foul-ball stalling didn't prevent the ninth inning from beginning, the Cubs rallied to score four runs and took the lead, 4–3, on Gabby Hartnett's double. Knowing that time was running out, though, "Hartnett retaliated for Boston's stalling by an attempted walking steal of third, and Blair struck out purposely" to end the half inning with time still left. At 5:55 the Braves went to bat. Once George Sisler singled, "time was consumed while Neun came in from a remote corner of the park to run for him." After

This cartoon in the *Boston Post* on July 14, 1930, poked fun at the Sunday law in Massachusetts that required professional baseball games on Sunday to stop precisely at 6:00 P.M. The Sunday curfew had the unintended consequence of encouraging stalling tactics in the second game of a doubleheader, such as Rabbit Maranville intentionally fouling off numerous consecutive pitches.

Buster Chatham fouled off a half-dozen balls before finally striking out, Jimmy Welsh doubled to put runners on second and third bases with one out when the clock struck 6:00. At this point, "Lieut. McCloskey of the commonwealth stepped in and ended the contest under the Sunday law which makes it wicked for ball fans to enjoy themselves after 6 P.M." Umpire Quigley halted the game and declared the Braves the winner, since the score reverted back to the last completed inning.[32]

The Cubs were miffed at the ruling that negated the four runs they scored in the top of the ninth inning, but no one had anticipated that 20 minutes wouldn't be enough time to complete a full inning. That was almost double the 12 minutes it usually took to play an inning at that time, according to the umpires interviewed after the game. Chicago protested the game, but got nowhere in the hearing before National League president John Heydler on July 17. "The Cubs, though greatly chagrined at the outcome, have no one to blame except the penchant of the magnates to drag in all the dough in sight," the *Chicago Tribune* commented the day after the curfew-shortened game. "The doubleheader was not a scheduled one, tomorrow's regular game having been moved up to swell the gate."[33]

Most of the curfew-shortened games in the 1930s occurred in Boston, rather than in Philadelphia and Pittsburgh where ballclubs seemed to have an easier time completing two games within the stipulated four-hour timeframe. One exception was the second half of the Sunday doubleheader at Baker Bowl on June 6, 1937, after St. Louis had posted an 8–2 lead in the third inning. "Umpire Ziggy Sears forfeited the second game of a doubleheader today for alleged dilatory tactics by the Philadelphia club in what appeared to be an attempt to prolong the game until the Sunday curfew would halt the contest before it became legal," one newspaper reported on the stalling.[34]

One of the more egregious uses of curfew-inspired stalling tactics occurred in the second contest of the Sunday doubleheader on September 3, 1939, between the Red Sox and the Yankees at Fenway Park. With the game tied, 5–5, after seven innings as the curfew neared, the Yankees rallied for two runs in the top of the eighth inning to take the lead, 7–5, with less than 10 minutes to the curfew. With two Yankee runners on base, Red Sox pitcher Joe Heving then tried to execute a stall tactic by intentionally walking Babe Dahlgren. Heving threw the first pitch wide, but Dahlgren, trying to execute a hurry-up tactic, swung at the wide serve to force the umpire to call a strike. After Dahlgren also swung at Heving's next wide throw, George Selkirk, the Yankee runner on third base, executed another hurry-up tactic when he "deliberately ran up from third base to be tagged out by catcher Johnny Peacock." On Heving's next pitch, "Gordon repeated the move" for the third out. Executing another time-proven stall tactic, Boston manager Joe Cronin immediately argued with the umpires about the validity of the two Yankee suicide outs at home plate. As Cronin jawed with the umps, the Boston fans showed their displeasure with New York's hurry-up antics by showering the field with bottles (drinks in paper cups were yet to come). As the curfew arrived, umpire Cal Hubbard declared the game forfeited to New York due to the unplayable field.[35]

While the ballclub owners debated the wisdom of the Level 3 Sunday doubleheader as a scheduling strategy, the advent of night baseball at the major-league level in 1935 put the Sunday doubleheader on the fast track to scheduling acceptability. In Cincinnati, Sunday doubleheaders had barely kept the ballclub afloat during the Great Depression. At the National League meeting in December 1934, Cincinnati owner Powell Crosley said, "In Cincinnati during 1934, 70 percent of the Reds' gross home attendance for the year was recorded on only fifteen playing days, these including opening day, Sundays and holidays." To Powell, and his innovative general manager Larry

MacPhail, Sunday doubleheaders were not enough to lift the ballclub out of its financial plight; they needed night baseball, which had saved the minor leagues after being introduced there in 1930.[36]

On May 2, 1930, the first regular-season professional baseball game played under a permanent lighting system was staged in Des Moines, Iowa, in a Western League engagement, before 8,000 paying customers. The Des Moines ballclub had installed the lights after witnessing crowds flock to football games played at night during the fall of 1929. "As the turnstiles whirled, believers were made—you could even say they saw the light," David Pietrusza wrote in his book *Lights On! The Wild Century-Long Saga of Night Baseball*. "Within weeks, such far-flung franchises as Joplin, Denver, Omaha, Lincoln, Buffalo, Rochester, Montreal, Indianapolis, and Fort Worth had installed lamps."[37]

While the minor leagues rapidly embraced night baseball in the early 1930s, major-league club owners flogged the concept as a passing fad and focused on its downsides—the late hours (games typically started at 9:00 P.M.), wet grass, the glare of lights, and the disruption of eating times for the players. However, as F.C. Lane pointed out in a *Baseball Magazine* article, there was no denying one huge positive attribute of night baseball. "The main advantage is, of course, the fact that many more patrons can attend night baseball than can possibly attend day baseball. In short, night baseball multiplies the prospective customers greatly, perhaps, as William Veeck suggested, even twenty-fold," Lane wrote. "Baseball does not belong to the owners nor to the players. It belongs to the public. And if the public want night baseball, you may rest assured they will get night baseball."[38]

At the December 1934 league meeting, MacPhail "prepared a forty-page brief on the virtues of night games, [and] spoke for three hours to convince his National League rivals." The ballclub owners approved night games in Cincinnati for the 1935 season, but limited the number to just seven. In retrospect the owners had startlingly limited vision in how to improve attendance and profitability through such games. "It was obvious that many people would attend night games who couldn't or wouldn't be there in the day time," Jules Tygiel observed in his book *Past Time: Baseball as History*. Tygiel cited ingrained caution and a sense of tradition for the owners' inability to see that night baseball created exponentially more opportunities for spectators to go to the ballpark. The first night games in Cincinnati showed how effective they were at increasing a ballclub's finances. The Reds attracted 124,000 spectators to the seven night games in 1935, which represented more than one-quarter of the total seasonal attendance that year. Thus, night contests were on their way to becoming the new Sunday, which had only recently become the new holiday.[39]

While the night games in Cincinnati helped to shore up the club's overall attendance, they also contributed to further deterioration in daytime attendance, especially on the following day. During 1935 and 1936, on the day after a night contest, Cincinnati regularly played an afternoon game, often to a dismally small crowd in contrast to the thousands that were at the night game. For example, 12,000 people attended the July 10, 1935, night game against the Brooklyn Dodgers, while at the afternoon game on July 11 between the same two clubs "about 3,700 fans were on hand ... and 2,700 of today's crowd were youngsters, admitted free." In 1937, Cincinnati began using a Level 2 doubleheader strategy in conjunction with its night games, to cancel the afternoon match following the night game in favor of playing a doubleheader either before the night contest or later in the season. For example, rather than play Pittsburgh as scheduled for the afternoon of July 1 after the night game on June 30, Cincinnati arranged to host the Pirates in a doubleheader on June 29 and make July 1 an open date. While this strategy ostensibly provided a needed breather for the ballplayers, it was designed to optimize attendance during the workweek and maximize ballclub profits.[40]

The term "Sunday doubleheader" began to appear more regularly in newspaper accounts in the mid–1930s, as well as acknowledging its heritage. "The Dodgers also are idle tomorrow, their scheduled game with the Phillies having been made into part of a Sunday doubleheader," the *New York Times* reported in August 1936. The term had been used occasionally in the years before, dating back to the headline "Reds and Cubs Split Sunday Double-Header" in a 1913 edition of the *Dallas Morning News*. But the widespread creation of synthetic doubleheaders advanced the term into general use. After an early morning rain in August 1934, "in the interests of a bigger and better attraction for tomorrow ... officials lost no time broadcasting a postponement," the *Chicago Tribune* reported. "The idea, of course, was to make possible a Sunday doubleheader which, it is hoped, will draw a quantity of customers."[41]

Owners gave up trying to regulate Sunday doubleheaders in 1936, when they decided "to leave the scheduling of Sunday doubleheaders to the individual whims of owners." When Brooklyn installed artificial lights to join Cincinnati as a second ballclub that would play night games in the 1938 season, the National League adopted an informal policy of moving the scheduled afternoon games following night games to create Sunday doubleheaders. "Games scheduled on days succeeding the [night] contests have been reset as part of doubleheaders," the Cincinnati ballclub announced after the 1938 National League schedule was published. "Following all night games the next afternoon will be an off-day," the Brooklyn ballclub announced in June when it commenced to play night games. "To make up for the off-days, Sunday doubleheaders have been scheduled." For instance, to replace the Cincinnati game slated for June 16 after the night contest on June 15, Brooklyn booked a Sunday doubleheader with the Reds for August 7.[42]

In 1939, with three teams playing night games, the National League put 12 Sunday doubleheaders on its initial schedule that related to the night matches to be played that season in Cincinnati, Brooklyn, and Philadelphia, rather than encourage date switching during the season. "As a result of the open dates which usually follow night games, an unusually large number of Sunday doubleheaders have been scheduled, to enable teams to provide for the engagements which otherwise would follow the nocturnal battles," *The Sporting News* observed about the radical change in preseason scheduling strategy.[43]

The first day-night doubleheader in the major leagues occurred on September 27, 1939, at Comiskey Park in Chicago, when the White Sox combined a scheduled night game with the Cleveland Indians with an afternoon contest to make up a postponed match. "Ticket holders for the afternoon game, which will start at 3 o'clock, may remain in Comiskey Park for the night game, or go away and come back on their rainchecks for the night game, which will start at 8:15 o'clock," the *Chicago Tribune* reported about the unusual single-admission status of the twin bill.[44]

Cardinals owner Sam Breadon proposed putting baseball on a six-day-a-week schedule, with Sunday doubleheaders allowing for an open date every Monday. "I'd rather have the twin bills placed in the regular schedule," National League president Ford Frick said in late 1939, "than let the teams call off a game at the last minute to make a synthetic doubleheader."[45]

Night baseball was an unqualified attendance success by 1940, which led to the need for more Sunday doubleheaders as more night games were carded. More than 1.5 million fans attended night games in 1940, for an average of 20,000 per game. Two of the largest crowds of the year were at contests on a Wednesday night in August—59,000 at Cleveland's Municipal Stadium and 54,000 at the Polo Grounds. If you "hazard a guess at what these same contests would have drawn on any work-day afternoon, you will understand why lighting systems have been welcomed by most of the baseball magnates."[46]

As more major-league ballclubs installed lighting systems to play night baseball, the preseason schedules began to feature numerous Sunday doubleheaders; in the 1941 schedules, there were 41 Sunday doubleheaders. "Taking official cognizance of the growing practice of some clubs in arranging Sunday double-headers after the season starts, the American League schedule sets a precedent this year by definitely charting 16 Sabbath twin-bills in advance," *The Sporting News* reported. "Paralleling the action of the American League in making definite advance provision for Sunday double-headers, instead of waiting for individual clubs to arrange such dates after the season starts, the National League went even farther in that direction by charting 25 Sabbath twin-bills." In an editorial, *The Sporting News* wrote that "fans once more can depend upon the annual chart issued in the spring ... their schedules will not look like Chinese puzzles before the season has progressed far" which will ensure "they need not alter their arrangements or run the risk of disappointment" in planning trips to the ballpark. With this relative plethora of Sunday doubleheaders on the 1941 schedule, for the first time ever more than 10 percent of scheduled major-league games were planned to be conducted via doubleheaders.[47]

One of the most memorable nonplaying moments in doubleheader history took place on July 4, 1939, when the New York Yankees held "Lou Gehrig Appreciation Day" at Yankee Stadium to honor Gehrig, who, just two weeks earlier, had been diagnosed with a terminal illness (amyotrophic lateral sclerosis). Between games of the scheduled holiday doubleheader, with more than 62,000 fans in attendance, Gehrig took the microphone to utter one of the most famous phrases in baseball history.

However, according to Gehrig biographer Jonathan Eig, the man who had played in 2,130 consecutive baseball games (including dozens of doubleheaders) dreaded going to his own Appreciation Day. Public displays of gratitude were just not within Gehrig's persona. During the first game of the doubleheader between the Yankees and the Washington Senators, Gehrig sat on the Yankees bench next to manager Joe McCarthy and reportedly begged him to get him out of the ceremony. With the players from both the Yankees and Senators lining the basepaths to converge at home plate, Mayor LaGuardia and other dignitaries awaited Gehrig's arrival at the microphone placed there.

Gehrig was so weak that he needed the assistance of Yankees general manager Ed Barrow to get to home plate. "When they drew near, Barrow released his grip, letting Gehrig complete the journey alone," Eig wrote. "He had about ten yards to go. He lowered his head, avoiding all eye contact. He walked slowly and awkwardly ... the fans stood and cheered. Gehrig never acknowledged them." The moment was the zenith of embarrassment for the congenitally shy Gehrig. He twisted his baseball cap throughout the ceremony, scratched the dirt with his baseball cleats, shifted his weight from one foot to the other, and stared at the ground. Originally, he demurred about speaking to the huge crowd in the stadium, but back in the dugout, McCarthy had convinced him to talk. When Gehrig approached the microphone, the crowd fell dead silent. "Every man and woman, every peanut vendor, every ballplayer and batboy, every photographer and writer seemed to stare and wait. Even the men in the press box stopped typing," Eig described the scene.[48]

Rick Ferrell, the Washington catcher and a future Hall of Famer, stood at the head of the line of Washington players closest to Gehrig. "I didn't know if he was trembling because of his sickness or because of the emotion of the day," Ferrell recalled 50 years later on the golden anniversary of the event. "Then Babe Ruth walked over and put his arm around Lou's shoulder to brace him. Lou gathered his strength and started talking. What a great speech. The players were stunned."[49]

Everyone was so awed that no one transcribed Gehrig's words, since he spoke extemporaneously. As Eig wrote, no one is sure *exactly* what Gehrig said between the games of that Fourth of July doubleheader, since even the newsreel companies saved only a few sentences on film. A transcript of Gehrig's speech has been spliced together from various newspaper accounts. One thing is for sure—Gehrig delivered his famous line in his second sentence: "Fans, for the past two weeks you have been reading about the bad break I got. Yet today I consider myself the luckiest man on the face of this earth." Three years after Lou Gehrig gave that farewell speech at Yankee Stadium, actor Gary Cooper delivered a different rendition of it in the movie *Pride of the Yankees*. The movie script rearranged the farewell speech to make its words more powerful to the movie audience. Gehrig's words were thus immortalized by Cooper not as the beginning of his talk but rather as the pause-strewn last line of a movie script: "People all say that I've had a bad break. But today, today I consider myself, the luckiest man, on the face of the earth."[50]

Gehrig died in June 1941, about four months before one of the most famous playing moments in doubleheader history when Boston Red Sox outfielder Ted Williams completed his quest for a .400 batting average in a Sunday twin bill on the last day of the 1941 season. Williams walked into Shibe Park for a single game on Saturday, September 27, possessing a .401 batting average, but he never considered sitting out the last three games of the season against the Athletics. "I want to hit over .400 but I'm going to play in all three games [even] if I don't get the ball out of the infield," Williams said before the Philadelphia series. "A batting record's no good unless it's made in all the games of the season."[51]

After going one-for-four in Saturday's game, Williams saw his average dip to .39955; although below the .400 mark, his average would officially round up to .400 if he sat out the Sunday doubleheader. Once again Williams didn't think twice about exercising that technicality, as he related about his conversation with Red Sox manager Joe Cronin in his autobiography *My Turn at Bat*. "The night before the game Cronin offered to take me out of the lineup to preserve the .400," Williams wrote. "I told Cronin I didn't want that. If I couldn't hit .400 all the way I didn't deserve it."[52]

Williams got additional inspiration for his goal on that cold Sunday in Philadelphia when he went to bat for the first time. Philadelphia catcher

Frank Hayes told Williams: "Ted, Mr. Mack told us if we let up on you he'll run us out of baseball. I wish you all the luck in the world, but we're not giving you a damn thing." Then, home plate umpire Bill McGowan called time, just as Williams was set to battle pitcher Dick Fowler. McGowan walked in front of home plate, leaned down, dusted off the already clean pentagon and said without looking up at Williams, "To hit .400 a batter has got to be loose. He has got to be loose."[53]

In the first game of the doubleheader, Williams went four-for-five before going two-for-three in the nightcap to complete a six-for-eight day at the plate and finish the season with a .406 batting average. "That's the fabulous figure with which Ted Williams finished the American League season today as the first major leaguer to hit .400 or better since Bill Terry accomplished the feat for the Giants 11 years ago," the *Boston Globe* reported in a front-page story. As it turned out over the next six decades, Williams was the last man to bat .400 in the major leagues.[54]

Two months later, Japan attacked Pearl Harbor on December 7, which forced the United States to enter World War II. With democracy at stake, suddenly Williams' remarkable season plummeted in importance. That twin bill on September 28, 1941, in Philadelphia was the last doubleheader before World War II completely changed the institution of baseball and modified how major-league ballclubs viewed the doubleheader.

11

Swing-Shift and Other Wartime Doubleheaders

THE JAPANESE INVASION OF Pearl Harbor on December 7, 1941, changed life for every person and institution in the United States for the next four years. Major-league baseball was no exception. America's entry into World War II resulted in an exponential increase in doubleheaders staged each season during the four years 1942 to 1945, one of the many changes that affected major-league baseball during those harrowing times.

Among those changes, one of the most visible was an increase in night games, spurred on by a sentence in President Franklin Roosevelt's "green light" letter sent to Commissioner Landis in mid–January. "I honestly feel that it would be best for the country to keep baseball going ... everybody will work longer hours and harder than ever. And that means that they ought to have a chance for recreation and for taking their minds off their work even more than before," Roosevelt wrote. "And incidentally, I hope that night games can be extended because it gives an opportunity to the day shift to see a game occasionally." While FDR fostered the continuation of professional baseball during the war, he was also clear that ballplayers would receive no favoritism when it came to military service.[1]

Both leagues responded by raising the limit on night games permitted for the 1942 season, allowing 14, double the previous limit of seven, with the Washington ballclub being given an exception to play 21. However, blackout restrictions on outdoor lighting imposed by the military resulted in a prohibition of night games at Ebbets Field and the Polo Grounds in New York City. One could hardly fashion a series of blackout curtains to mask the floodlights for night contests at the two baseball venues. Boston was not affected, since lights had yet to be installed in either Braves Field or Fenway Park; Yankee Stadium was similarly not affected, and Washington and

Philadelphia were far enough inland so that night games there were not hindered.

Enticing spectators to the ballpark was a challenge in 1942, especially those fans looking to travel by car to the game. Tire rationing began in January, since the Japanese military controlled more than 95 percent of the U.S. crude rubber supply (tires were then made from real rubber, not today's synthetic material). Tire rationing was a forerunner to the institution of gasoline rationing in May. The limit of four gallons of gasoline per week for car with an "A" sticker enabled people to go to work, but didn't leave much in the gas tank for pleasure trips. "Driving to baseball games was out in the East. Most families could not afford to squander their meager gasoline ration on trips to the ball park," William Mead wrote in *Even the Browns: The Zany, True Story of Baseball in the Early Forties*. "The basic gasoline ration was enough to drive about 240 miles a month, less than one-third of the average norm for most families."[2]

To dampen an expected decrease in attendance at major-league ballgames during wartime, the number of scheduled doubleheaders in 1942 nearly doubled relative to 1941, the previous high-water mark for scheduled twin bills (see Appendix C for details). This expansion of scheduled doubleheaders meant that one-fifth of the scheduled major-league ballgames in 1942 were planned to be conducted on a two-per-day basis. By season's end, two-fifths, or 40 percent, of the games actually played were staged through nearly 250 twin bills, which eclipsed the previous high established in both 1933 and 1935.

To replace their expunged night games, the New York Giants and the Brooklyn Dodgers substituted twilight games, hoping to attract many of the same spectators that would have attended the night games. Brooklyn began its first twilight encounter of the 1942 season on May 8 at 4:45 P.M. and soon moved the starting time of its twilight games to 6:00 P.M., giving the club about two hours to complete a game. Then, the club appealed to authorities to begin a twilight contest at 7:00 P.M. and conclude it under the lights before the outdoor lighting affected visibility at sea. Because the contest would then qualify as a night game, the Dodgers could do this under league rules; otherwise, matches started in the daytime could not be concluded under the lights.

However, the later start with a fixed ending time (when the lights were turned off) created some sticky moments for the Dodgers, the Giants, and their fans. At the Polo Grounds on August 3 before a crowd of 57,000 people, the game with the Dodgers was halted in the ninth inning with the Giants mounting a rally to overtake a Brooklyn lead when the lights were turned off. The crowd booed vociferously when it was announced that the score reverted to the last completed inning, giving the Dodgers the victory. Giants president Horace Stoneham announced after the game that, following the next day's twilight game with the Dodgers, there would be no more such games at the Polo Grounds for the duration of the war. However, the August 4 game also ended in controversy. At the end of nine innings, the game was tied, 1–1, and went into extra innings. Pee Wee Reese of the Dodgers hit a grand slam in the top of the tenth inning to put Brooklyn ahead 5–1, but the inning couldn't be completed before the appointed time for the lights to be extinguished. So the game went into the books as a 1–1 tie. The booing of patrons was "another indictment of twilight baseball" under dimout regulations.[3]

With restrictions on automobile travel and people working longer hours, ballclubs needed to exercise some creativity to attract spectators to the ballpark, so one of the first wartime innovations in major-league baseball scheduling was the twilight-night doubleheader. With this type of twin bill, spectators paid one admission to watch a twilight game followed by a night game. The first twilight-night doubleheaders were played in the American League on July 24 in St. Louis and Cleveland. Because at the time, a day game couldn't be completed under lights and thus needed to be finished before the night game began, the starting times for the two games were usually about three hours apart. "There will be something new and novel in the local baseball picture this evening," the *St. Louis Post-Dispatch* reported, "a twilight-night doubleheader between the Browns and the Red Sox, with the first game to start at 5:30 and the second at 8:30." This schedule gave the two clubs enough time to play nine innings in the first game and a few extra innings if need be.[4]

The innovative doubleheader attracted a big crowd to watch the attendance-challenged Browns. "Twilight-floodlight doubleheader baseball had its premiere at Sportsman's Park last night, and it was a smash hit," the *St. Louis Post-Dispatch* reported. "More than 20,000 persons paid at the gate, and the show, lasting five hours and 52 minutes, was all that the most critical could have demanded." The biggest concern for spectators was when and how to eat dinner. The Browns seemed to anticipate this in their business planning by stocking up on hamburgers and hot dogs as well as box lunches and fish-and-cheese sandwiches. The intermission between games was nearly 45 minutes long, at which time "the gathering took on a basket picnic color." The twilight-night doubleheader attracted the largest crowd for a Browns game in more than two years.[5]

After Cleveland and St. Louis initiated the concept, the three other American League ballclubs with lighting systems in their home parks immediately imitated the twilight-night doubleheader concept. A popular opponent to schedule for these doubleheaders was the New York Yankees, "who reluctantly or otherwise, are lending themselves to the various innovations that the war has brought about in baseball, [and] agreed today to play one of those twilight-night doubleheaders in St. Louis." The Yankees played twilight-night doubleheaders in Chicago on July 29, in St. Louis on July 31, and in Washington on September 5.[6]

Detroit was also a popular opponent for the twilight-night doubleheaders, playing them in Cleveland on August 11 and in Philadelphia on August 26. However, the hazard of darkness ending the first contest before a victor emerged reared its ugly head in the Cleveland twin bill on August 11, when the Indians' game with the Tigers went 14 innings and ended in a scoreless tie when darkness set in. Detroit went on to win the nightcap under the lights.

Since spectators clearly loved the new doubleheader concept, the twilight-night doubleheader became a staple of wartime baseball, especially in St. Louis.

The St. Louis Browns continued to experiment with the new doubleheader idea. On September 4, the Browns hosted the Indians in a single-admission, day-night doubleheader dubbed a "passout check special," with "the first game starting at 3 o'clock, the second scheduled for 8:30, with the customers free to leave the park between games with return privileges." However, as the *St. Louis Post-Dispatch* noted, "split-shift, passout check baseball didn't burn up any turnstiles at Sportsman's Park." Attendance at the afternoon contest was 2,126; of those, 1,851 took advantage of the passout privilege for the night game while another 3,885 paid just to see the night game.[7]

Another innovative aspect of wartime baseball was the dedication of the proceeds from certain games to benefit war-relief agencies, such as the May 8 twilight game at Ebbets Field. However, all of the dedicated dates for the war-relief games initially were day games during the workweek, which didn't optimize proceeds for the war effort as much as night games or Sunday doubleheaders would have. American League president Will Harridge stepped in and convinced some ballclub owners to have three Sunday doubleheaders in August targeted to war-relief efforts. On Sunday, August 23, proceeds from the doubleheaders in New York, Philadelphia, and Detroit went to war relief, as huge crowds thronged Yankee Stadium, Shibe Park, and Briggs Stadium to see the twin bills.

The preliminary event at the August 23 doubleheader between the Yankees and the Washington Senators at Yankee Stadium was a home-run–hitting exhibition with 55-year-old Walter Johnson pitching to 48-year-old Babe Ruth. On Johnson's fifth pitch, "the Babe swung, the ball arched and came to rest among the fans in the lower [right-field] stand, who fought for a priceless souvenir." The appearance of the two old-time greats helped to pack Yankee Stadium; the announced attendance was 69,136 people. As the *New York Times* commented, "They helped immeasurably in bringing an estimated $80,000 to the funds of dependents of the nation's heroes ... as much toward this as did the double-header, perhaps more."[8]

Similar warm-up performances before a Sunday doubleheader, or in between games of a doubleheader, were standard fare during the war years. Other war-related activities were often connected to Sunday doubleheaders, such as a scrap-metal drive conducted at a Sunday doubleheader at the Polo Grounds on September 24, 1942. In exchange for ten pounds of scrap metal, fans could get free admission to the ballgame; thus, "556 scrap iron guests" watched the two games between the Giants and the Phillies.[9]

Another interesting aspect to Sunday doubleheaders during the war years was the "Sunday pitcher," a ballplayer who pitched just once a week on the Lord's Day due to age or wartime commitments. Ted Lyons of the Chicago White Sox was the epitome of the Sunday pitcher. During the 1942 season, the 41-year-old Lyons, then in his 20th season with the White Sox, won 14 of 20 starts and produced a league-leading 2.10 earned run average. Thirteen of those 20 starts came on a Sunday during a stretch between May 17 and August 30, in which Lyons won 10 ballgames. During that three-and-a-half-month time period, Lyons pitched the first game of the Sunday doubleheader every week, except on August 2 when the rain canceled the twin bill. Seven of those 13 Sunday contests were home games at Comiskey Park, where Lyons posted a 6–1 record, including career victory number 250 on June 21. After the 1942 season ended, Lyons, like many major-league ballplayers, decided to serve his country in the military. The *Chicago Tribune* headlined the decision made by the once-a-week Sunday pitcher as "Lyons Asks to Pitch Against Axis Every Day." In 1955, Lyons was enshrined in the Baseball Hall of Fame.[10]

In addition to losing ballplayers like Lyons who entered the service, stocking a ballclub for the 1943 season became even more challenging when it was announced early in the year that "baseball players could not expect an occupational deferment" from the military draft, since being a baseball player was not considered an "essential" job. "The usefulness of the sport [to national morale] is a separate question from the 'essentiality' of individuals who play it," Manpower Commissioner Paul McNutt explained. "Thus it may well be that it is desirable that Blankville have a ball team. But Blankville may lose certain members of that team to higher priority industries—even members that might be 'essential' to winning the pennant. The pennant is not 'essential.'"[11]

Business prospects for baseball dwindled further when the Office of Price Administration announced a ban on all pleasure driving by limiting gasoline rations for people with an "A" sticker to three gallons per week (war workers had larger rations, as these employees had "B" stickers that permitted them eight gallons of gasoline per week). Gasoline rationing, naturally, was a challenge for the government to enforce. As Richard Lingeman wrote in *Don't You Know There's a War On? The American Home Front 1941–1945*,

"OPA men took to hanging around race tracks and athletic stadiums, copying down license numbers of out-of-county cars on the theory that just getting to the athletic spectacle was per se pleasure driving." Of course, after-hours visits to the infamous Mr. Black, for black-market refueling, or borrowing cars with a "C" or "X" sticker that afforded unlimited gasoline use, were not unheard occurrences in 1943. For the most part, though, getting to the ballpark during the war years required the use of public transportation rather than driving a private automobile.[12]

Besides the traveling issues for spectators, ballclubs also experienced their own transportation challenges in 1943. The federal government put pressure on major-league baseball to curtail traveling, since train accommodations were in short supply due to the large number of military personnel that needed them. Responding to initial concerns that the season might have to be shortened by at least two weeks, the *New York Times* reported that "the lost two weeks would be made up by scheduling additional doubleheaders, some probably twilight-night twin bills." Commissioner Landis was able to keep the playing season at the same 154-game length by negotiating with Joseph Eastman, the director of the Office of Defense Transportation, to forego spring training trips and eliminate one east-west road trip to minimize travel requirements.[13]

In response to the restricted travel conditions, ballclub owners tried to encourage attendance at the ballpark by scheduling nearly 200 doubleheaders in 1943, almost three times the number just two years earlier during the prewar 1941 season. Close to one-third of the 1943 major-league schedule was comprised of twin bills; almost one-half of all ballgames played in

The scheduled Sunday doubleheader was a career-extender for Chicago White Sox pitcher Ted Lyons. In 1942 Lyons pitched almost exclusively once a week in the first game of the Sunday doubleheader, as the 41-year-old hurler rested his arm the other six days of the week. (National Baseball Hall of Fame Library, Cooperstown, New York)

1943 were part of a doubleheader. Both percentages (32 percent and 48 percent, respectively) smashed the previous highs set just the year before. On average, one of every three playing dates for a major-league ballclub in 1943 consisted of a doubleheader. Assisting in the increase in doubleheaders was the popularity of the twilight-night twin bill; one was even carded on the initial American League schedule, on July 22 at Washington.

With the abundance of doubleheaders played in 1943, still-standing records were established for most doubleheaders played in a season by ballclubs in both leagues. The Chicago White Sox set the American League record with 44 doubleheaders, while the Philadelphia Phillies set the National League mark with 43 twin bills.[14]

The American League schedule called for the White Sox to play 27 doubleheaders in 1943, 22 on Sundays, three holidays, and two mid-week. Chicago was slated to play every Sunday during the season, except for the day before Labor Day (September 5) and the last day of the season (October 3). As it turned out, the White Sox wound up playing doubleheaders on both those dates, with the latter being the key to establishing the major-league record. Chicago's Saturday, October 2, game in Boston was rained out, which led to the club's 44th twin bill being played the next day, Sunday, on the last day of the season. In addition to establishing a major-league record, the season-ending doubleheader in Boston was also a memorable occasion for six-year-old Bill Kirwin, who grew up to become a historian and editor of the scholarly baseball publication *NINE: A Journal of Baseball History and Culture*. In an interview after his retirement, Kirwin reminisced about that October 3, 1943, doubleheader:

> My first memory of great interest in baseball was the day after my sixth birthday in 1943. It was October 3, and my father took me to see a doubleheader between the White Sox and the Red Sox at Fenway Park. It was a small crowd, the last game of the regular season, and what I remember is sitting in the right-field pavilion seats in the bottom of the eighth inning when the Red Sox scored their only run. The Red Sox lost both games, but to me that run was some sort of victory, and I always kept that in the back of my mind. The first day I retired, I went to the library and looked up that game in the *New York Times* archives. Sure enough, it was just as I remembered, with the Red Sox scoring that one run in the bottom of the eighth inning, preventing a shutout. It was a moral victory in [my] eyes.... To me, after all these years, it is still clear as a bell.[15]

The 1943 White Sox exemplified the type of scheduling that ballclubs needed to use to attract spectators to the ballpark during the war years. The White Sox hosted 13 Sunday doubleheaders and 14 night games (the maximum permitted by the American League, with the exception of 21 for Washington). This helped to minimize the number of weekday afternoon games, which were inconvenient for war workers to attend and thus typically drew small crowds. Bad weather helped to further minimize the weekday single-game calendar by creating a number of Level 1 doubleheaders. The dramatic difference in attendance during a two-week homestand at Comiskey Park in early July illustrated the scheduling impact.

On Wednesday afternoon, June 30, a war-fund benefit doubleheader drew nearly 30,000 spectators to see the Great Lakes Naval Training ballclub play an opener followed by the scheduled game between the White Sox and the Washington Senators. This was ten times the size of the 2,000 or so spectators that went to each of the two afternoon contests with the Senators on July 1 and 2. A twi-night twin bill with the Philadelphia Athletics on Saturday, July 3, attracted 10,000 on a rainy evening (the second game being canceled after two innings). A preholiday Sunday doubleheader with the A's on July 4 drew 18,000. The Independence Day holiday twin bill with the Boston Red Sox on July 5 attracted 22,000, in stark contrast to the crowd of 3,000 at the afternoon game on July 6. A night game with the New York Yankees on Thursday, July 8, attracted 31,000, while doubleheaders with the Yankees on Saturday, July 10, and Sunday, July 11, drew crowds of 17,000 and 12,000, respectively.[16]

Playing so many doubleheaders in 1943 was tough on the ballplayers not only physically but also nutritionally. Rationing began in early 1943 to equitably distribute the limited supply of meat and cheese; sugar and coffee had already begun to be rationed in 1942. "Food shortages caused perhaps the most pervasive rationing nuisance. Traveling baseball teams often encountered beefless menus; athletes accustomed to their nightly steak settled for fish instead," Mead wrote in *Even the Browns*. Ballparks might have enticed a few spectators looking not to just watch a ballgame but also to eat a hot dog or hamburger at the concession stand that they might not otherwise be able to buy at the local butcher shop. For example, the crowd of 37,792 at a June 27, 1943, Sunday doubleheader at Wrigley Field in Chicago "stowed away no less than 35,000 red-hots—nearly one to a spectator." Hot-dog consumption may have been larger than usual, since the Cubs couldn't stock hamburgers or roast-beef sandwiches due to rationing restrictions. The thirsty crowd at the June 27 doubleheader also drank 32,000 bottles of beer, 30,000 bottles of soda pop, and 5,400 glasses of lemonade.[17]

Another wartime scheduling innovation was the morning game, which debuted on May 3, 1943, when Cincinnati hosted Pittsburgh in a game that started at 11:30 A.M. The early start was designed to attract war workers on the swing shift, who normally couldn't attend a ballgame during the workweek because they worked from 3:00 P.M. to 11:00 P.M. (the swing shift contrasted with the day shift, referenced in FDR's "green light" letter, which was normally 7:00 A.M. to 3:00 P.M., and the night shift, which ran from 11:00 P.M. to 7:00 A.M.). "I hope that these games at odd hours work out and draw the crowd that baseball deserves," Manpower Commissioner McNutt said in mid-May. However, attendance was usually fairly light for these morning games.[18]

One of the largest crowds at a major-league morning game in 1943 occurred when the Cubs hosted the Reds on June 11. "War time morning baseball, tried out for the first time in Wrigley Field yesterday, was adjudged a success from the viewpoint of attendance—there were 8,707 present—but a flop artistically," the *Chicago Tribune* reported, "inasmuch as the Cubs appeared especially dull and drowsy as they absorbed a 7 to 4 whipping at the hands of the Cincinnati Reds." The paid attendance was 5,307 people, since it was ladies day and several thousand female fans took advantage of the free admission.[19]

The Phillies, in setting the National League record for doubleheaders in a season, hosted several morning-afternoon twin bills in 1943 that were dubbed "swing-shift" doubleheaders. The morning game at Shibe Park began at 11:00 A.M., to allow war workers to see one game before heading to work to begin their shift. On June 15, the first swing-shift doubleheader in the major leagues occurred at Shibe Park, when the Phillies hosted the Boston Braves. "The ladies day crowd of 6,679 (4,567 paid) was considered evidence in favor of 11 A.M. baseball here," the *Boston Globe* reported. Two days later, the Phillies staged "another of their swing shift bargain bills that are making ordinary, afternoon games a sensational novelty." This second swing-shift doubleheader attracted an even bigger crowd than the first one, with 7,379 spectators (6,002 paid).[20]

Philadelphia was the most prolific purveyor of the swing-shift doubleheader concept. The Phillies conducted several other swing-shift doubleheaders, including morning-afternoon twin bills on August 11 against the Pittsburgh Pirates and September 15 against the New York Giants. The Athletics also staged swing-shift doubleheaders on September 22 and 27, with two elements contributing to the success of these contests. The Phillies promoted the events, which also often included a ladies day feature that might be attractive to the Rosie the Riveters among the war workers. Secondly, Philadelphia baseball fans still had lively memories of morning games on a holiday, since the city was the last to succumb to the single-admission holiday afternoon doubleheader trend. The Athletics continued to stage separate morning and afternoon games on a holiday as late as 1934, whereas most other major-league ballclubs had discarded the concept in the 1920s.

Interestingly, the traditional holiday scheduling format that had gone out of fashion in the late 1920s suddenly reappeared in 1943. Several ballclubs used a variation of the swing-shift doubleheader concept by conducting a separate-admission two-game set with one game in the morning and the other in the afternoon. The Boston Red Sox first experimented with this format on May 27, while the Cleveland Indians hosted two-game sets on July 8 against the Senators and August 18 against the Yankees.

After the Red Sox game with the Indians was rained out on May 26, Boston management decided to reschedule the postponed game for 10:30 A.M. on May 27 prior to the scheduled afternoon contest that day. "But it will be no bargain—they'll be a separate admission charge for each game," the *Boston Globe* reported. "The Red Sox are to play baseball this morning right after breakfast. The morning game was scheduled so that war workers who go to work on the 3–11 P.M. shift can take in a game. Whether they'll roll out of bed sufficiently early to take it in remains to be seen." They didn't. Only 2,027 fans showed up for the "first nonholiday morning game in the professional baseball history of Boston." The *Globe* assigned blame for the meager attendance to the Sox management "because the Red Sox—with an amazing lack of promotional flare—kept the game a secret until the last moment." The *Globe* also noted another flaw in the plan for the morning game: "Guys who have worked all night and other guys who've jumped out of bed on six hours sleep don't like frankfurters for breakfast."[21]

The Cleveland Indians had a bit more success attracting spectators to their separate-admission morning-afternoon twin bill on August 18 against the Yankees. "Embroiled in their first morning game in many years, with an 11 o'clock start," the Yankees lost to the Indians before 5,673 fans. "They came back at 3:30 P.M. thoroughly rested and lightly fed," only to lose in 14 innings before 7,500 spectators.[22]

Another wrinkle introduced in 1943 was the suspended game, which was designed to avert situations like the lights-out fiascos at the Polo Grounds in 1942 and a more pervasive issue—the Sunday curfews in Massachusetts (now extended to 6:30 P.M.) and Pennsylvania. The rule "aims to eliminate stalling and similar acts of skullduggery so frequently practiced while the clock is running out on a helpless adversary." Rather than have the score revert to the last completed inning when a game was prematurely stopped by unnatural conditions, the game was suspended at that point and resumed the next time that the opponent visited the home team. The first application of this National League rule came on July 18, when the second contest of the Sunday doubleheaders in Pittsburgh and Boston were both stopped by a Sunday curfew. Both were resumed at a later date, the Boston game not until two months later on September 13.[23]

The Dodgers–Braves match at Braves Field was stopped in the sixth inning with the score tied, 4–4. The Braves caught a break, since they had scored three runs in the bottom of the sixth inning and had the bases loaded with one out "when the gong struck at 6:29 and the umps called it a day for fans and ball tossers alike." If the game had occurred in 1942, the score would have reverted to a 4–1 victory for Brooklyn. "The boos compared favorably, however, with the pop bottles that might have flown through the air if the game had reverted in Brooklyn's favor," the *Boston Globe* remarked. There also were no shenanigans that sometime occurred in curfew-curtailed contests. "It really worked out great compared with some of the games we used to have. There wasn't any stalling," umpire Bill Stewart said after the game. "Everything Brooklyn did was strictly legitimate. Knowing the game was going to be finished anyway [at a later date], nobody was under pressure."[24]

In 1944, war workers came to Sunday doubleheaders not only to watch the games but also to play in them as part-time players, as many ballplayers who hadn't entered the service had obtained jobs that contributed to the war effort, which was the primary source of draft deferment in 1943. The St. Louis Browns utilized several war workers to play weekend games in 1944. After they converted to full-time players in mid-season, these players helped the Browns win the American League pennant that year for the only time in the club's half-century, generally moribund, history.

Browns outfielder Chet Laabs worked at a defense job during the week in St. Louis, after starting the season working in a war plant in Detroit. "Bill [DeWitt] got me a job in his father-in-law's plant in St. Louis," Laabs said after his playing days were over. "I got to St. Louis about the first of June. I worked days. Whenever the club was at home, I could play at night and on Saturdays and Sundays."[25]

Denny Galehouse became a Sunday pitcher for the Browns. Galehouse commuted between his job at Goodyear Aircraft in Akron, Ohio, and the location of the Browns Sunday doubleheader. "On Saturday, I'd get an overnight train to wherever the Browns were playing. You knew the schedule way ahead and made the reservations way ahead, so most of the time I'd get an upper berth [to sleep in on the train]," Galehouse recalled. "I'd get there at 7:30 or 8 o'clock in the morning. I'd have breakfast and go to the ball park. I'd pitch the first game and then I'd leave and take the train and go back home."[26]

On May 14 in Philadelphia and May 21 in New York, Galehouse pitched in relief. He then started the succeeding four Sundays, three in St. Louis and one in Detroit—and lost all four games. "It was a little tiring because I was on the go all the time. At first I pitched pretty good. I wasn't winning, but I kept the opposition low," Galehouse recalled about his Sunday pitcher experience. "From a pitching standpoint, the hitters were a little easier to pitch to than prior to World War II. But then the fielders weren't quite as good, either, so it would kind of balance." After taking off a few weeks, Galehouse rejoined the Browns on a full-time basis in late July, helped the club win the pennant, and was the starting pitcher in the first game of the World Series that fall.[27]

Transportation challenges continued to haunt major-league baseball in 1944. Several ballgames in 1944 were purposely cut short to enable ballclubs to make train connections. On May 16, the Philadelphia–St. Louis match was called after seven innings to allow the Phillies to catch a train. On August 1, the Pittsburgh–Boston game was stopped at 5:00 P.M. after eight innings so that the Pirates could catch a 6:00 train to New York in order to get to Pittsburgh for its August 2 game. Both were considered suspended games and were completed at a later date. Sunday curfews also continued to plague the two leagues. Pittsburgh, in particular, had challenges completing the nightcap of several Sunday doubleheaders during the 1944 season. The second contests on July 2 and July 9 had to be suspended; on July 5 the Pirates completed a suspended game from May 21.[28]

Twilight-night doubleheaders expanded in number in 1944 after the lifting in July of the restriction on the number of night games that a ballclub could play during the season. Washington had already been granted permission to play 43 night games in 1944, while the two St. Louis clubs could play 21 games apiece. The twi-night twin bills were played mostly in the American League, though, since the majority of National League ballclub owners frowned on the concept.[29]

After a slight decrease in number during 1944, doubleheaders reached their zenith of major-league utilization in 1945. More than 300 twin bills were played in the two leagues, which represented 49 percent of all games played during the 1945 season. The initial 1945 schedule had called for 198 doubleheaders, or 32 percent of all games. Both were high-water marks for the doubleheader in major-league history.

In 1945 the Chicago Cubs established a major-league record by winning both games of a doubleheader 20 times. The Cubs set the record on September 16 by sweeping a twin bill from Brooklyn for its 18th sweep of the season, eclipsing the record set by the St. Louis Cardinals just the year before. The Cubs went on to sweep doubleheaders against the Reds on September 27 and against the Pirates on September 29 on the way to clinching the National League pennant on the latter date.[30]

The Cubs doubleheader-sweep streak in 1945 ran contrary to baseball's generally accepted principle that there was a greater probability that a twin bill would be split than swept. Various analyses have shown that the probability is at least equal. An examination by *Baseball Magazine* in 1928 of the 185 doubleheaders played during the 1927 season (those without any ties) showed that 94 were split and 91 were swept. A more sophisticated analysis in the *American Statistician* in 1969 concluded that 58 percent of doubleheaders were swept during the 1964 season so that "we may safely accept the hypothesis that more double-headers are swept than are split."[31]

The doubleheader helped to save major-league baseball during World War II, as the two-for-one technique provided an incentive for war-weary fans to attend ballgames when it was convenient for them, on the weekends

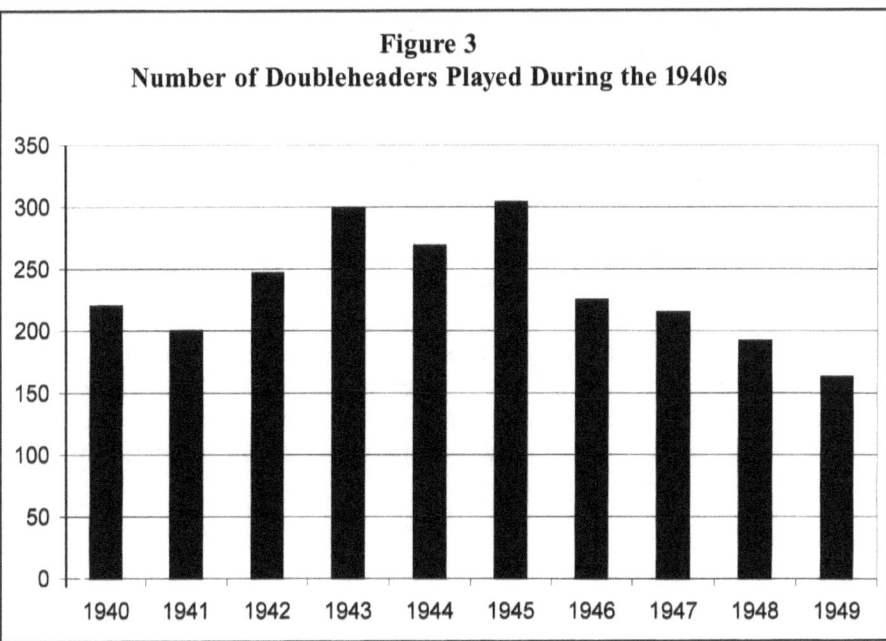

Doubleheader usage in the major leagues reached its zenith during the wartime years in the 1940s, as ballclub owners used the two-for-one promotion as an incentive for weary war-plant workers to attend ballgames. (Source: Retrosheet database.)

and in the early evening. Overall ballpark attendance did fall during 1942 and 1943, but it would have been worse had it not been for the doubleheader and other promotions (including admitting stateside servicemen for free, who weren't included in the attendance counts). However, the great fear of ballclub owners in decades past came to fruition as spectators came to expect a doubleheader on Sundays, since single games generally only attracted large crowds when played as night games.

"The natural avenue of escape for those engaged in their daily tasks is not even Sunday any longer, although it still holds a high place on the recreation calendar," *The Sporting News* editorialized in 1943. "Instead, a war-busy civilian population turns to the evenings for respite from everyday toil." The editorial added, "Club owners have come to the belief that doubleheaders were the attraction that brought out the patrons. In view of the single-game night crowds, one is prompted to ask, 'What price doubleheaders now?'"[32]

Baseball Magazine posed similar concerns. "The scheduling of other than Sunday and holiday double features in 1944 has been another practical war time measure that has won at least the temporary approval of the fans," the monthly periodical editorialized. "But would it be desirable to continue on such a basis after the war? Taking a long range view, would it be to the best interests of baseball?" The editorial concluded that "the doubleheader will gradually lose its appeal as other interests mount."[33]

By 1945, the doubleheader had become a staple of other sports besides baseball, in particular college basketball at major arenas such as Madison Square Garden in New York. The double feature was also the norm at the movie theater, where it was estimated that three-fourths of the nation's theaters were dedicated to two-feature shows.[34]

Because two-for-one was becoming engrained in the mind of the American consumer, ballclub owners couldn't just immediately jettison the doubleheader concept. However, those "other interests" that *Baseball Magazine* mentioned would lessen the appeal of the doubleheader soon began to appear in the early 1950s. But they were not what anyone in 1944 expected them to be.

12

Twi-Night and Day-Night Doubleheaders

ATTENDANCE AT MAJOR-LEAGUE ballparks soared in 1946, as Americans celebrated the end of World War II and compensated for the lost years of normalcy in everyday life. "Yes, indeed, America has certainly gone baseball conscious in the first post-war campaign in a manner that promises to send attendance figures soaring into 'gastronomical figures,'" John Drebinger waxed about the crowds at the ballpark by mid-season. "For there is no getting away from it. Mr. and Mrs. Gus Fan, Gus Jr. and Sister Fannie are determined to make this the most amazing, and at the same time, the most lucrative season in all baseball history." Attendance topped 18 million during the 1946 season, nearly double the prewar attendance level of 9.5 million in 1941, to establish a high-water mark for spectatorship at major-league ballgames.[1]

Baseball fans feasted on doubleheaders in 1946, as the two-for-one bargain was offered in every major-league ballpark on all three holidays, just about every Sunday, and several times during the season to make up postponed games. Fans could also sample night games more often, as the Braves and Yankees installed lights for the 1946 season and the Red Sox and Tigers for the 1947 season. Every major-league ballclub, with the sole exception of the Chicago Cubs, was able to play home games at night by 1948.

Drebinger espoused caution regarding the abundance of doubleheaders. He wrote that owners should consider "a reduction of the innumerable 'bargain' features which the magnates found so necessary to arouse flagging interest in less prosperous times—such as booking synthetic doubleheaders on the slightest provocation, scheduling doubleheaders for all Sundays and overcrowding the schedule with night games." The concern was fan complacency. "In some cities in recent years a fan came to regard a doubleheader as such a regular and commonplace offering he scarcely would bother to come out for a single game," Drebinger wrote. "It was the automatic Sunday doubleheader that all but wiped out the once profitable Saturday afternoon." The love affair with the single afternoon ballgame headed for an abrupt ending.[2]

The widespread acceptance of night baseball forever changed the nature of the doubleheader. The first casualty was the basic Level 1 doubleheader, two games during the afternoon, which had been used to make up postponed games for five decades. For dates when night games were scheduled, ballclubs couldn't just tack on another night game as they easily could do to an afternoon game, since spectators would not tolerate the second game starting at 11:00 P.M. Thus ballclubs more often used the twilight-night doubleheader concept, a variation of the Level 1 doubleheader, which was spawned in the war years. The problem with the twilight-night doubleheader was that the night game component was likely to attract a large attendance by itself, and thus didn't need the lure of the second "free" game to be economically viable like the weekday afternoon game needed.

A technique to substitute for the Level 1 doubleheader idea arose in 1946. When the New York Giants game with the St. Louis Cardinals was rained out in St. Louis on June 1, the Cardinals announced that it would be made up on August 28 as part of a day-night doubleheader, or as Cardinals president Sam Breadon put it, "two single games on the same date." Breadon had cooked up a variation of the defunct morning-afternoon separate-admission holiday two-game set. In the new version, the night game played the role of the holiday afternoon game with its big attendance, while the ballclub tolerated the smaller crowd at the holiday morning game (the afternoon game in the new version). Of course, technically, the day-night concept wasn't a doubleheader at all because there were separate admissions for each game, but that didn't stop anyone from promoting the concept as a doubleheader.[3]

Breadon was precluded by National League rules from playing a twilight-night doubleheader to make up a rainout, since the league had agreed to prohibit such events at its winter meeting in December 1945. Short of moving the scheduled night game to the afternoon to create a conventional doubleheader—which club finances would dictate against—the only other option was a separate-admission afternoon contest as a prelude to the scheduled night game.[4]

Branch Rickey, the president of the Brooklyn ballclub, was actually the first to implement the day-night doubleheader, after a Dodgers game with the Giants was rained out at Ebbets Field in mid–August. "The powers-that-be in Brooklyn immediately borrowed a page out of Sam Breadon's book and scheduled one of those new-fangled doubleheaders for today, except that one of the games will be played at 2:30 in the afternoon and the other at 8:30 at night," the *New York Times* reported, adding, "Of course, two admissions will be charged." There was no spectator backlash at the time, in what the *Times* called an "unprecedented doubleheader" and "the longest day in Flatbush history." Indeed, the two games on August 14, 1946, set a record for attendance on one day in Brooklyn, when 57,224 entered the ballpark at both games. "The Dodgers asked for and received with virtually no complaints double admission prices and since 26,970 fans paid to witness the afternoon contest and 30,254 followed suit at night, the exchequer was handsomely enriched." With results like that, the day-night doubleheader was soon duplicated at many major-league ballparks.[5]

While the day-night doubleheader was a financial success for the ballclubs, it was a huge inconvenience for the ballplayers, who spent the entire day at the ballpark to play games starting at 2:30 P.M. and 8:30 P.M. "Of course, there is the change in living habits of the athletes to be considered," the *New York Times* commented. "They completed the opener at 5:17 P.M. and retired to their dressing rooms, where specially catered dinners were served. They then rested and relaxed until it was time to take batting practice and none looked any worse for their experience." However, Arthur Daley of the *Times* summed up the situation from the ballplayer's perspective: "The Brooks and the Giants spent approximately twelve hours at the ballpark in one day, much too long for as highly keyed a machine as an athlete." It was far too long for any human being, for that matter. Daley called them "split twin bills." The day-night doubleheader soon became a bone of contention between the ballplayers and the ballclubs.[6]

Contrary to the National League, the American League did permit twilight-night doubleheaders to make up postponements. The St. Louis Browns hosted the first postwar twilight-night doubleheader on August 13, 1946, against the Chicago White Sox. The technique was quickly copied by other American League ballclubs; 10 days later the Washington Senators hosted the Detroit Tigers in another twilight-night twin bill.[7]

The National League resisted playing twilight-night doubleheaders until the 1950 season, after the league voted to authorize the technique in December 1949. The key to staging a twi-night doubleheader was to be able to complete the twilight portion under the lights without having a lengthy delay between the twilight game and the night game, which occurred during such twin bills before 1950. Because the National League also permitted a day game to be completed under the lights for the first time in 1950, the twilight-night doubleheader now morphed into the twi-night doubleheader, where the second game could begin shortly after the completion of the first game and not have to wait an hour or so in order to leave time for potential extra innings to be played in the first game. On April 16, 1950, spectators at Braves Field saw the first major-league game to be started in daylight and completed under lights. The American League was slower to allow this to happen, waiting until August 29, 1950, at Yankee Stadium.[8]

Brooklyn pitcher Don Newcombe nearly entered doubleheader pitching immortality when he pitched both games of a twi-night doubleheader at Shibe Park on September 6, 1950, when the Dodgers were in a neck-and-neck battle with the Phillies for first place. "Big Don Newcombe tried to do it all by himself last night at Shibe Park," the *Brooklyn Eagle* reported. "The Dodger righthander made a bold bid too. Not for 20 years had it been attempted—a pitcher hurling both ends of a doubleheader. It's an iron man stunt that requires an arm of tempered steel." After Newcombe pitched a three-hit shutout in the first game, manager Burt Shotton, with few live arms available among his pitching corps, joked with Newcombe that "a big guy like you should be able to pitch two." To the surprise of Shotton, Newcombe nodded his concurrence and told Shotton, "Give me the ball. If we've got to have it, I'll pitch." Newcombe then hurled the first seven innings of the second game, before departing with the Dodgers losing, 2–0. Brooklyn rallied for three runs in the ninth to win, but too late for Newcombe to gain credit for it and thus claim a double-victory for the day. "It was a foolish thing to do," Newcombe said years later. "But the club needed the win, and we had some pitchers with sore arms. I was young and strong." Newcombe was one of the last pitchers (who didn't rely on a knuckleball) to start both games of a doubleheader.[9]

The twi-night doubleheader was such a novelty that it inspired rhetorical discourse in an academic journal. Willis Russell included the term in an article in *American Speech* about new words (which included "shoo-in" and "automation"), defining it as "pertaining to a doubleheader the first game of which begins during twilight." The term also spawned literary metaphors by writing luminaries such as George Plimpton. "The Twi-Night Doubleheader is hardly anything to get riled up about—being a small cinch worm. The worm sometimes makes a loop or so forward, and then often backwards, so that to the imaginative observer the creature appears to have two heads," Plimpton penned. "He emerges in the evening, most usually in the months of August and September. Heavy rains in the summer are apparently instrumental in the Twi-Night Doubleheader's appearance later on."[10]

While the twi-night doubleheader enjoined popularity, the day-night doubleheader also became a staple of both leagues in 1947. In the American League where clubs could reschedule a postponement as part of either a day-night or twi-night doubleheader, the selection between the two techniques depended on the judgment of which would produce the larger incremental attendance. Since day baseball during the workweek was essentially dead in St. Louis—both the Browns and the Cardinals played a higher number of night games relative to the other ballclubs—the Browns usually opted for the twi-nighter. In Boston, where night games were judiciously scheduled, the Red Sox usually opted for the day-night affair.

Both techniques likely would have died a quiet, early death had not attendance begun to drop in 1949 and continue to tank throughout the 1950s. After hitting a height of 21 million in 1948, attendance plunged to 17.5 million in 1950 and plummeted to 14 million by 1953. Reduced attendance resuscitated the Sunday doubleheader, rendered viable both alternative forms of the doubleheader, and virtually killed the traditional afternoon doubleheader during the workweek (except, of course, at Wrigley Field, which had no lighting system). During the 1950s, day-night and twi-night doubleheader thrived even though, much like the early history of the Sunday doubleheader, they rarely appeared on the initial season schedules.[11]

The St. Louis Cardinals tried a few variations on the day-night doubleheader. The Cardinals attempted to schedule a day-night doubleheader for Sunday, July 16, 1950, before the commissioner stepped in to nix the ploy to maintain the Lord's Day as night-game-free. On September 13, 1951, there was an unusual day-night doubleheader in St. Louis involving three ballclubs. In the first game, the Cardinals played the Giants in the afternoon to make up a rainout the previous day; in the nightcap the Cardinals played the Braves in a scheduled night game.[12]

The day-night doubleheader made its first appearance on a preseason schedule in 1955, when the American League included two. "There are two unusual items in the schedule, however, a pair of day-night games. In the past this sort of thing had been resorted to only to take care of postponed games, for which suitable dates could not be found." One was on June 17 in Boston, for the Bunker Hill Day holiday unique to that major-league city. The second was on June 1 in Kansas City to accommodate the New York Yankees, who wanted to travel by train after their Memorial Day twin bill in Washington rather than fly by airplane to Kansas City.[13]

Day-night doubleheaders worked best on a Saturday, when a ballclub could maximize the attendance at both the afternoon and evening segments. Twi-night doubleheaders worked best on mid-week evenings when attendance was expected to be light. By the end of the 1950s, the day-night doubleheader was an accepted method to economically make up a postponed game. "Two games for the price of two games was the big bargain the Yankees advertised yesterday," one wag reported in 1958.[14]

The day-night doubleheader was so successful that the Brooklyn Dodgers extended the concept to reinstitute separate admissions for holiday games at Ebbets Field in 1947 in a quest to maximize revenue for the ballclub that played in one of the smallest ballparks in the league. The Dodgers' Independence Day twin bill in 1947 consisted of a morning game starting at 10:00 A.M. and an afternoon game starting at 2:00 P.M. However, only eight innings could be completed in the first game "before the 1 o'clock curfew humanely put an end to the struggle," a 16–7 Brooklyn victory. "At the outset it had been agreed to start no inning after one in order that there would be ample time to clear the park for the afternoon crowd." There was no fan backlash for the separate-admission holiday fare, as more than 50,000 spectators attended the two games at Ebbets Field, 20,565 in the morning and 32,332 in the afternoon.[15]

Three years later in 1950, though, the New York state legislature tried to stop the Dodgers from charging separate admissions for games played on the same day, through the passage of the Murphy-Rosenblatt bill. The bill, proposed by two Brooklyn legislators, Assemblyman Lawrence Murphy and Senator William Rosenblatt, prohibited major-league ballclubs from starting a game before 1:00 and, if two games were being played, the second one couldn't start or continue after sundown. "The Dodgers have been putting on one game in the morning and another in the afternoon, and sometimes one in the afternoon and another at night," Murphy said after the State Assembly passed the bill by an overwhelming majority, 136 to 4. "These are normally doubleheaders and there's no reason why the fans should pay two admissions." After the State Senate passed the bill by a 52 to 4 vote, the bill went to Governor Thomas Dewey for signature.[16]

As the governor deliberated whether or not to sign the bill to make it law, the Brooklyn Dodgers filed a legal memorandum opposing the bill. Walter O'Malley, part owner of, and attorney for, the ballclub, wrote the memo, in which he argued that the bill was "unconstitutional," "discriminatory," and an "improper exercise of police power." O'Malley went on to argue that "the purpose of the bill is not to promote the public health, safety or morals." Seeming to take O'Malley's arguments into consideration, Governor Dewey vetoed the bill. In a memorandum that accompanied the veto, Dewey wrote, "It is not the business of the state to determine by law when baseball games shall be played in the absence of any showing that the health, welfare or safety of the people is involved." As Dewey observed, "This is still a free country."[17]

The separate-admission doubleheader concept almost made its way to the Supreme Court to determine its continued legality. "The impertinence of legislators in wrongfully butting into other people's business was recognized by Governor Dewey when he vetoed the bill which would have prevented the Dodgers from staging split double-headers at two admission prices," sportswriter Arthur Daley commented the day after Dewey's veto. "Baseball men will breathe easier from now on. They were firmly convinced that the proposed law could be proved both unconstitutional and discriminatory but appealing their case to the Supreme Court would have consumed both time and money." Daley thought the appeals process unnecessary, though, since history had shown that this kind of doubleheader was uneconomical. "It was common practice in the old days for holiday bills to consist

BROOKLYN EAGLE

16 PAGES OF COLOR COMICS — **5¢ EVERYWHERE**

WEATHER—Partly cloudy, windy and somewhat warmer today.

109th YEAR—No. 91—DAILY and SUNDAY BROOKLYN 1, N. Y., SUNDAY, APRIL 2, 1950

PRESENT AND ACCOUNTED FOR—Census taker Marion Reilly, left, asks Mr. and Mrs. Pignoloni the pertinent questions at Emidio's Bar and Grill. Scow Capt. Ernest Selvek, center, holding his dog, Rita, was probably the most surprised man in America when John Labi reached his barge with census forms. Capt. W. R. Cooke, U. S. N., commanding officer of the U. S. Naval Receiving Station, right, is shown being questioned by Leon R. Poley.

Reds Paid Jessup Institute $3,500, McCarthy Asserts

Hickenlooper Blasts Atom Board; 'Clean Bill' for Accused Envoy

RUSH ALASKAN DEFENSE JOB, IKE DEMANDS

Calls for All-Around Modernization of U. S. Land, Sea, Air Arms

Census Tabulators Discover Brooklyn Is Full of Surprises

Indians, Gypsies and Barge Dwellers All Grist for Mill of Tally Scouts

By JEANNE TOOMEY

MAN'S WOUND TIPS COPS TO HOLDUP PAIR

2 Admit Robberies —Others Hunted in Series of Crimes

More Foot Police Sought by O'Brien In War on Crime

'Can't Win Without Them,' He Says, Comparing Them to Infantry

MEETING SEALS ATLANTIC PACT DEFENSE PLAN

Ministers of Eleven Nations Approve Master Strategy

TRUMANS ANSWER QUIZ

CITY PUTS OFF 2 BORO TRANSIT IMPROVEMENTS

Utica Ave. Subway, IRT Nostrand Extension Must Wait, Board Says

Flying Couple Hop for Paris In Round-World Record Try

PALM SUNDAY STROLLERS FACE GUSTY WINDS

House Group Lists 9 Steps to Curb Reds

Dodgers Urge Veto Of Doubleheader Bill

APRIL FOOL'S DAY, BUT IT WAS NO JOKE

WHERE TO FIND IT

The term "doubleheader" was rarely seen in front-page headlines, such as page one of the *Brooklyn Eagle* on April 2, 1950. The headline in the lower right-hand corner, "Dodgers Urge Veto of Doubleheader Bill," referred to the recently passed bill in the New York legislature that would have mandated single-admission doubleheaders and outlawed separate-admission two-game sets. New York Governor Thomas Dewey did veto the legislation.

of morning and afternoon games," Daley explained. "They were stopped only when the magnates discovered that they could draw more clients with genuine twin bills than split ones."[18]

While the Memorial Day holiday bill at Ebbets Field in 1950 was a separate-admission two-game set, it was the last holiday ballgame in Brooklyn under Rickey's tenure. When O'Malley assumed the leadership of the Dodgers later that year, the ballclub reverted to conducting single-admission holiday doubleheaders during the 1951 season (although the ballclub continued to use the separate-admission concept for day-night doubleheaders).

Forecasting how holiday ballgames would change in the 1950s and 1960s was the makeup of the Bunker Hill Day holiday bill, one of the two Boston-specific holidays on the major-league schedule that the Red Sox and Braves alternated hosting each year. Just as changes to the Bunker Hill Day games in 1921 had been an auricle of the rise in holiday doubleheaders, the postwar changes to the Bunker Hill Day bill were a harbinger of the decline of holiday doubleheaders.

After more than four decades of staging two games on the Bunker Hill Day holiday—first as a morning-afternoon two-game set and then as a single-admission doubleheader—in 1947 the Red Sox opted to play just one game on the holiday. The Braves reverted to the traditional doubleheader in 1948, which was the last two-for-one bill on the holiday. In 1949, the Red Sox staged a separate-admission day-night doubleheader on the holiday, which drew 7,264 spectators for the afternoon game but filled Fenway Park in the evening with a crowd numbering 31,446. Following a brief hiatus in 1950 and 1951 when the holiday fell on the weekend, the Braves scheduled a twi-night doubleheader for the holiday in 1952. Rainy weather kept the crowd below 10,000 and eventually led to canceling the second game. The Red Sox scheduled a single game on the holiday in 1953, the year the Braves left Boston to relocate to Milwaukee. The Bunker Hill Day holiday tradition ended when Boston ceased to be a two-club major-league city. The last time two games were played on the holiday was June 17, 1955, when the Sox played a day-night event that attracted 10,612 in the afternoon and 33,104 at night. The trials and tribulations with the Bunker Hill Day holiday signaled that the custom of playing of two afternoon games on a holiday was in serious trouble as a viable scheduling technique.[19]

The separate-admission morning-afternoon Patriots Day holiday twin bill—with the break in between so fans could watch the runners in the Boston Marathon—was dropped from the schedule after the 1955 two-game set. While the Patriots Day twin bill had a brief revival from 1963 to 1967 (including as a single-admission doubleheader with return-entry privileges in 1966), the holiday's lasting legacy today is the 11:00 A.M. start for the single game that the Red Sox play every year on Patriots Day. This tradition began on

April 19, 1968, and continues now that the holiday occurs on the third Monday in April.[20]

While the number of twi-night and day-night doubleheaders increased during the postwar era, the Sunday doubleheader began a three-decade-long decline in popularity. Before there was even evidence of a postwar attendance boom, the Brooklyn Dodgers jettisoned the Sunday doubleheader from its schedule in 1946 in favor of playing 14 night games. The only doubleheader slated for Ebbets Field in 1946 was on Memorial Day. The trend to night baseball was most evident in St. Louis where the Cardinals scheduled 38 night games in 1946, the highest number in the National League. Along with its steady slate of Sunday doubleheaders, there were very few afternoon ballgames during the workweek for Cardinals fans.[21]

One factor that accelerated the change in Sunday scheduling was the creation of a new social institution in America—the "weekend"—as the normal workweek contracted from six days to five, providing most working people with a full day off on Saturday in addition to the conventional Sunday day of rest. Attending a ballgame on Saturday became much easier for many fans, particularly those who desired to bring their family along, thus eroding a portion of the demand for Sunday ballgames.

On Easter Sunday, April 21, 1946, only four of eight matchups that day were contested as doubleheaders, with the rest played as single games. The doubleheader in Boston between the Red Sox and the Athletics, however, equaled just a game and a half, since the second game lasted just five innings due to the Sunday curfew under the Massachusetts Sunday baseball law. That five-inning loss to the Athletics set into motion the political wherewithal within the state legislature to finally remove the legal impediment that affected the completion of Sunday doubleheaders in Boston. On May 17, the Massachusetts governor signed the law eliminating the Sunday curfew, which removed a potential obstacle to the Red Sox who were on their way to winning their first American League pennant in nearly three decades.[22]

The Sunday doubleheader got a reprieve from widespread elimination by other ballclubs duplicating the Brooklyn strategy when the postwar attendance boom lasted just three years. As attendance declined, ballclubs used the two-for-one Sunday twin bill as a promotion to attract spectators and stem their sagging attendance figures. In 1952, the *Wall Street Journal* noted that "the number of fans turning out for professional games has been going downward each year since 1948" and that the attendance in the National League was running 13 percent below 1951 figures. "Baseball's biggest problem, of course, is to hold on to old fans and cultivate new ones," the *Journal* noted. "One result is that lots of club owners are stepping up promotional activities," notably Bill Veeck, owner of the St. Louis Browns. "Mr. Veeck has been mixing up baseball activities with occasional fireworks displays, roving bands, circus acts and free orchids for the ladies." The *Journal* concluded by saying some clubs disdained promotions in favor of the game on the field. "Our policy is to put the best possible team on the field," a Detroit Tigers publicist was quoted, to which the *Journal* wryly commented, "The Tigers, incidentally, are in last place." The second free ballgame of a Sunday doubleheader was no longer enough to fill seats in the ballpark.[23]

Declining attendance led to the first franchise shifts in major-league baseball in a half century. The Boston Braves began the process when they moved to Milwaukee for the 1953 season. Milwaukee offered a new stadium a few miles from the center city, acres of parking for the cars of suburban fans, and a large Midwestern area from which to draw fans. After trading schedules with Pittsburgh for the 1953 season to more easily accommodate the shift to Milwaukee, the Braves jettisoned the bulk of their Sunday doubleheaders from the 1954 schedule in favor of single games on the Lord's Day. By leading the National League in attendance in 1954 with over two million fans, Milwaukee's one-game-on-Sunday strategy helped to accelerate the decline in Sunday doubleheaders that Brooklyn had commenced in 1946. When the Browns moved to Baltimore for the 1954 season and the Athletics to Kansas City for 1955, neither ballclub used the Sunday doubleheader to a large extent. By 1956 the typical midseason Sunday schedule had atrophied to four or five doubleheader matchups from the typical full slate of eight that had dominated the major-league calendar for the previous decade and a half. The Sunday doubleheader was quickly becoming an anachronism during the month of September as professional football began to dominate the post–Labor-Day sports scene on Sunday.

Ironically, with the decline in the number of ballpark spectators came a shift in ballclub economics away from gate receipts toward television rights fees. The increase in financial dependence on TV rights fees contributed to the decline of the doubleheader, both the Sunday and holiday varieties. At first, TV stations, seeking low-cost productions to fill air time, telecast both games of a doubleheader. For example, WPIX in New York reserved the entire afternoon of June 30, 1949, to telecast a doubleheader at the Polo Grounds between the Giants and the Braves. However, the arrival of a national "Game of the Week" telecast in 1953 started to diminish the value of the second game from a television perspective. Because ballclubs received greater TV rights fees from the number of televised dates, pressure soon came to bear to minimize doubleheaders and maximize single-game dates on the schedule.[24]

The percentage of ballclub revenue associated with radio and television broadcasts nearly quintupled from 3 percent in 1946 to 17 percent in 1956. That was the average for all 16 major-league ballclubs. The percentage of Brooklyn Dodgers revenue from broadcasts rose from 6 percent in 1946 to 26 percent in 1956, as home-game receipts declined from 72 percent of total revenue in 1946 to 53 percent in 1956 when attendance nearly halved over that time period.[25]

Much like the Cubs ownership who advocated radio broadcasts of baseball games in the 1920s, the proponents of televised baseball in the 1950s believed that "in the long run television will increase interest and bring to the parks scores of thousands who never before would have bothered to see 'live' major league baseball." As attendance sank at the ballpark, owners hungry for revenue permitted one-third of all ballgames to be televised by the mid–1950s. Rights fees from these telecasts helped to offset lost revenue from lower gate attendance.[26]

Baseball clearly had to compete with leisure activities such as golf and other entertainment options such as horse racing and air-conditioned movies, which increasingly nipped away at baseball's traditional spectator base. Attendance at race tracks to watch horse racing steadily increased during the 1950s as track owners remodeled their once-dingy facilities to attract new customers. "Take a look around the newer race tracks," Jim Murray wrote in a 1956 *Sports Illustrated* article, "escalators, a multiplicity of restaurants and cocktail lounges (real hot chef's food, not hot-water frankferters and soupy mustard), cushions on seats, clean-up crews constantly at work, plenty of police for your protection and a setting as relaxing and beautiful as the center of Central Park on a summer afternoon. A baseball park ought to be a facsimile of same." Murray postulated that baseball's *homo spectator* was on the way to becoming merely the backdrop to a TV athletic show because of deplorable conditions at big-league ballparks. "The ball park? That filthy hole? Not on your life!" Murray illustrated a wife's lament to her husband. "We're going down to Loew's High where they have Rossano Brazzi kissing Katherine Hepburn's hand in Technicolor on a Wide Screen with Stereophonic Sound, and where they have those big, comfortable loge seats with air-conditioning and hot popcorn and cold Coke if you feel like it." Sweating and cheering on hard wooden seats at the ballpark, too many with poles obstructing views, became much less appealing.[27]

Baseball's traditional spectator base began to abandon the ballpark in the postwar era. "By mid-century, urban growth had extended the market for professional sports to metropolitan areas, as people and jobs spread to the suburbs at an accelerating rate," Michael Danielson wrote in *Home Team: Professional Sports and the American Metropolis*. "Among those moving outward were professional sports' most attractive customers, relatively affluent white males and their families." Because many ballparks were in "decaying areas undergoing racial transition," the now-suburban baseball fan "saw these areas as undesirable and dangerous" and, even when safe, "sports facilities in older cities offered insignificant parking for a metropolitan population addicted to automobiles." Ebbets Field in Brooklyn was a classic example.

Its limited seating (30,000 seats), too many obstructed views, few amenities, and inadequate parking (barely 700 cars) in an increasingly rundown neighborhood inspired the perspectives that it was "a cherished tradition [that] had become an inconvenient obsolescence" and "had lived by the trolley and was going to die by the car."[28]

To try to attract new customers to deteriorating ballparks, owners devised more twi-night doubleheaders and giveaways at Sunday doubleheaders. "Premiums and panaceas to lure baseball fans from television set to ballpark are being called in like relief pitchers at a slugfest," one writer wryly noted. Clubs sponsored days in the name of a town, a player, or a large organization. For the 1952 season, the Dodgers slated a number of ladies' days and one ladies' night in addition to "no fewer than fourteen knothole days, three twi-night doubleheaders, a veterans' day, a father-and-son day and a batch of autograph days when, after the game, Dodgers players will sit in booths under the grandstand where they will oblige freely with their signatures."[29]

By the end of the 1950s, the Sunday doubleheader continued to decline in popularity. While the weekend, franchise relocations, night baseball, and television had precipitated a downward spiral for the Sunday doubleheader, the expansion of consumerism on Sunday accelerated this trend. "During the 1950s and 1960s commercialism and materialism intensified their pressure on all aspects of American life, including Sunday," social scientist Alexis McCrossen observed in *Holy Day, Holiday: The American Sunday*. "Blue laws were amended to provide more time for commercial activity." Although leisure activities for decades had presented attractive alternatives to attending a baseball game, the novel opportunity to shop on Sunday heightened the competition to sway spectators from attending Sunday doubleheaders.[30]

The "free" second game of a Sunday doubleheader was no longer enough of an attraction to fill the ballpark. Other promotions were needed to fill the seats. The savviest promoter of the twin bill was Bill Veeck, who instituted numerous giveaways and promotions when he took ownership of the Cleveland Indians in 1946 and advanced the art to new heights when he purchased the St. Louis Browns in 1951. Veeck's most famous promotion occurred at a Sunday doubleheader on August 19, 1951, at Sportsman's Park when midget Eddie Gaedel strode to the plate as a pinch-hitter for the Browns.

Veeck had arranged for a 50th anniversary celebration of the Falstaff Brewery (to coincide with the 50th anniversary of the founding of the American League that year). The efforts of Falstaff's distributors and dealers to hawk tickets all over the state of Missouri resulted in a paid attendance of 18,000, the largest crowd to see the Browns in four years. Veeck gave every spectator a can of beer, a slice of birthday cake, and a box of ice cream as they entered the park, along with salt-and-pepper shakers in the shape of a Falstaff bottle. Between games, Veeck arranged for a parade of old-fashioned cars, circus performers, and troubadours in Gay Nineties costumes roaming through the stands. To cap the festivities, a seven-foot-high cake was rolled on the field and Gaedel popped out of it, being announced as "a brand new Brownie." In the bottom of the first inning, Gaedel emerged from the dugout as a pinch-hitter for George Saucier. After Detroit pitcher Bob Cain walked Gaedel on four pitches, a pinch-runner substituted for Gaedel. Writers called Veeck's promotion "baseball burlesque" and "a mockery of the sport," but Veeck gained national publicity through the publication of Gaedel's photograph at bat, which spurred people to attend future Browns games.[31]

When Veeck became owner of the Chicago White Sox in 1959, he brought to Comiskey Park the showmanship skills he had exhibited with the St. Louis Browns. Veeck pioneered the exploding scoreboard, and made extensive use of the Lucky Seat promotion, where a spectator won 10,000 cupcakes or 1,000 cans of beer. "On Mother's Day, we opened the gates to any woman who could show a picture of a child, preferably her own. Almost 4,000 mothers passed through the turnstiles," Veeck recounted in his autobiography *Veeck—As in Wreck*. "Between games on one Sunday doubleheader, we presented the whole Christiani Brothers Circus, complete with the parade of elephants and a high-wire act."[32]

To honor National Dairy Week, Veeck conducted one of his more novel promotions at the June 7, 1959, Sunday twin bill against Boston. "The Red Sox won a cow-milking contest and a ball game before 25,844 here today as they split a doubleheader with the White Sox," the *Boston Globe* reported. After losing the opening game, "the Red Sox started their comeback when a three-man team of Jim Busby, Pete Runnels and Gary Geiger won a cow-milking contest—and $500—among them between games." Early Wynn, Ray Moore, and Nellie Fox of the White Sox provided the opposition. "All the cows submitted in good spirit except for the one drawn by Nellie Fox, who was on his way to winning the award as the league's Most Valuable Player," Veeck recalled. "The cow kept kicking, and Nellie kept trying and I started writing mental headlines again. This one read: Fox in Hospital in Critical Condition as Result of Veeck Gag. Nellie's cow lost no milk that day, and I lost no more than three buckets of blood."[33]

Sometimes baseball itself was enough of a draw for a Sunday doubleheader. Stan Musial gained doubleheader immortality when he set a major-league record by hitting five home runs in a Sunday twin bill on May 2, 1954, at Busch Stadium in St. Louis (the renamed Sportsman's Park). Musial hit three homers in the first game—then munched on a sandwich between games and gulped down a glass of milk—and hit two more homers in the second game to set the record. A crowd of 26,662 sat through rainy weather to watch the seven-hour doubleheader, waiting to see if Musial could stroke a sixth homer. He popped out in his last at-bat. "Jansen got me out on a bad pitch—a high fast ball inside," Musial said after the game. "Yeah, I was going for one that time." Musial had clubbed his fifth homer off Hoyt Wilhelm in the fifth inning. "My fifth home run that day went even higher over the back screen of the right-field roof, even farther out toward right-center," than his third homer of the day in the first game, Musial wrote in his autobiography. "I'm especially proud that it was hit off a knuckleball. Not just any old knuckleball—but a great knuckler's, Wilhelm's." Musial was a bit dumbfounded after the game that he had set a record, telling reporters, "I still can't believe it. You mean, real sluggers like Babe Ruth, Lou Gehrig, Ralph Kiner—men like them—never hit five homers in a doubleheader?"[34]

The Pennsylvania Sunday curfew, now extended to 7:00 P.M., also hurt interest in Sunday doubleheaders in Pittsburgh and Philadelphia. While the suspended game concept "eliminated stalling in games about to be halted by Sunday curfew," the *New York Times* reported in 1949, it "fell out of favor because it also brought about considerable confusion when the schedule became cluttered up with unfinished encounters." A suspended game was resumed at the point the curfew stopped the game when both teams met again in the same place. This was often weeks away, though, since Sunday was usually the last game of a series between two teams.[35]

With games taking a longer time to complete, more and more second games of Sunday doubleheaders in Philadelphia ended in suspended games, resulting in considerable fan confusion. For instance, the suspended game from the April 28, 1957, Sunday doubleheader between the Philadelphia Phillies and the New York Giants wasn't finished until 16 weeks later on August 16 when the Giants next returned to Philadelphia for a single game (the July 4 date in Philadelphia was already scheduled as a doubleheader). The Giants were ahead, 8–7, in the last of the seventh inning of the April 28 game, with the Phillies at bat and the tying run on second base, when the Sunday curfew under Pennsylvania law stopped the game. It was an unsatisfactory finish for Philadelphia fans at the game or listening on radio, as well as for New York fans since the Giants had lost the first game, 11–2, and they had to wait almost four months before they could claim victory in the second game. When the suspended game was finally resumed on August 16, New York pitcher Marv Grissom retired eight straight Philadelphia batters to preserve the 8–7 New York victory, unchanged from the score sixteen weeks earlier.[36]

By midseason 1958, the second game of four of five Sunday doubleheaders in Philadelphia couldn't be completed by the 7:00 curfew and thus resulted in suspended games. In 1959, the Pennsylvania legislature finally eliminated the last Sunday curfew in major-league baseball. Governor

Lawrence signed the bill on July 31, ending the baseball stoppages to ensure that "an activity not deemed sinful at 3 P.M. doesn't become so at 7:01 P.M." One wag noted that the Sunday curfew "probably did more to provoke sinning in terms of anger and profanity than it ever did to encourage less worldly activities." The last implementation of the Sunday curfew was at the July 12 Sunday doubleheader in Pittsburgh.[37]

Attendance for holiday doubleheaders began to decline in the 1950s. The last year that major-league baseball had a full slate of holiday doubleheaders for all three national holidays was 1956. Night baseball, along with franchise relocations, hastened a swift decline in holiday doubleheader scheduling. Working people, now with a standard 40-hour five-day workweek, could attend games on Saturday and during the week at night, greatly lessening the promotional value of the second "free" game of a doubleheader. A wider variety of holiday leisure activities also drew fans away from attending holiday doubleheaders.

The doubleheader's grip on the holiday schedule began to slip in 1954. After seven decades of carding two games on nearly all holiday dates, there were two single contests scheduled on holidays in 1954—a Memorial Day game between the Dodgers and Phillies in Philadelphia and a Labor Day match between the Cardinals and Reds in Cincinnati. In 1957, the Baltimore Orioles scheduled a single game on Independence Day. The Orioles had a larger attendance at the night contest on July 3 (11,506) than they did at the holiday game on the afternoon of July 4 (9,530). Of even greater interest to Orioles executives were the gates earlier in the week against the New York Yankees. At the Monday night game on July 1, 45,276 people paid to watch the Orioles take on the Yankees in what the *Baltimore Sun* called "the largest crowd ever at Memorial Stadium." On Tuesday afternoon, another 24,293 saw the second contest with the Yankees. Despite the long tradition of holiday twin bills, the ballgame on Independence Day in Baltimore was, in the larger picture, just not that important to the financials of the ballclub, or to the Orioles' fans. The holiday doubleheader thus began a rapid decline in popularity that would occur over the next two decades.[38]

The relocation of the Giants and Dodgers from New York City to the West Coast for the 1958 season accelerated the decrease in doubleheaders. Both clubs carded a few Sunday doubleheaders during the 1958 season, but abandoned them entirely for the 1959 season in favor of more night games during the workweek. For example, on August 31, 1959, 60,000 people packed the Los Angeles Coliseum, the Dodgers' temporary home, for a Monday night game, a significant increase over the 44,000 attendance for its single game on Sunday, August 30. The Dodgers took an even more radical approach to holiday scheduling. For the Independence Day holiday in 1958, the Dodgers chose to play a twi-night doubleheader on July 3 and take the day off on July 4, not even playing a single game on the holiday. In 1959, the Dodgers played the first night game on a holiday, a single game on Labor Day, and followed that up in 1960 with another first, a twi-night doubleheader on Labor Day. The Dodgers also popularized the scheduling of twi-night twin bills on the preseason schedule in 1958, with four that year. This was fitting since the ballclub had pioneered the strategy when it was in Brooklyn with three twi-night doubleheaders on the 1952 schedule.

With the declining popularity of Sunday and holiday doubleheaders, in 1959 major-league baseball experienced its fewest doubleheaders played in more than 50 years (1906). The percentage of all games conducted via twin bills dropped during the 1950s from roughly one-third in 1950 to just one-fifth in 1959. While the decline was generally good news for the ballplayers, the increase in travel to the more far-flung franchise locations combined with an increase in twi-night and day-night doubleheaders posed continuing hardships.

In the early years of the Players Association, which was formalized in 1954, the primary concern of the players was the pension plan that had been established in 1946. Concerns such as doubleheaders following night games or day-night twin bills were discussed by the players and their legal representatives at ballclub-owner meetings, but were generally left unresolved given the players' paramount emphasis on the pension plan. Doubleheader concerns predated the pension plan. In July 1946, a group of players met with Boston Braves owner Lou Perini at the behest of Robert Murphy, who was trying to organize the players into the American Baseball Guild. The players voiced "their requests for a minimum salary, spring training expenses, and the prohibition of daytime doubleheaders after night games." To forestall Murphy's attempt to create a players union, the owners established a pension plan for the players and set the minimum salary at $5,000. Restrictions on doubleheaders had to wait.[39]

As the number of twi-night and day-night doubleheaders increased during the late 1940s and early 1950s, player concerns were gruffly dismissed by the ballclub owners as simply the result of how the schedule was devised. "A more pertinent question, in pointing to the numerous day-night and twi-night atrocities that have popped up on the skeds," writer Dick Young posed in 1950, "would be: 'When you make up the original schedule, doesn't the possibility of a certain amount of rain falling ever occur to you?'" Young considered it "a Utopian notion" that postponements would never occur and then be converted into day-night and twi-night doubleheaders. In 1957, the Players Association garnered improvements in the pension plan, including an increased benefit formula, which effectively limited their ability to negotiate changes in other issues such as excessive doubleheaders following a night game.[40]

12. Twi-Night and Day-Night Doubleheaders

With a pension plan, minimum salary, and a few other perks, players during the 1950s grumbled privately about the hassles associated with the new-style doubleheaders but had little leverage with the owners to change the situation. At an owners' Executive Council meeting in 1959, the players once again voiced their concerns with playing a twin bill following a night game. Although the owners verbally agreed to minimize this scheduling situation, there was no written agreement or assurance of its implementation by all owners. This raised the ire of the players during the 1960 season.[41]

When the June 4, 1960, game between the Pirates and Phillies in Philadelphia was rained out, the two ballclubs rescheduled the makeup contest to be part of a Sunday doubleheader on July 10. However, there was already a night game scheduled for Saturday, July 9, so the Pirate players voted not to play the second game of that July 10 twin bill. "We feel that this doubleheader is coming at an important time of the season when we are making a run for the pennant," said Bob Friend, the Pirates player representative in the Players Association. "The players are up in arms and unanimously agreed not to take the field for that second game." The Pirates had leverage in the situation, since they were contending for the National League pennant. "There are three open dates in September when that game could have been rescheduled. Even the owners and the ballplayers had agreed that a doubleheader should not be played after a night game," Friend said in regard to that 1959 verbal agreement. Philadelphia owner Bob Carpenter agreed to reschedule the makeup game on September 20 to avoid having a doubleheader after a night game.[42]

However, when the same situation occurred in 1962, the Pirates, then in fourth place and not in first, were rebuffed by the owners when the players objected to playing a day-night doubleheader on Saturday, August 25, in St. Louis the day before a Sunday doubleheader. Friend, still the Pirates player representative, had suggested that the Pirates play a traditional afternoon doubleheader on both days, or move the night game from Saturday to Monday, which was an open date for both teams. National League president Warren Giles concluded that the day-night doubleheader should be played as originally determined by the two ballclubs (without consulting the players); he also refused to compare the 1962 situation with the one two years earlier that had concluded differently.[43]

"Baseball owners have moral scruples against taking any man's dollar when there is a chance to take a dollar and a quarter," sportswriter Red Smith railed about the Pirates situation. "They insisted on their plan to offer two games for the price of two. All it cost the players was their rights and their sleep. For a regular doubleheader it is customary to report for work about 11 A.M. Saturday's games consumed four hours, 18 minutes. Starting at 1:30 P.M. with a half-hour intermission, the players could have got to the showers a little after 6 P.M. Instead they remained at the park all day without a square meal, got to the hotel for a sandwich and beer around midnight, and may have made the sack by 3 A.M. Assuming that they were now relaxed and at peace, they could count on something like six hours rest."[44]

But the Pirates had it easy compared to the Yankees, who experienced an even worse scenario the same weekend. After playing an afternoon game in Los Angeles on Thursday, August 23, they flew cross country to play five games within 48 hours. The *New York Times* described their itinerary: "Arriving by plane in Baltimore tomorrow morning at 6:00 A.M., the Bombers will plunge right into a five-game series with the Orioles that will open with a twilight-night doubleheader. Day and night games will be played Saturday, with a single game following on Sunday." Not surprisingly, the Yankees lost all five games.[45]

There was little compunction for the ballclub owners to avoid scheduling doubleheaders that inconvenienced ballplayers. Despite the gripes by ballplayers, back-to-back twin bills were not uncommon, and even produced occasional exceptional hitting displays. In consecutive twi-night doubleheaders on July 17 and 18 in 1961, Bill White of the St. Louis Cardinals collected 14 hits in four games to boost his average 28 points from .289 before the games on July 17 to .317 after the games on July 18. White accomplished this feat despite getting less than an hour of sleep between the twin bills. White stayed up with an ailing child after the first doubleheader, had a baseball clinic to attend the following afternoon, and "grabbed 45 minutes rest on a dressing room table just prior to the second doubleheader." Six weeks later in the second installment of consecutive doubleheaders on September 4 and 5, Lee Thomas of the Los Angeles Angels collected nine hits in a twi-nighter to tie a major-league record.[46]

In 1961 the doubleheader received a shot of adrenalin to sustain its existence when the American League expanded to ten clubs from the traditional eight-club lineup that had existed for the previous six decades. The uneven number of home and visiting clubs, compounded by a balanced schedule where ballclubs played each other 18 times during the season (and trips to the West Coast to play the Los Angeles Angels), required the increased use of doubleheaders to make the new 162-game schedule work. The 1961 American League schedule "offers several commendable points," one sportswriter noted about the replacement for the 154-game schedule. "If nothing else, it seems to provide a better balance. Also a lot more doubleheaders." This increase in doubleheaders came in the form of twi-night and day-night doubleheaders, not Sunday or holiday ones. There were a dozen twi-nighters on the 1961 schedule and three day-night twin bills (two in Baltimore and a Labor Day session in Minnesota), compared to zero of both types on the 1960 schedule.[47]

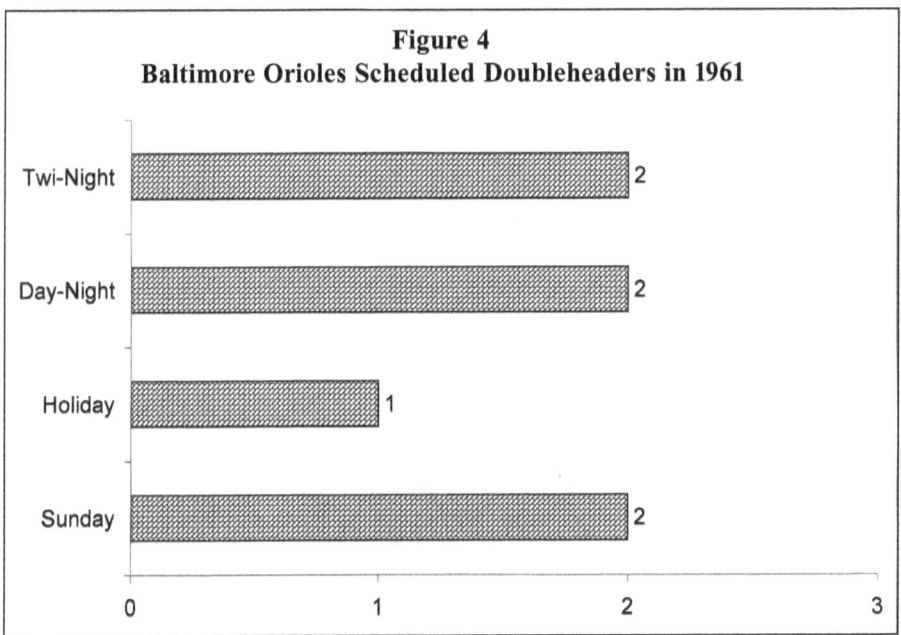

The diversity of types of doubleheaders scheduled by the Baltimore Orioles in 1961 illustrates the changing nature of the doubleheader in the 1960s—predominantly twi-night and day-night doubleheaders, with fewer Sunday or holiday ones—compared to the early 1950s when doubleheaders dominated the schedule on most Sundays and every holiday for most major-league ballclubs. (Source: American League schedule, *New York Times*, February 10, 1961.)

When the National League expanded in 1962 to bring Houston into major-league baseball along with the New York Mets, the twi-night doubleheader increased in popularity as a scheduling technique to squeeze in the eight extra games on the schedule. By 1963 there were three dozen twi-nighters on the initial major-league schedule. As *The Sporting News* reported, "The twi-night doubleheader, which was once a contrivance used only when other efforts to reschedule a game failed, now appears as a standard part of the schedule." Signaling a change in the type of spectator at the ballpark, even the New York Yankees, who normally frowned on promotions because they expected a championship ballclub to fill the seats, carded a twi-nighter in 1963 at Yankee Stadium.[48]

The day-night doubleheader also garnered increased space on the major-league schedule in the mid–1960s at the expense of the single-admission doubleheader (both twi-night and Sunday). The Atlanta Braves, newly transplanted from Milwaukee, scheduled day-night doubleheaders for six Saturdays on their 1966 schedule. The Houston Astros, now playing in the

Astrodome, carded three day-night events on their 1966 schedule. And those were just the *scheduled* day-night doubleheaders, not including the makeup ones. With this expansion of the "two games for the price of two" concept, limitations on doubleheaders gained priority on the negotiation agenda of the Players Association.[49]

Even seemingly innocuous doubleheaders began to impede the lives of ballplayers, not just the inconveniences associated with day-night doubleheaders. The thrill of a twin bill also waned with spectators, as the time to complete them had expanded from four hours in the 1940s to five or six hours in the 1960s. Then there were the marathon doubleheaders—in reality tripleheaders in length—that tested the determination of both ballplayers and spectators.

On May 31, 1964, the Giants and the Mets played a Sunday twin bill that established the major-league record for longest doubleheader in terms of elapsed time (nine hours and 52 minutes) as well as innings played (32). Both records have never been eclipsed. "At 1:05 P.M. at Shea Stadium yesterday a crowd of 57,037—the largest in the major leagues this season—settled down for what was to become the longest day in baseball history," the *New York Times* reported. "By 11:28 P.M., the crowd had dwindled to about 8,000 ... there were no traffic tie-ups and the IRT station was not jammed after the game."[50]

On June 17, 1967, the Tigers and the Athletics played a 28-inning doubleheader at Tiger Stadium, which lasted from 2:21 P.M. until 12:17 A.M. The nine-hour, five-minute, elapsed playing time for both games established an American League record, which has never been eclipsed. Commissioner William Eckert spent a dozen hours at the ballpark that day, doing a pre-game TV interview and sitting through both ballgames. After a short rain delay in the first game, the second game began at 6:37 P.M. and lasted 19 innings before catcher Dave Duncan (substituting for Phil Roof who had caught the first 17 innings) hit a home run to win the nightcap for Kansas City. There were about 1,000 spectators left in the stands at the end, including Eckert. In the clubhouse afterward, Eckert shouted "Quite a game" to Detroit manager Mayo Smith, who then quipped, "Congratulations for staying through it all. It's pretty late to keep everybody up for a split doubleheader."[51]

Two months later on August 29 at Yankee Stadium, the Red Sox and Yankees engaged in a 29-inning marathon. Although the first game of the twi-night doubleheader finished in a little more than two hours, the second contest went 20 innings and lasted more than six hours before finally ending at 1:57 A.M. Both teams returned to the ballpark a few hours later to play an afternoon game starting at 2:00 P.M.[52]

While the franchises playing in newly constructed ballparks or in newly minted major-league outposts did quite nicely without the single-admission doubleheader, those ballclubs still playing in an aging stadium in a deteriorating urban area needed something extra to boost attendance beyond the second "free" game of a Sunday or twi-night doubleheader. Bat Day became a very popular promotion in 1964, and was adopted by the Yankees for their Father's Day Sunday doubleheader in 1965. The promotion was exceptionally popular, as 40,000 Little League model bats were distributed to youngsters among the 72,244 crowd that entered Yankee Stadium. "The gates had to be closed at 1:15 P.M., ten minutes after the doubleheader with the Minnesota Twins began. Many who had entered the park could not find seats or adequate standing room; they got their money back and left." It was a good deal for the ballclub as well. "The bats retail at $1.75; the Yankees paid perhaps half that for bulk purchase but probably got back at least the same amount ($30,000) from increased concession sales from so large a crowd."[53]

Giveaway days like Bat Day soon replaced the doubleheader as the promotional technique that best brought spectators to the ballpark, though attracting fans was no longer the quest—attracting anyone who would be a paying customer increasingly was the challenge in ballpark economics. More importantly, expanding the audience that watched the ballgames on television was the new challenge. Both trends marginalized the doubleheader, which remained popular with die-hard fans but was ineffective or obstructive with casual spectators and TV audiences and loathed by the Players Association.

13

Decline of the Doubleheader

WHILE THE HIRING OF Marvin Miller in the spring of 1966 as executive director of the Players Association helped to reroute the course of major-league baseball history, Miller's hiring also set into motion the ultimate demise of the doubleheader. The reduction during the 1960s in the number of single-admission twin bills on Sundays and holidays accelerated in 1968 after the signing of the first collective bargaining agreement between owners and ballplayers, a document known as the Basic Agreement. The initial negotiation target in the doubleheader area was the so-called "split doubleheader," more commonly known as the day-night doubleheader.

Because the split doubleheader had been a complaint of the ballplayers since Sam Breadon and Branch Rickey first popularized the concept back in 1946, Miller put it on the list of major negotiation priorities for the players in addition to an increase in the minimum salary and improved travel conditions. "I would say the players' greatest concern centers around schedules, especially the long season," Miller told the *New York Times* in an interview in February 1967. Miller said there was a growing concern that the current schedule with its tight travel schedules might damage the health of players and cut their careers short. "A tired player is more likely to get hurt," Miller said. "I'm not at all sure the fans get the top quality baseball in this kind of situation."[1]

During the summer of 1967 Miller issued a policy statement outlining the players' negotiation position, which "sought a revision to the reserve clause, a voice in determining the length of the season, and a hard-and-fast standard contract binding on both parties" in addition to an increase in the minimum salary already under discussion. "The historic manifesto called for nine detailed scheduling rules," of which the top three concerned twin bills: no day doubleheaders following a night game, no split doubleheaders, and no twi-night doubleheaders preceding a day game. Miller also slipped into the policy statement some wording about the implementation of a grievance procedure.[2]

The ballclub owners chaffed at introducing limitations on scheduling rules in the Basic Agreement. "Owners traditionally believed that to be the 'heart of their function,'" John Gaherin, the labor representative of the owners, said in early 1968, "but that Miller wanted to sit down with them as an equal to determine the character of the schedule." Miller responded by saying: "Nothing is more basic to the players than how long he must play. The owners raised the season from 154 games to 162 games with various incidental abuses without consulting or paying the players. Now there will be further expansion and the players want to have their say on the schedule." Despite the owners' reluctance at negotiating scheduling rules, Miller was able to achieve a minor victory in the negotiations leading to the first Basic Agreement.[3]

Economic provisions in the 1968 Basic Agreement included an increase in the minimum salary to $10,000, increased meal money (from $12 to $15 per day), increased allotments for spring-training expenses, and a reduction in the maximum salary cut. Among the non-economic provisions were a grievance procedure and "the adoption of a set of scheduling rules and guidelines with respect to the 1968 and 1969 championship seasons." Those scheduling rules included a limit on split doubleheaders, a concept that continues to survive in the text of the most-current version of the Basic Agreement: "Split doubleheaders shall not be scheduled in the original schedule." In a few years the Players Association negotiated limits on using the day-night doubleheader concept to reschedule postponed games.[4]

The 1968 Basic Agreement ended the short life of the scheduled day-night doubleheader that had begun in 1955. There was a 100 percent decrease in the number of day-night doubleheaders on the 1968 schedule compared to the number listed in 1967, as there were zero on the 1968 schedule. Another casualty was the longer life of the morning-afternoon twin bill on the Patriots Day holiday in Boston, sandwiched around the Boston Marathon, which had made a comeback on the American League schedule. The last two-game event on Patriots Day was scheduled for 1967, but was rained out.

While the victories for the Players Association in the 1968 Basic Agreement were relatively minor in nature, they laid the groundwork for bigger wins in the future. "It was another landmark in many ways, and not just because of the economic improvements for the players," Miller wrote in his book *A Whole Different Ball Game*. "We had put real restrictions on the power of the owners either to change rules unilaterally or to ignore established ones when it suited their whims." The 1968 Basic Agreement set the stage for reforming the reserve clause that restricted a player from negotiating with other clubs to secure a better contract. Once player salaries increased, the desire for ballclubs to eliminate doubleheaders increased as well.[5]

Scheduled doubleheaders dropped by one quarter from 1967 to 1968. In a sign of things to come, the biggest users of the day-night concept in the National League, Atlanta and Houston, had no scheduled twin bills whatsoever during the 1968 season—no Sunday doubleheaders, no holiday doubleheaders, and no twi-night doubleheaders. The doubleheader was also virtually extinct in the city that had pioneered the Sunday doubleheader, St. Louis. With the St. Louis Cardinals having only two scheduled twin bills in 1968, one observer wryly noted "the doubleheader, once as much a must in St. Louis as anywhere, is fast going the way of the nickel cigar, the five-cent phone call, and the longie skirt." While the 1968 Basic Agreement was the beginning of the end for the doubleheader, it took another quarter-century before the scheduled doubleheader was virtually extinct and the makeup doubleheader was a much less frequent occurrence on the major-league baseball calendar.[6]

The general contraction in number of twin bills was led by the accelerated decline of the holiday doubleheader. By 1967 only half of the major-league matches for the three national holidays consisted of doubleheaders, with the rest being single games, many played as night games. When the Monday holiday law went into effect in 1971, the observance of Memorial Day shifted from May 30 to the last Monday in May. Because Labor Day and Memorial Day were now the foundation for a three-day weekend, they began to lose much of their original meaning as well as their secondary appeal as a double-bill ballpark attraction.[7]

Fewer people like Frank Rinella created memories by attending a holiday doubleheader. "On Labor Day, 1934, I traveled from McKeesport, Pennsylvania, my hometown, to Forbes Field in Pittsburgh on a street car to attend my first ever baseball game along with my older brother," Rinella recalled several decades later. "I was 12 years old. I bought a program for ten cents. I kept score the best I could as I wanted to remember that glorious day forever. However, my mom cleaned house as they do, and my precious program was gone." The ballclub owners were now disposing of the holiday doubleheader much as Rinella's mother did with his Labor Day scorecard.[8]

Even Independence Day lost its luster at the ballpark. Fewer people agreed with sportswriter Clifford Bloodgood's assessment in 1946 that "the anniversary date of the signing of the Declaration of Independence is observed in baseball by the playing of doubleheaders because it is a national holiday that comes during the season and gives millions of fans a chance to celebrate in the manner they like best, by attending the games." The Fourth of July was now more about beach and barbeque than baseball.[9]

The number of holiday doubleheaders dropped precipitously in 1968, as there were only two scheduled for each of the Memorial Day and Independence Day holidays, with six carded for Labor Day. The Mets-Pirates twin bill in Pittsburgh was even a morning-afternoon affair, reminiscent of the swing-shift doubleheaders played in 1943. By 1973 there were no doubleheaders played on Memorial Day, only single games. However, there was a game-and-a-half played; before the regular holiday game the Chicago White Sox finished a suspended game with the Cleveland Indians that had been stopped on Saturday night after 16 innings.

Wilbur Wood, a knuckleball pitcher with the White Sox, not only pitched both games for Chicago on Memorial Day in 1973 but also won both games. Wood pitched five innings of the suspended match and all nine innings of the second contest, a 4–0 shutout, to achieve two wins on one day. However, Wood didn't tie the record of the legendary Iron Man McGinnity, since the first victory, in the windup of the suspended match, was neither a complete game nor officially played on the holiday. In the record books, Wood is credited with a victory for a game on Saturday, May 26, and a victory in the holiday contest on May 28. Two months later, Wood did start and try to win both games of a doubleheader on July 20, 1973, but lost both games in his quest to equal McGinnity's feat.[10]

For the remainder of the 1970s, only one or two doubleheaders were slated for Memorial Day. The last scheduled Memorial Day twin bill was in Seattle in 1981. Having a second game on Labor Day remained appealing for a few ballclubs through the 1970s, as three to four doubleheaders were typically carded on the last holiday of the baseball season. The last scheduled Labor Day doubleheader was played in Pittsburgh in 1980. Independence Day was the final casualty of holiday doubleheader scheduling. Like Memorial Day, only one or two doubleheaders were played on the Fourth of July during the 1970s, until none were scheduled in 1979. In 1982, there were no twin bills scheduled on any of the three national holidays. After two doubleheaders were scheduled for the Fourth of July in 1983, the last scheduled Independence Day doubleheader—indeed, the last scheduled holiday doubleheader—was played on July 4, 1984, at Candlestick Park in San Francisco.[11]

Expansion of both the American and National Leagues from 10 to 12 ballclubs in 1969 caused a slight blip in the percentage of doubleheaders, similar to the impact that expansion had earlier in 1961 and 1962. Because both leagues moved to a two-division format for the 1969 season, they also decided to play an unbalanced schedule. Ballclubs played the other five clubs in their own division 18 times a year and the six clubs in the other division 12 times per year. The use of an unbalanced scheduled didn't necessitate the use of doubleheaders to resolve scheduling complications as much as the balanced schedule did with expansion earlier in the decade.

The addition of the Montreal franchise to the National League in 1969 also contributed to the decline in holiday doubleheaders, since only one U.S. holiday—Labor Day—overlapped the Canadian holidays observed in Montreal during the baseball season. The other two major Canadian holidays were proximate on the calendar to U.S. holidays, but not identical, as Canada Day on July 1 was close to Independence Day and Victoria Day on the Monday preceding May 25 was near Memorial Day.

Negotiations between the owners and the players over the pension agreement in 1972 created the next big step that contributed to the eradication of the doubleheader. Although the eventual agreement between the two parties didn't explicitly refer to doubleheaders, the settlement had a direct impact on the future of the two-games-for-one-price-of-admission institution. The players went on strike on April 1, 1972, when the owners took an intractable stance in the pension negotiations. The strike was ostensibly about increasing pension benefits for the players, but what it was implicitly about was resisting the owners' desire to reclaim power that they had ceded to the players in the 1968 Basic Agreement. "The more I read the more I was persuaded that the owners were not only out to break the union, but also intent on achieving a 'victory' over me," Marvin Miller wrote years later. "After all, I had cost them a fair sum of money" in increased minimum salaries, millions in benefit plan costs, but more importantly he had achieved an "ability to defend players' rights." The owners thought the players would fold after a few days on the picket line. They were wrong.[12]

Because the players showed their solidarity, the owners caved in on April 10. However, there was a snag concerning the makeup of the lost games during the strike, since the season had expected to open on April 5. "The owners wanted us to make up all the games lost during the strike *without pay*," Miller wrote about the aftermath of the strike. "The hardliners [among the owners] didn't give up easily. They suggested extra doubleheaders and games on scheduled off-days. The players scorned the plan." Indeed, the owners suggested that "the players would be paid for separate-admission make-ups—on open dates or as part of day-night doubleheaders—but would not be paid for games that are rescheduled as part of a one-admission doubleheader."[13]

Miller said the players' initial position on making up the lost games, offered on April 10, was to not reschedule any of the games. The owners rejected this position, not because they were concerned about the sanctity of the 162-game playing season, but rather because they wanted to recapture some of the $5 million that they had lost during the strike. Miller said that he offered an alternative to make up the lost games with neither the players nor the owners receiving any compensation. "Make admission to those games free as a way to make it up to the fans, and have the proceeds from concessions, parking, and radio-television go to mutually agreed upon charities." Miller said the owners' lead negotiator thought he was nuts. On April 13, the owners and players agreed to not make up any of the lost games, rather than agree how to divvy up the revenue from doubleheaders. After nine days on strike during the season, 86 games were canceled. The result was that ballclubs played a varying number of games during the 1972 season, from 153 to 156 games. The uneven schedule probably cost the Red Sox the American League Eastern Division title when they finished a half-game behind the Detroit Tigers.[14]

The doubleheader could have preserved the entirety of the 1972 playing season, yet neither the owners nor the ballplayers, nor seemingly Commissioner Bowie Kuhn who refused to engage in the debate, cared enough about the sanctity of the 162-game season to bend in the negotiations. The doubleheader was just a business tool to the owners, and a hindrance to the players. These fundamental positions on the idea of the doubleheader set the stage for the diminishing number of doubleheaders to be scheduled, and played, in the coming years.

One player who didn't mind doubleheaders in 1972 was Nate Colbert, first baseman for the San Diego Padres. In a twi-night doubleheader on August 1, 1972, Colbert hit five home runs against the Braves in Atlanta Fulton County Stadium to tie Stan Musial's major-league record set in 1954. Besides tying the record for most home runs in a doubleheader, Colbert established major-league records for most total bases in a doubleheader (22) and most RBIs in a doubleheader (13). Ironically, Colbert had been an eight-year-old spectator at Busch Stadium during the doubleheader when Musial hit five homers in 1954. "I grew up in St. Louis. I lived close to old Busch Stadium, and I sat in the bleachers with a glove, trying to catch batting practice home runs," Colbert recalled in a 1989 interview. "Stan was my idol after that day (the five home runs). Now when I see him, he says, 'We're the only ones to do it.'"[15]

Colbert hit two home runs in the first game and three in the nightcap, off five different pitchers. He only needed to see six pitches to hit those five home runs. "The first one was a three-run homer off Ron Schueler. The second was a solo shot off a left-hander, Larry Jaster, and it went to straightaway center. I got all of it. I hit both on the first pitch," Colbert remembered. "In the second game, I hit one with nobody on off Jim Hardin, then I hit a grand slam off Pat Jarvis on a 1–0 pitch. I did look at a pitch that time. Finally, I hit a two-run shot off Cecil Upshaw—on the first pitch again." The fifth homer came in the ninth inning of the second game. "I wasn't thinking homer when I went up against Upshaw. I don't like to bat against him—I was just thinking about a base hit," Colbert said a few days after the event in 1972. "But he threw me a high fast ball and I hit it. When I saw it go over the fence, I knew I had the record, and all I could think about was Musial's five homers. It was unreal."[16]

During the 1972 season, the owners tested the resolve of the Players Association to enforce the provisions of the 1970 Basic Agreement that it had negotiated to restrict the rescheduling of doubleheaders, which included limitations on the use of both day-night doubleheaders and night games before a day doubleheader. After the New York Mets unilaterally rescheduled a May 9 rainout with the Los Angeles Dodgers to be part of a day-night doubleheader on May 11, the Players Association took the offensive.[17]

When the Montreal Expos rescheduled a rainout with the Mets to be part of a day-night doubleheader on July 1—the Canada Day holiday—Miller called the move "an outrageous example of ignoring a contractual obligation." If the Expos hadn't used the same tactic two years earlier to reschedule a rainout with the Phillies to be part of a doubleheader on Canada Day, they might have had a better chance of pulling off the stunt in 1972. "Under normal circumstances, I am opposed to split doubleheaders," John McHale, president of the Expos, said. "I think there were many factors in this scheduling arrangement which made it not only feasible but preferable." However, the ability to attract two large crowds on a holiday wasn't one of the factors in the Basic Agreement. Miller reminded the press that "the Basic Agreement says a split doubleheader may be scheduled only when there is no practicable alternative to doing so, bearing in mind the nature of the pennant race, seating capacity of the park, and tradition of split doubleheaders in the city involved." The Expos eventually relented and rescheduled the rainout to be part of a doubleheader in October, not on the Canada Day holiday.[18]

When the Atlanta Braves tried to reschedule a rainout with the Giants to be part of a twi-nighter on Saturday, July 29, the day before a scheduled Sunday twin bill for each club (the Braves at home, the Giants in Cincinnati), in violation of the rule that no night game precede a day doubleheader, Miller had no trouble getting the postponement rescheduled for mid–September when the Giants next returned to Atlanta. But Miller had to ask, the owners didn't agree automatically.[19]

To cure these ills in the 1973 Basic Agreement, Miller negotiated a prohibition on twi-night doubleheaders on getaway days and a provision that "any rule about rescheduling games may be waived if approved by a majority of the players on each club." Players now had a contractual hand in decisions about rescheduling postponed games into doubleheaders. For instance, the Chicago Cubs players elected to play a getaway-day twi-nighter in Atlanta on June 12, 1975, rather than reschedule a rainout for later in the season.[20]

The prohibition of staging a night game prior to a day doubleheader was the death knell for the Sunday doubleheader, since Saturday night games had became increasingly popular with ballclubs and fans. By the mid–1970s, the Sunday doubleheader had disappeared from the schedules of a number of big-market ballclubs like the Boston Red Sox and Los Angeles Dodgers. "The Sunday doubleheader, once the meal ticket for every team in baseball, may be on its way out. If it isn't, it should be," one writer commented. He noted the problem wasn't the mass of people coming to the ballpark, but rather the large number seeking to leave after the first game. By 1979, other franchises had abandoned the Sunday doubleheader and just small-market ballclubs like the Pittsburgh Pirates, Cleveland Indians, and Oakland Athletics continued to schedule Sunday twin bills. By 1984, only a half dozen ballclubs had a Sunday doubleheader on their playing schedule; with the exception of the Giants with two, it was just one Sunday doubleheader per ballclub.[21]

Other language in the Basic Agreement also stifled the scheduling of doubleheaders. Twi-nighte doubleheaders were limited to three per season. The provision to limit off-days to no more than two in any seven-day period, while seemingly detrimental to the ballplayers, was designed to block northern-situated ballclubs from switching early-season games to doubleheaders during warmer months. The Players Association also approved of another seemingly detrimental provision in the 1980 Basic Agreement that extended the number of allowable consecutive playing dates from 19 to 20 because it reduced the need to schedule twin bills. While one day wouldn't seem to be that important to scheduling, the 20-day rule allowed for a full three weeks of scheduling, whereas the previous 19-day rule often required the use of doubleheaders to not violate the 19-playing-date rule within a 20-day period.[22]

One impetus for the change in number of consecutive playing dates was the "Lost Wednesday" one-day road trip for the Yankees to play a doubleheader on June 30, 1978, in Milwaukee. The Yankees lost both games to the Brewers. "Because the doubleheader came on what would have been the 20th consecutive playing day the Yankees would have played, the players had to waive the rule in the Basic Agreement that says a team cannot be scheduled to play in more than 19 days in a row," the *New York Times* explained at the time. "The players voted during spring training to play the doubleheader in June rather than go to Milwaukee in September." The one-day road trip came about because the original Wednesday game with the Red Sox was moved to Monday night so that ABC could televise it to a national audience, and Milwaukee owner Bud Selig wanted a warm-weather date with the Yankees. Marvin Miller said the decision made sense at the time, to play the games in June rather than September when the schedule would be tight and Yankees might be in the middle of a hot pennant race. "You place the players in a hole," Miller said. "Here are two very undesirable situations and the players have to decide which, at the time they're voting, would be the less undesirable."[23]

Free-agency provisions in the 1976 Basic Agreement, in the wake of the McNally and Messersmith decisions, were ultimately the tipping point for the future decline of the doubleheader. To pay the skyrocketing salaries that ballplayers commanded in the era of free agency, ballclub owners needed

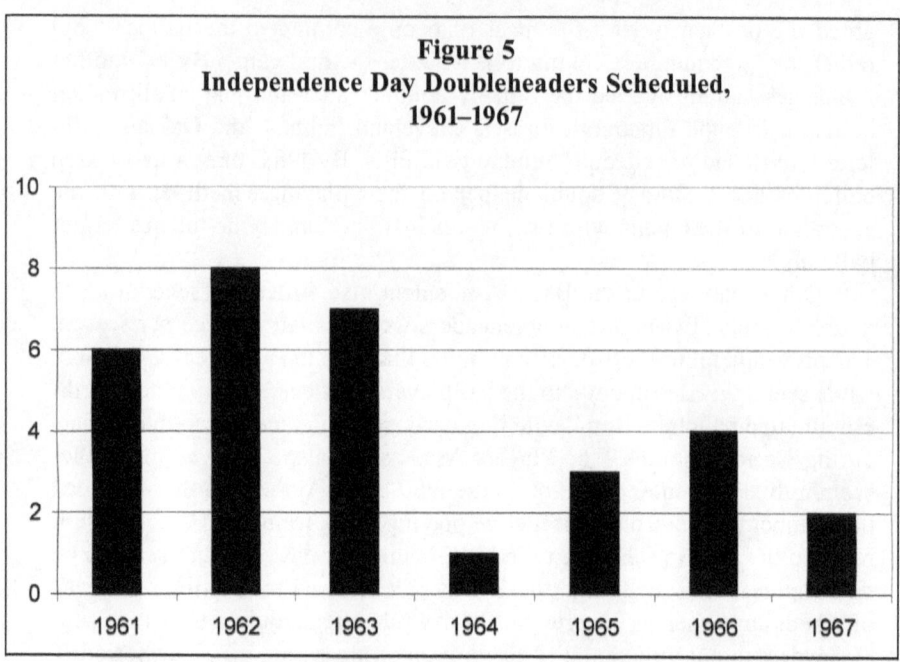

The popularity of scheduling holiday doubleheaders dropped during the mid–1960s, as other entertainment alternatives on the holidays increasingly enticed spectators away from the ballpark. (Source: Retrosheet database.)

increased revenue from television and the gate, which put additional pressure to eradicate the doubleheader. There were several trends that assisted the owners in accomplishing this objective.

As the average game time lengthened from two hours to three hours, fewer spectators were willing to sit through both games of a doubleheader. "In a television world, people don't look forward to spending seven hours in a ball park, as my generation of kids used to, with another couple of hours of travel time," one writer observed about the completion time for a doubleheader increasing 50 percent from about four hours in the 1940s to six or seven hours in the 1980s.[24]

Those spectators that could tolerate such a long day at the ballpark often exhibited unruly behavior due to their beer consumption "since guzzling beer for 18 innings proved too much even for the most stout-hearted drinkers." This factor played out in one of the biggest fiascos in doubleheader history, Disco Demolition Night at Comiskey Park in 1979. The promotion cooked up by Mike Veeck, son of legendary ballgame promoter Bill Veeck, was to "admit for 98 cents anyone who brought a disco record to the park" to watch a local disk jockey blow up disco records between games of a twi-night doubleheader. Some 50,000 people packed the park, while 20,000 others milled around outside the stadium. However, the promotion got out of control as thousands of spectators stormed onto the smoke-filled field. "The haters of disco tore up the playing field, stole bases, and destroyed a batting cage," one writer described the situation. "While this was going on a bonfire continued to burn in center field." When Chicago police in riot gear appeared wielding nightsticks, the rowdy crowd dispersed. "Not surprisingly, the second game was not able to begin at its scheduled time. In fact, over an hour after the second game was scheduled to start, the field was deemed unplayable." After the White Sox forfeited the second game, the Veecks were roundly criticized in the Chicago newspapers. Bill Gleason of the *Chicago Sun-Times* called it "the most disgraceful night in the long history of major league baseball in Chicago." David Israel of the *Chicago Tribune* concluded, "It would have happened any place 50,000 teenagers got together on a sultry summer night with beer and reefer."[25]

While some baseball executives contended that "increased concession sales make doubleheaders almost as profitable as two separate admissions," most believed that twin bills were money-losing propositions in an age of robust ballpark attendance, to the extent that "one doubleheader instead of two single dates costs a club between $75,000 and $100,000." For example, since the Los Angeles Dodgers averaged 40,000 spectators a game in the early 1980s at 56,000-seat-capacity Dodger Stadium, "no wonder the Dodgers have no scheduled twin bills this year."[26]

Promotional giveaways (other than Disco Demolition Night) also made far more economic sense than doubleheaders. Bat Day had morphed into Cap Day, Helmet Day, and Just About Anything Day. One White Sox executive noted that caps in bulk cost about $1 apiece, while at a doubleheader the club lost the $6 gross spent by each fan. That was if the club bought the items given away. "The White Sox, like many other teams, hold promotions that are *fully* sponsored by a corporation, like Chicago's Clorox Beach Towel Day," one commentator reported. "All of the Sox's 32 promotions are fully sponsored; they don't pay one cent."[27]

In many cities people no longer needed any incentive—a two-for-one doubleheader or a giveaway promotion—to attend a ballgame. As new facilities such as Veterans, Three Rivers, and Riverfront Stadiums were erected to replace aging edifices Connie Mack Stadium (Shibe Park), Forbes Field, and Crosley Field, respectively, modern ballparks were attractions in themselves. "On average for baseball teams, moving into a new stadium increased attendance by 62 percent—over 600,000 per year—during the first five years a team was in a new stadium, as compared to the previous five-year period," James Quirk and Rodney Fort concluded in their book *Pay Dirt: The Business of Professional Team Sports*. "Part of the increase in attendance associated with new baseball stadiums was due to the curiosity of fans, coming as much to see the new park as to see the team."[28]

Even attracting people to the ballpark was much less of a consideration in the 1980s for many ballclubs, since revenue from ticket sales now represented only about one-half of total ballclub revenue, down from three-fourths in the 1950s. Television and radio broadcast revenue now represented about one-third of ballclub revenues, up from one-sixth in the 1950s. Proceeds from the national television contract made ballclubs more dependent on the TV networks. This escalated in 1983 when NBC and ABC agreed to pay $1.1 billion in TV rights fees during the 1984–1989 period, which represented nearly a fivefold increase from the previous $190 million deal. Getting people in front of television sets, not into ballpark seats, was becoming more paramount to ballclub finances. This dependence on television revenue helped to further kill off the doubleheader. Because television executives wanted certainty of starting times in prime viewing times, they could not tolerate a twinight doubleheader where the unwanted first game (from the television perspective) created an estimated starting time for the telecast of the desired second game. While the first game of a Sunday or holiday twin bill worked fine for television, executives had no interest in the second game, figuring few in the audience would continue watching beyond three hours.[29]

During the 13-year period from 1968 through 1980, the percentage of both scheduled and played doubleheaders dropped in half. In 1980, less than six percent of all scheduled major-league games were part of a doubleheader, the lowest level since 1938; less than 10 percent of all major-league games played were part of a doubleheader, the lowest level since 1888. In addition to the decline in Sunday and holiday doubleheaders, there were fewer makeup twin bills due to the artificial turf used in many new stadiums that drained better than grass fields and cut back the number of postponements. Expansion or relocated clubs located in dry climates also contributed to fewer game cancellations. By 1980 the acronym "DH" was associated more with the designated hitter in the American League, a new position that the league had instituted in 1973, and less with the doubleheader.

After the Players Association and the ballclub owners agreed to the 1985 Basic Agreement—following a two-day strike by the ballplayers—the doubleheader tumbled to a new low. The strike year of 1985 was the last year that at least a dozen twin bills (or one percent of all games) were scheduled in majors; 1985 was also the last year that at least 50 doubleheaders (or five percent of all games) were played in the majors. Because the owners "gave up their hard-won player compensation scheme for top-level free agents and permitted free agents to entertain offers from any clubs," the players gained increased flexibility in free-agent negotiations which resulted in even higher salary costs to be dished out by the owners. The ballclubs needed as many of their available 81 home dates to be played as single-admission games to maximize both their ballpark-related and television revenues. For most ballclubs, that meant *all* of their 81 home dates. Only nine doubleheaders were scheduled in 1986, two twi-nighters and seven Sunday twin bills. Five of the seven Sunday doubleheaders were planned for the Bay Area, with three at San Francisco and two at Oakland. The scheduled baseball doubleheader was clearly on sport life-support, an endangered species destined for extinction.[30]

In 1990 the doubleheader found a new role in major-league baseball, not at the ballpark but rather on the television screen. Cable network ESPN paid baseball $400 million for a four-year deal to televise 175 regular-season ballgames on four nights each week. ESPN had scored the first national cable rights to televise major-league baseball beyond network coverage, even though only about half of the nation's households were wired for cable television. CBS, the winner of the bidding rights for network coverage over that four-year period, paid baseball $1.1 billion to televise a dozen regular-season games in addition to the plums of the package, the All-Star Game, the playoffs, and the World Series. ESPN televised six games each week, headed by exclusive rights to televise *Sunday Night Baseball* and semiexclusive rights for a game on Wednesday night. The other four weekly games were combined in twosomes: "On Tuesdays and Fridays, ESPN will present doubleheaders." ESPN also televised tripleheaders on the holidays. The ESPN television deal ushered in a new era where the baseball doubleheader became "let's televise two" rather than "let's play two."[31]

14

"Let's Play Two"

No BALLPLAYER IS MORE identified with the doubleheader than Ernie Banks, the Hall of Fame shortstop-first baseman who played for the Chicago Cubs from 1953 to 1971, who is famous for his frequent exultation of "Let's play two." *The New Dickson Baseball Dictionary* refers to this phrase as Banks' dictum and defines it as a line that "captures the spirit and joy of the game of baseball." This three-word phrase has become not only indelibly associated with Banks but also an iconic expression in the lexicon of baseball.[1]

When a statue of Banks was unveiled outside of Wrigley Field in the spring of 2008, this phrase was immortalized on the base of the statue, albeit initially with a grammatical error as the word "lets" was inscribed rather than the contraction "let's." The statue's sculptor was unapologetic. "I'm the sculptor, I'm not a writer," Lou Cella said. "I just read it the way I heard it in my mind." An apostrophe was quickly etched onto the base of the statue to correct the punctuation in the first word of the legendary saying.[2]

Banks was one of the first power-hitting shortstops. He won back-to-back Most Valuable Player Awards in 1958 and 1959 while hitting 47 and 45 home runs, respectively, for a fifth-place ballclub. In 1961 Banks moved to first base, where he completed his playing career with a .274 batting average, 2,583 hits, and 512 homers. He never played in the World Series, though; his closest opportunity came in 1969 when the Cubs led the Eastern Division of the National League in August but were eventually overtaken by the New York Mets. Banks was one of the last daytime ballplayers, playing all of his home games at Wrigley Field in sunshine in the last major-league ballpark to install lights. The prime of his career also occurred during the height of the doubleheader; his most productive doubleheader was on June 25, 1967, when he had four hits in four at-bats in the second game against Houston (including two home runs) after collecting one hit in four at-bats in the first game.

Banks first received national recognition for saying "Let's play two" in 1977, a few days following the announcement that he had been elected to the Baseball Hall of Fame. Dave Anderson wrote a column in the *New York Times* in January 1977 whose opening paragraph extolled the positive attitude of Banks: "In his 19 seasons with the Chicago Cubs, the phrase never changed. 'It's a beautiful day for a ball game,' Ernie Banks would say. 'It's such a beautiful day, let's play two.' Or when a doubleheader was scheduled, 'let's play three.'" The publication of Anderson's syndicated column in newspapers across the country began the legend of Ernie Banks and "Let's play two."[3]

A week after the publication of Anderson's column, *Time*, the influential weekly newsmagazine, wrote a piece about Banks that extended the legend:

> Ernie Banks has not been heard from much since he retired as an active player with the Chicago Cubs in 1971. But he never lost the sunny disposition that made him one of the best-loved players in baseball. "It's a beautiful day for a ball game," he would often say. "Let's play two." Last week, Banks, 45, enjoyed his most beautiful day yet. He was elected to baseball's Hall of Fame.[4]

The legend accelerated six months later on August 8, 1977, when Banks spoke at the Hall of Fame induction ceremony in Cooperstown. "We've got the setting. We've got the fresh air," Banks began his speech. Looking at the two dozen Hall of Fame ballplayers seated to his left and right, Banks said, with a sweeping gesture of his hand, "We've got the team." Pausing a few seconds to accentuate the moment, Banks then said, "Let's play two." And with that statement, Banks cemented his legacy.[5]

Banks first spoke his immortal phrase about 10 years earlier. A precise date has been lost to history, perhaps intentionally. The usually meticulous Banks, who can remember the pitchers who surrendered many of his 512 career home runs, has cited several different dates when asked to describe the first time he said "Let's play two." In most instances, Banks pinpointed the first time as occurring during the 1967 to 1969 time period.

In the 2007 book *Once Upon a Game: Baseball's Greatest Memories*, Banks told author Alan Schwarz that the first time was July 18, 1967, after he had driven to Wrigley Field for that day's game through some of the city's low-income neighborhoods.

> It was about 105 degrees that day, and as I walked into our locker room, my Cubs teammates were really worn down. But I was feeling so great. So lucky. I was getting paid to do something I loved. So I walked into the locker room and I said, "Boy, it's a beautiful day—let's play two!" Everybody kind of raised up and looked at me. They were saying to themselves, "This guy is crazy."[6]

Four years earlier, in the foreword to the 2003 book *The Golden Age of Baseball*, Banks wrote that the first time was July 3, 1969, but recounted a similar story to the one he later told Schwarz.

The temperature was over 100 degrees. The team was tired and we hadn't even played yet. I looked around, scanning the solemn faces of my teammates. It was just like a wake or something. And then, it just came out: "Let's play two!" A couple of writers wrote it down and it stuck. I was just trying to remind my teammates how fortunate they were to be playing that day, on that field, for the Cubs.[7]

Glenn Stout, in doing research for his 2007 book *The Cubs: The Complete Story of Chicago Cubs Baseball*, discovered several other less-easily-retrieved references to Banks citing 1969 as the first time that he said "Let's play two." Since there are also a few contemporary accounts to substantiate the timing, the 1967–1969 time period seems to be a good candidate for the phrase gaining its initial popularity. Stout, however, also located a *Chicago Tribune* article published in 1990 where Banks recalled that he first said the phrase to broadcaster Jack Quinlan before the 1960 All-Star Game in Kansas City. The provenance of the phrase's initial utterance will probably never be conclusive.[8]

"Let's play two" was already part of Banks' persona by the late 1960s, long before the phrase ever found its way into mainstream print. "'It's a lovely day — let's play three games today' is an answer Banks will give to any number of unrelated questions," David Llorens wrote in an *Ebony* magazine profile in 1967. "Most of these stock phrases that pour forth from the tongue of Ernie Banks are without the import that would warrant their repeating, the manner in which they invariably come. The style (or script), to be sure, is influenced by the only matter of consequence related to the event: the offering of the hero's voice. It meets the needs of those, both old and young, who besiege him."[9]

Banks' now-famous phrase started out as just random talk. Naturally, as Llorens implies in his *Ebony* article, few writers would have been inclined to write about it in a serious article. Then there was the issue of whether, in his random talk, Banks was being sincere or disingenuous. Former teammate Fergie Jenkins took Banks at face value, saying, "Ernie was a pretty good guy, didn't have a bad word to say about anybody, always wanted to play two." Catcher Randy Hundley thought the opposite: "Ernie gave you 'Let's play two' and all that stuff, and we know that a bunch of it was BS." Many ballplayers, however, just didn't know how to take Banks. In a 1969 profile of Banks in *Sports Illustrated*, writer Mark Kram related a story about Banks jawboning with Henry Aaron during batting practice before a Cubs–Braves game in which Banks says the famous phrase. "Henry Aaron! The most dangerous hitter who ever lived," Kram quotes Banks talking to Aaron. "Hall of Fame here he comes. Henry, let's play two today." Kram then writes that "Aaron, shaking his head, looks at him curiously." Author Peter Golenbock put the situation in perspective in his book *Wrigleyville*: "Even if his teammates could never figure out whether Ernie was sincere, the fans didn't care ... the fans, unlike any skeptical teammates, loved that Banks always had a kind word for the inept Cubs organization and a corny phrase or slogan for the media and fans."[10]

The genesis of "Let's play two" may have even predated Banks' arrival with the Cubs in 1953 from the Kansas City Monarchs of the Negro Leagues. After legendary Negro League ballplayer Buck O'Neil died in 2006, Banks told the *Kansas City Star* about his famous saying, "I learned that from Buck O'Neil." Banks said that O'Neil told him, "Son, you've got to love this game to play it." A week later, Banks told the *Chicago Sun-Times*, "Buck had so much love for everybody, in my life I became the same way. Let's play two. Buck was a role model for my life." O'Neil was at least the inspiration for the saying, and he may well have coined a variation of it himself.[11]

Besides the questionable origination of "Let's play two," there is also a dubious connection between the phrase and an actual doubleheader, because doubleheaders were declining in popularity during the 1967–1969 period. Banks played in his first major-league doubleheader on September 22, 1953, at a time when the Cubs played two games on every Sunday and holiday, and were often scheduled for a few twi-night doubleheaders on the road (there were no lights at Wrigley Field then) in addition to the usual coterie of ad hoc doubleheaders to make up a postponed game. The Cubs played 30 twin bills in 1954; they were involved in just 15 in 1969 (and only 11 in Banks' final season in 1971). So it seems illogical that the foundation for Banks' famous line was the actual playing of a doubleheader.

A contemporary newspaper account unearthed by Stout, which was originally published on March 14, 1969, in the *Chicago Daily News*, provides a hint about the possible genesis of the line. The syndicated story by Ron Sons, which discussed what the 38-year-old Banks did in spring training to prepare for the upcoming 1969 season, contained this conclusion: "Then he trots back on the field to take one more exercise or that one more lap of running to win his personal fight for another day. And he hollers to anyone who will listen: 'Let's play two games today. It's too nice a day for just one.'"[12]

The terms "personal fight" and "hollers to anyone who will listen" can be seen to signal a reference to Banks' cool relationship with Cubs manager Leo Durocher. "The union between Durocher and Banks, which began in 1966, was that in name only," Kram wrote in the 1969 Banks profile in *Sports Illustrated*. "Their disparate attitudes and personalities promised sudden conflict." Durocher was abrasive and could be insensitive in his remarks, while Banks was placid and always upbeat, forever flashing that smile of his.[13]

Durocher thought Banks—known as Mr. Cub—was washed up as a ballplayer and wasn't bashful about sharing his attitude with the media. "For three years the virtually peerless leader of the Chicago Cubs has made an

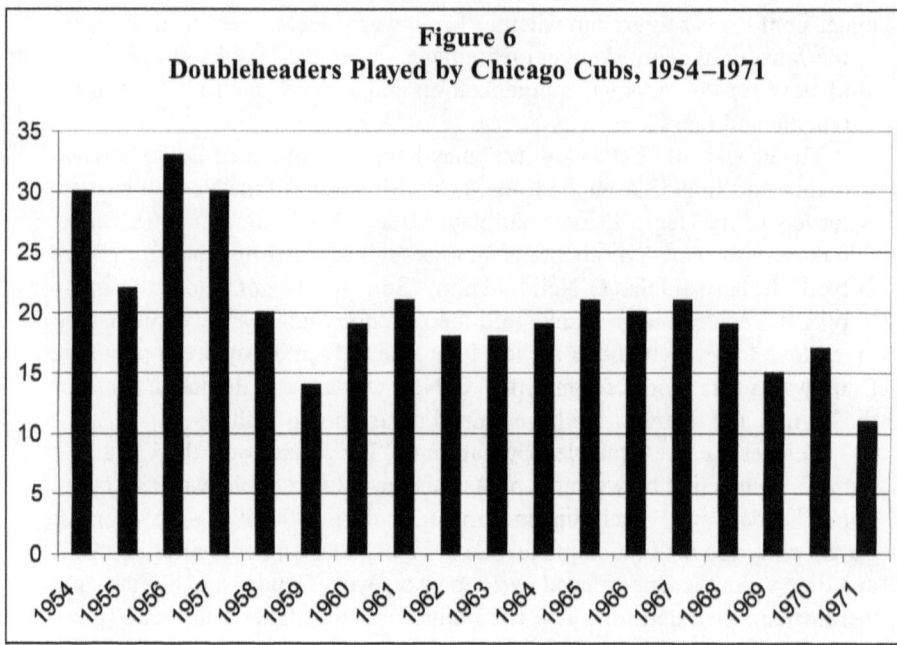

**Figure 6
Doubleheaders Played by Chicago Cubs, 1954–1971**

The number of doubleheaders that the Cubs played each season, which served as the backdrop to Ernie Banks' famous saying "Let's play two," declined over the course of Banks' playing career. (Source: Retrosheet database.)

effort to replace Ernie Banks as his first baseman on the presumption that Ernie is in the twilight of his career," one newspaper reported before spring training in 1969. Durocher also wasn't subtle at all about his remarks about Banks. Later that year Durocher said, "We've got a good young team. Except for Ernie Banks—how old is he now, 38?—we're young with everybody under 30." Durocher understandably disliked Banks.[14]

Jenkins remembers the clash between Banks and Durocher. "Ernie and Leo were constantly feuding. Leo was always giving Ernie Banks's job away," Jenkins recalled. "Every spring he'd give it to John Boccabella or George Altman or Lee Thomas, and Ernie would win it back again ... Ernie would get in there and get some hits and get back in the lineup, and you couldn't take him out. He was a hitter." Banks understandably disliked Durocher.[15]

It wasn't in Banks' personality to publicly battle Durocher, since Banks was one of the first ballplayers to follow in the footsteps of Jackie Robinson. "Banks kept his good nature and held his tongue along with the few other black players," Steve Jacobson, author of *Carrying Jackie's Torch: The Players Who Integrated Baseball—and America*, wrote. Said Banks: "It also labeled us with the next wave of players who came into the majors and we were called 'Uncle Tom' because we didn't question anything." Banks made his statement with his bat on the field, however, continuing to drive in runs at a prodigious pace and help lead the Cubs in 1969 in their failed quest for a first-place finish for the first time since 1945.[16]

The fact that Banks was usually saying "Let's play two" to a crowd of people and/or in a public place can be viewed as a subtle rebuke of Durocher's negative attitude toward Banks. "Let's play two!" could be translated as "Leo, I can still do my job!" In his autobiography *Nice Guys Finish Last*, Durocher told several stories about Banks that create a basis for acknowledging that "Let's play two" served that purpose.

For example, Durocher derisively wrote that Banks couldn't remember baseball signals, but he never forgot a newspaperman's name. "All he knew was, 'Ho, let's go. Ho, babydoobedoobedoo. It's a wonderful day for a game in Chicago. Let's play twooo.'" Durocher went further to say. "We'd get on the bus and he'd sit across from the writers. 'A beaoootiful day for twooo.' It could be snowing outside. 'Let's play three.'" In his last years with Cubs, Banks had major problems with his left knee. Writers always asked Banks about his playing status, and he'd say he felt great and could play. "Then he'd tell Doc Sheuneman, the trainer, that he couldn't play, and I'd write him out of the lineup," Durocher wrote. "'How come you didn't play today, Ernie?' the newspapermen would ask him. 'The knee bother you?' He'd shrug and give them a significant look. 'The man says I play, I play.' Aha! Leo Durocher doesn't want Banks to play because Leo Durocher has decided that it would be a wonderful day in Chicago to lose a game or two, scoobedoobedoo."[17]

Durocher was in a no-win situation with Mr. Cub. "A couple of times I said to him, 'I ask you if you can play and you're always ready to play a doubleheader, a tripleheader if we'll let you, but you get into the clubhouse and I see them wrap your knee and it's that big. I know you can't play, and I don't play you and I catch hell from the newspapermen about it. Ernie, if your knee hurts, why don't you tell them? ... 'Well,' he'd say, 'you're the manager, Leo. I don't think it's my place to tell you who to play.'"[18]

Matters came to a head in a doubleheader in Atlanta on July 20, 1970. "In comes Ernie. He wants to play both games," Durocher wrote. "'All right,' I said. 'Let's have an understanding then. I'm sick and tired of taking the abuse. You want to play? You're playing.' I called in the newspapermen. 'Banks just asked to play and he's playing both games. A doubleheader tonight. Both games!'" By the sixth inning of the first game, Banks could hardly walk and needed medical attention. "Don't you think the writers came bombing in afterwards wanting to know why I hadn't played Banks in the second game like I'd promised?" Durocher wrote. "All Ernie knew was that the manager hadn't written his name on the card. Shrug, smile, what-are-you-gonna-do? The next day we had to put him on the disabled list."[19]

Was Banks needling Durocher with his "Let's play two" remarks? We'll likely never know. "Banks still responds to the Durocher matter with that enigmatic smile," one writer has succinctly put it about Banks' thoughts about Durocher. The timing of 1967–1969 as the initial dating of the phrase certainly adds credence to that perspective. But what year Ernie Banks first said "Let's play two," and whether or not its foundation was connected to doubleheaders, getting back at Leo Durocher, or any other rationale, is inconsequential. The embedded sentiment in the phrase is what is important today, as the phrase is used in countless newspaper and magazine stories that talk about a doubleheader—in baseball as well as other sports—or anything that has to do with two events occurring at the same time.[20]

As Banks told author Alan Schwarz, "I did a lot of things in my career on the field—500 home runs and everything—but the best part was sharing my joy for baseball with so many people. Every day of my life I wake up thinking, 'Let's play two!' That will never change." Banks added, "I love it—it's become a part of me. It seems like athletes are remembered for just one thing. With Ted Williams, it's his .406 batting average. With Willie Mays, it's his over-the-shoulder catch. But people remember Ernie Banks for 'Let's play two.'"[21]

Banks' attitude helped to establish the romance surrounding the doubleheader as the concept entered its demise phrase in the 1980s, when players and fans alike rapidly fell out of love with the seven-hour marathon that the doubleheader had become. "I've never heard anybody say they like doubleheaders, except Ernie Banks," Mike Hargrove said in 1991. "And I think he was lying." Just 10 years after Banks was inducted into the Baseball Hall of Fame, the doubleheader was nearly extinct on the major-league baseball schedule.[22]

15

Extinction of the Scheduled Doubleheader

DURING THE DECADE OF THE 1980s, the number of scheduled doubleheaders in the major leagues shriveled from five dozen in 1980 to less than two dozen by 1984 and to just three in 1989. Despite valiant attempts to eradicate the twin bill from the schedule in the early 1990s, one or two found their way onto the initial schedule each year. However, in 1997, the doubleheader did completely disappear from the major-league schedule.

Elimination of the scheduled doubleheader was clearly an objective of Henry Stephenson, major-league baseball's official schedule-maker in the 1980s. "When I draft the schedule, one of the standards it has to have is no doubleheaders whenever possible," Stephenson said in 1989 after inserting three doubleheaders into the schedule that year. The primary reason to schedule a doubleheader was to satisfy Players Association rules as stipulated in the Basic Agreement.[1]

Two of the three scheduled doubleheaders in 1989 were created to comply with the Basic Agreement. The July 28 twin bill in Detroit was needed to avoid having the Tigers play 39 games in 39 days and thus run afoul of the maximum number of consecutive playing dates (20). The April 16 doubleheader in San Francisco was required to give the visiting Braves a mandated nontravel day off as the ballclub flew cross-country for its next game on April 18 in Atlanta. The third doubleheader, August 11 in San Diego, was necessary to avoid a stadium-use conflict with an NFL preseason game. Another possible reason to schedule a doubleheader would be if a ballclub requested one, but according to Stephenson "nobody does [that] anymore."[2]

With the paucity of scheduled doubleheaders in the 1990s, the Level 1 or makeup doubleheader was the last bastion of the two-for-the-price-of-one bargain bill. However, even those single-admission twin bills were far fewer than they used to be. While the priests of baseball were administering the last rites to the scheduled doubleheader, the baseball gods—the ballclub owners and the Players Association—were resurrecting the separate-admission day-night doubleheader from its burial plot in the baseball cemetery.

On June 24, 1989, the Boston Red Sox revived the day-night doubleheader with two separate-admission ballgames with the Minnesota Twins at Fenway Park. "Call it a Rocket tax, a Wade tariff, or a Dwight, Geddy or Marty assessment, a reflection of the Boston Red Sox' need to bring in the most bucks possible to pay the hefty salaries of Roger Clemens, Wade Boggs and the rest of New England's boys of summer," Art Turgeon of the *Providence Journal* wrote. "The popularity of day-night doubleheaders, never high to begin with, has all but disappeared in recent years. Indeed, the Bosox, who will be staging their 15th since 1971, are the only team in the major leagues to use them since 1973. Even they haven't scheduled one since 1982."[3]

The Red Sox positioned the two games for the price of two as good for the fans, since Fenway Park had a small seating capacity and a large percentage of seats were sold for every game. Oh, yes, and the ballclub had a ticket policy of no refunds, only exchanges. "People go out of their way to buy choice seats early," Red Sox president John Harrington said. "If they get rained out, then all we can offer them for another game is bleacher seats or high grandstand because other people have bought up that game early." Despite the economics to the ballclub, the Red Sox owners still had to secure the cooperation of the ballplayers on both teams to conduct a day-night doubleheader, in accordance with the terms of the Basic Agreement. While the Red Sox players approved the idea, the Twins didn't. Reportedly, another vote of the Twins players okayed the idea after the Red Sox promised to make a $20,000 contribution to a charity chosen by the players. In August, the Red Sox conducted another day-night doubleheader with the Baltimore Orioles; no publicized word on the tribute demanded by the Orioles players to waive the clause in the Basic Agreement.[4]

The day-night doubleheader, once the much reviled split doubleheader, was now an acceptable technique in the eyes of the Players Association. It was a small gesture by Donald Fehr, who now headed the Players Association, to help the ballclub owners pay the million-dollar salaries of the Association's membership. In the 1990 Basic Agreement, Fehr even allowed a concession that gave the Red Sox and the Chicago Cubs the right to play one day-night doubleheader without having to obtain the approval of the ballplayers, as conveyed in this clause of the agreement:

> This will confirm our understanding that notwithstanding the requirements of Article V (D)(1), when there is no practical alternative to doing so, one postponed game scheduled to have been played in Fenway Park and one postponed game scheduled to have been played in Wrigley Field may be rescheduled as a

split doubleheader to be played in such parks in each championship season covered by this Agreement. Scheduling a postponed game as part of a conventional doubleheader will not be considered a practical alternative.[5]

Due to better drainage systems in the ballparks, artificial turf, and covered stadiums, there were now far fewer postponed games that needed to be rescheduled, either as the second game of a single-admission twin bill or the second installment in a day-night doubleheader. The concession in the 1990 Basic Agreement set the stage for a further reduction in "true" doubleheaders as the scheduled doubleheader dwindled in number.

Although there were no doubleheaders in the original release of the 1991 schedule, the Cleveland Indians wound up with one on August 16 in a subsequent schedule revision. "We didn't have any control over it," said Indians president Hank Peters. "That was the schedule they gave us. Some other team must have needed an open date and we got stuck with it. It wasn't something we asked for." Peters added, "Years ago the doubleheader was a staple of baseball, especially on Sunday afternoons. But that was before TV revenues became so important. No wants to televise both games of a doubleheader."[6]

In the 1992 schedule, Cleveland was saddled with another doubleheader, which demonstrated that scheduled twin bills were not only rare, but increasingly wacky as well. The first problem with the April 12, 1992, doubleheader between the Indians and the Red Sox at Municipal Stadium was that the two ballclubs played fewer innings in the two games of the Sunday doubleheader than they did in one game on Saturday night. On April 11, the Indians and Red Sox engaged in a 19-inning contest that lasted six and a half hours, in which the two clubs used 15 pitchers and 39 players. The Red Sox flew in ace pitcher Roger Clemens from Boston, where he had stayed to rest, expecting to pitch the Sox home-opener on Monday. Instead, Clemens was thrust into the role of hurling the nightcap of the Sunday twin bill; he responded by tossing a two-hit shutout. The stranger part of the doubleheader was the first game, when Sox pitcher Matt Young tossed a no-hitter but lost the game. Young walked seven and allowed the Indians to steal six bases in the eight innings he pitched. "Bizarre? Intriguing? Unbelievable? Young's outing was all of that," the *Boston Globe* described Young's unusual pitching feat, which because he didn't complete nine innings technically didn't qualify as a no-hitter under major-league rules. But the strangest part of the doubleheader was that the Red Sox set a major-league record for fewest hits allowed in a twin bill, as the Indians had reached Young and Clemens for just two hits in 52 at-bats.[7]

Young was sanguine about not getting credit for a no-hitter. "They didn't get any hits. The game's over. People can make rules all they want. It doesn't matter to me," Young said after the game. "I thought when you throw a no-hitter, you're supposed to strike out the last guy and the catcher comes out and you jump around. When you have to go back into the dugout and see if your team can score another run, it's kind of anti-climatic." Sixteen years later when two California Angels pitchers combined to throw a no-hitter for eight innings and lose the game, Young was reflective about his feat on that chilly Sunday in Cleveland. Because he had already thrown 125 pitches in that game, he wasn't sure he would have made it out to the mound for the bottom of the ninth had the Sox tied the game or gone ahead in the top of the ninth inning. "I wasn't the same the rest of the year," Young told the *Los Angeles Times* in 2008. "They're not going to take you out with a no-hitter, but I threw a complete game my next start too. That was too many pitches too early in the season." As for making it into the record book, Young joked, "We gave up two hits in a doubleheader, the lowest ever, and we split."[8]

Despite the oddities, doubleheaders were lauded in the media for their nostalgic value, as a throwback to another era, with accounts accentuating the phrase "the only regularly scheduled doubleheader of the major league baseball season." Romanticized memories also periodically surfaced. "Some of my best baseball memories as a kid in Southern California were doubleheaders in the Dodger Stadium bleachers," Larry Stone wrote in a *Baseball Digest* article. "On one unforgettable Sunday, I saw Sandy Koufax and Don Drysdale, an overdose of baseball royalty that almost killed me with excitement. It seemed like cheating, getting two games for the price of one, as if I had pulled a fast one on Dodger management." Tom Verducci had similar East Coast memories. "You paid one price, the same price you would pay for a single game, but you saw two games. In effect, the second game was free," Verducci recalled. "So my brothers and I would take a bus and the subway to either Yankee Stadium or Shea Stadium. Yankees or Mets, it didn't matter to us. Two games for the price of one was what counted."[9]

Old-time ballplayers weighed in with their happy recollections. "We loved the game, even doubleheaders—especially doubleheaders. Oh how I loved them!" Dom DiMaggio remarked in the mid–1990s. "They gave us the chance to play two games instead of only one. If they had wanted us to play three, we would have been happy to." Modern ballplayers were much less enthusiastic. "I hate them," infielder Joe Morgan said. "You can't give that pure performance for 16 innings or more. After five swings of the bat, that's enough." Catcher Joe Girardi sided with Morgan. "It kills you. It's physically demanding on players, and I don't know if the fans really like them either. Kids may like it, but parents probably hate it."[10]

Quickly dispelling the romanticism for the doubleheader in the 1990s was the dismal reality of actually sitting through two ballgames in one day. For example, the Chicago Cubs hosted a holiday doubleheader on July 4, 1994—augmenting the scheduled single game at Wrigley Field with a second contest to make up a previous rainout—that lasted an agonizing 10 hours. The second game spanned seven and a half hours, due to three rain delays and six extra innings. "It's the longest doubleheader I've ever been involved in," Cubs catcher Rick Wilkins said after the game. "We even ran out of food. That's a long day right there." A *Chicago Tribune* sportswriter quipped, "Some marriages don't last as long as the doubleheader the Cubs and Colorado Rockies played Monday at Wrigley Field." Very few of the 37,000 people in attendance endured the entirety of the doubleheader experience; the *Tribune* reported that about half of the spectators left after the Cubs won the first game and only a thousand or so hardy fans remained when the second game concluded.[11]

Six weeks after that doubleheader marathon at Wrigley Field on July 4, major-league baseball came to a standstill as the ballplayers went on strike in August 1994 when negotiations broke down for a new Basic Agreement as the ballclub owners tried to implement a salary-cap structure. A month later the work stoppage forced the cancellation of the rest of the 1994 season, the playoffs, and the World Series. The strike continued into spring training in 1995, as the owners and Players Association haggled over how to apportion the riches of the baseball business. Only a ruling in March 1995 by federal judge Sonia Sotomayor, a future U.S. Supreme Court justice, to apply the provisions of the expired 1990 Basic Agreement saved the 1995 baseball season; negotiations for a new labor contract spilled into 1997.[12]

Scheduled doubleheaders went the way of the dodo bird and the rotary telephone as the ballclub owners sought to generate as much revenue as possible to alleviate their strike losses. There were just two twin bills on the 1995 schedule and only one in 1996; the latter turned out to be the last scheduled doubleheader in the twentieth century. On June 8, 1996, the Minnesota Twins hosted the Oakland Athletics in a twin bill at the Metrodome. "We were originally scheduled to play a three- or four-game set against the A's in September, with one game on Monday, September 9," a Twins representative explained in the *Minneapolis Star Tribune*. "We look at it two ways. One, it's nice to give fans something that hasn't been a part of baseball scheduling for quite a while. And two, it gives our team a day off in September and Oakland liked it because it gave them an extra day at home. It's good for everybody." In true Bill Veeck style, the Twins had the Minnesota Zoo's World of Birds show in the dome between the two games. The Saturday afternoon-evening doubleheader in the Metrodome attracted a crowd of 22,164 to watch the ballclubs split the two games, which was roughly a 50 percent increase over the 14,799 that attended the single game between the two clubs on Friday night.[13]

A new Basic Agreement was finally agreed upon in March 1997, which included a high-profile scheduling provision regarding interleague play.

Little publicized was another concession by the Players Association concerning the use of day-night doubleheaders to make up postponed games. The day-night twin bill—long banned from the initial season schedule at the insistence of the Players Association—gained enhanced life in the late 1990s, as more ballclubs were unilaterally allowed to use this technique rather than the conventional two-for-one doubleheader.

In the 1997 Basic Agreement, the Cubs and Red Sox obtained unlimited usage of the day-night doubleheader concept to make up postponed games, as the limiting word "one" was replaced by the more expansive "a" in the legal language: "When there is no practical alternative to doing so, the Boston Red Sox and the Chicago Cubs shall have the right to reschedule a postponed game as a split doubleheader to be played in, respectively, Fenway Park and Wrigley Field, even if the criteria set out in subparagraph (a) above are not met." The other ballclub owners gained enhanced rights to employ day-night doubleheaders, capped at two per club per year, through the following language in that subparagraph (a):

> Each Club shall have the right to reschedule any postponed game as a split doubleheader when ticket sales for the game at the time of postponement exceed, in any respect, the number of comparable tickets available to be exchanged by the Club for the balance of the championship season, and both the postponed and rescheduled game occur in the last regularly scheduled series between the two Clubs at the Club's park.[14]

Also making the use of day-night twin bills easier for the ballclub owners was a change in the procedure to secure a waiver of a contract provision. Rather than having to obtain a majority vote of the affected ballplayers, as had been the condition for many years, the new contract provided for the waiver to be granted by the Players Association: "The Association shall have the exclusive right to approve the additional rescheduling of postponed games as split doubleheaders in circumstances that are not automatically permitted by subparagraph (a) or (b) above." Interestingly, the waiver by the Players Association only applied to split doubleheaders, as all other waivers under the Basic Agreement continued to be subject to a vote by the ballplayers.[15]

In the 1997 Basic Agreement, the Players Association clearly supported the use of day-night doubleheaders to make up postponed ballgames (in exchange, of course, for other provisions deemed more valuable, such as a weaker salary-cap measure than originally proposed by the ballclub owners, among other provisions). Almost immediately when the 1997 baseball season opened, the new clause was put to use. When the April 10 game in Denver between the Rockies and the Reds was snowed out, it was rescheduled for August 25 as part of a day-night doubleheader.[16]

In the new millennium, as the single-admission twin bill appeared destined to soon die a quiet death, a small resurgence of interest in the doubleheader concept appeared. However, it was the oddball separate-admission doubleheader that drew the attention, not the traditional single-admission one. A home-and-home doubleheader and a three-club doubleheader were both staged during the 2000 season as part of concerted efforts to make up rainouts. Home-and-home games on the same day had not been experienced in the major leagues since 1903, while the three-club doubleheader was last seen in 1951 (and not on a widespread basis since 1899).

The two New York ballclubs, the Yankees and the Mets, were the combatants in the home-and-home doubleheader conducted on July 8, with a day game at Shea Stadium and a night game at Yankee Stadium. The novel situation, which was dubbed a "split-park doubleheader," arose when the June 11 game between the two clubs was rained out. Postponed interleague games posed a big challenge for rescheduling, especially an intracity matchup because the two ballclubs are rarely at home at the same time. While the rained-out game could have conceivably waited until after the season ended to be replayed, both clubs were contending for a playoff spot. And, naturally, the intracity rivalry was too big a revenue-generator to forego during the regular season if at all possible. There were a host of logistical challenges to work out, including major ones such as transporting the clubs between the two ballparks, and minor ones such as when players don their uniforms for the second game of the day.[17]

The *New York Times* wrote that the games "promise to be part sports novelty, part transit brain-teaser and, of course, an all-out example of New York City excess as police escorts accompany both teams along what is likely to be the chosen route down the Grand Central Parkway, over the Triborough Bridge and up the Major Deegan Expressway." The Mets decided to eat at their home ballpark after the first game, then dress in their road uniforms for the bus trip to Yankee Stadium for the second game. "It'll be like American Legion again," said Glendon Rusch. "It's not too often that you see a big league team get off the bus in uniform." While the novelty of the split-park doubleheader was good publicity, the day's events were taxing for the players, as all day-night doubleheaders were. "Maybe in years to come, to look back and say, yeah, in the year 2000 we had a day in which we played two games in two separate parks, it might be something to talk about," said pitcher Al Leiter. "But Saturday, for the most part, guys are going to view it as an inconvenience." It didn't take years for people to begin talking about the July 8 split-park doubleheader. What people remember most about those two games is not so much playing two games in two ballparks, but rather how a pitch from Roger Clemens hit Mike Piazza.[18]

The Cleveland Indians were the focal point of the three-club doubleheader, which was played on September 25, 2000, at Jacobs Field in Cleveland. The genesis of this novel arrangement for a day-night doubleheader was the rainout of the Indians game with the White Sox on September 10. Because the Indians and the White Sox were both in contention for a playoff spot, there was concern about rescheduling the game on an "if necessary" basis after the season concluded, given the tight scheduling for the playoff games. The Twins were already scheduled to play in Cleveland that night. Cleveland general manager John Hart was adamantly opposed to the three-club doubleheader on the 25th, because the Indians were already slated to play two day-night doubleheaders in Boston a few days before the appointed date. However, the three-club spectacle was carded for September 25 "to avoid complications." Cleveland defeated Chicago in the 12:05 afternoon game, but then lost to the Twins in the 6:05 evening encounter. The *Minneapolis Star Tribune* recounted for its readers some of the logistical problems of "one ballpark, three teams, two games," especially two teams sharing the same visitor's clubhouse. For instance, the last White Sox player left the visitor's clubhouse at 4:48, and just two minutes later at 4:50 the Twins equipment bags were delivered and unloaded. The first Twins players started to arrive in the visitor's clubhouse at 4:57, which was roughly three hours after players would normally have begun to get ready for a 6:05 game.[19]

The last scheduled doubleheader in the major leagues occurred on May 26, 2001, when the Minnesota Twins hosted the Oakland Athletics in a twin bill at the Metrodome. They were the same two ballclubs that had participated in the last previously scheduled doubleheader five years earlier in 1996 in the same location. The occasion was the 100th anniversary of the first two-game set in American League history, on May 30, 1901. Back then, the two clubs' predecessors, the Washington Senators and the Philadelphia Athletics, played morning and afternoon games on the Memorial Day holiday. The *Minneapolis Star Tribune* headlined the event as: "Let's Play 2! The Twins turn back the clock this weekend not only by wearing the 1901 Washington Senators uniforms but by bringing back a baseball tradition—the doubleheader." This doubleheader was the idea of former Twins executive Chris Clouser, who was seeking ways to increase attendance at Twins games. "We thought this would be a nice addition to the first holiday weekend of the season," a Twins representative told the media. "There's a lot of baseball history when it comes to holiday doubleheaders. Chris Clouser was on board, and this is something he really pushed for. He believed that doubleheaders were one of the magical things missing from the game of baseball today."[20]

There were the usual pre-game romanticisms uttered about doubleheaders. "I loved doubleheaders," said Tom Mee, the Twins official scorer and former public relations director. "We used to play a day game on Saturday. The farmers would come in, catch that game, go out on the town, then catch two on Sunday before heading home." However, Twins coach Paul Molitor expressed a more balanced viewpoint. "I still do like the concept of the doubleheader being part of the game. It's still unique to the sport and it's still fun," Molitor said. "Although I don't know how many fans will have the attention span to come out and sit still for two games anymore, with all that's going on." *Star Tribune* writer Jim Souhan added a more sobering assessment of the doubleheader, writing that management doesn't like them (costs revenue from one home game), television doesn't (few people likely to watch both games), and neither do the team managers (alters pitching rotation and depletes the bullpen). Souhan invoked the essential Banks quote for the occasion—"It's a beautiful day, let's play two!"—but followed it with the comment that "today, if Banks said that, he would get muzzled, beat up or sued."[21]

After all of the pre-doubleheader buzz, the reality set in as usual after the two games were concluded. "There might not be a movement for another doubleheader anytime soon," the *Star Tribune* pondered. "Each game took 10 innings and required a total of seven hours and 45 minutes to complete." The newspaper added, "Fans in the left field upper deck paid $5 for tickets—or 25 cents an inning." What a bargain for a rabid baseball fan. However, that was exactly the problem.[22]

It is not just fans that attend baseball games any more, as there are legions of casual observers that buy tickets as well, and not just spectators at the ballpark that matter, as the number of television viewers and advertisers affects ballclub finances nearly as much, if not more so. A large part of the aurora of going to a ballgame now is the so-called "baseball experience" that is nearly impossible to quantify. "The culture of baseball changed from peanuts and hot dogs to cinnamon rolls and sushi," Kevin Ausmus wrote, "from buying a game program to receiving a promotional bobble-head doll, from cheesy organ music between pitches to Metallica roaring from a state of the art sound system, from following balls and strikes to laying money on the bratwurst to win the wiener race." Sophisticated marketing is also de rigueur. "Fans, however, are only part of the spectator or viewer base of professional sports, and generally a declining part," Michael Danielson wrote in *Home Team: Professional Sports and the American Metropolis*. "Much of the intensive marketing by teams is designed to attract customers who are not particularly interested in the game being played."[23]

With all major-league ballclubs expecting to play 81 separate-admission home games during the season (and several, such as Tampa Bay that play indoor in a domed stadium, virtually assured of it), promotions are selectively used to increase ballpark attendance rather than a scattergun approach of synthetic doubleheaders in the 1930s or bat-day add-ons to Sunday doubleheaders in the 1960s. Ballclubs read studies like "Does Bat Day Make Cents? The Effect of Promotions on the Demand for Major League Baseball," which conclude that "promotions have a discernible 14% impact on attendance." Ballclubs execute variable ticket pricing, which studies find increase attendance from three to seven percent, by selling an outfield seat as high as $21 for a "marquee" game and as low as $11 for a "value" game in a four-level system that varies ticket prices by quality of the opponent, day of the week, and month of the year.[24]

All this sophisticated marketing by major-league ballclubs reinforces the need not just to ban single-admission doubleheaders from the initial schedule but also justifies the need for separate-admission day-night doubleheaders to make up any postponed games. The traditional twin bill seems to have no place in major-league baseball. Followers of the sport will have to be content with their romanticized notions of the doubleheader, as the concept is unlikely to experience a comeback. There is too much money at stake in television contracts for ballclubs to consider hosting a doubleheader when the second game is perceived as unlikely to attract a sufficient number of either viewers or advertisers. Given the average three-hour length of the ballgame today, there isn't the demand from spectators to sit through a minimum of six or seven hours of baseball at the ballpark.

Sportswriters started writing obituaries for the doubleheader even though rigor mortis had yet to materialize in the 120-year-old concept. "The main culprit is simple economics. The game grew too popular (and salaries too expensive) for owners to forfeit an entire gate," one writer explained. "Something in the fabric of the game, however, was lost with the death of the doubleheader."[25]

It was always about money, though, from the very beginning in 1882 when Harry Wright of the Providence ballclub sized up the attendance potential for a morning game in the early autumn against the last-place Worcester club and suggested, long before Ernie Banks, "let's play two" in the afternoon and perhaps the extra game for free will attract more customers. Doubleheaders allowed for schedule expansion to 154 games, and then to 162 games in 1961. Separate-admission holiday two-game sets converted to single-admission status when Sunday gates started to propel ballclub economics. Sunday doubleheaders during the Great Depression were staged to keep the ballclubs afloat, by getting as many bodies into the ballpark as possible, as were the twilight-night and swing-shift doubleheaders invented during World War II.

In many ways, it was astounding that the doubleheader lasted as long as it did, before petering out in the 1970s. Sure the fans loved them, but the ballplayers despised them, and once they no longer served any economic utility, the ballclub owners cast them aside in favor of a more television-friendly approach to staging ballgames. If they needed to play two games on one day to make up a postponed game, the day-night doubleheader became the preferred answer—for ballclubs as well as ballplayers—rather than the twi-night twin bill.

While a doubleheader in a domed stadium seems preposterous, and a scheduled one even more ludicrous, the Metrodome was the stage for the last two scheduled doubleheaders in major-league baseball history. The last ones, that is, barring a sudden, unforeseen revival of the concept, which is extremely unlikely. Resurrection would perhaps be a more appropriate term.

Future collective bargaining sessions between the ballclub owners and the Players Association are likely to produce a mandate for the day-night doubleheader as the preferred, if not only, method to make up a postponed game and outlaw the single-admission twin bill. At that point, we could say "doubleheader, rest in peace."

When the final extinction of the true, single-admission doubleheader occurs, perhaps as soon as 2015, we need to honor its past and not relegate it to the trash bin. The doubleheader saved baseball during the Great Depression and World War II, and established the foundation for a huge spectator base that fueled baseball's success in the 1970s and 1980s. Even when "doubleheader" becomes synonymous with the separate-admission day-night variation, and "Let's play two" means "two for two" and not "two for one," we need to revere the legend and lore of the single-admission doubleheader for what it did for major-league baseball.

Appendix A: Doubleheader Milestones

July 4, 1881	Buffalo and Detroit host the first separate-admission morning-afternoon two-game sets on the Independence Day holiday.
May 30, 1882	Troy hosts the first separate-admission morning-afternoon two-game set on the Decoration Day holiday (now called Memorial Day).
September 25, 1882	Worcester hosts Providence for two afternoon games in the first single-admission doubleheader in major-league history.
October 9, 1886	Philadelphia hosts Detroit in a season-ending doubleheader that popularizes the single-admission concept for two games on one day as a technique to make up postponed games.
September 3, 1888	Boston and Brooklyn host the first separate-admission morning-afternoon two-game sets on the Labor Day holiday.
September 9, 1888	Brooklyn hosts the first Sunday doubleheader, with the second game representing a makeup of a postponed game.
September 2, 1889	Two Philadelphia ballclubs, one in the National League and the other in the American Association, host the first single-admission doubleheaders on the Labor Day holiday.
September 1, 1890	Brooklyn hosts the first time that three games are played on the same day in the major leagues, with a combination of a separate-admission morning game

	and two afternoon games staged as a single-admission doubleheader.
October 2, 1892	Cincinnati hosts a Sunday doubleheader, with the second game representing the moving up of the scheduled Monday game the next day.
July 21, 1898	The first-ever scheduled nonholiday doubleheaders on a major-league schedule are played in six National League cities.
August 24, 1902	The Chicago Cubs host the first scheduled Sunday doubleheader ever played, sparked by competition from the newly created American League.
July 4, 1908	The St. Louis Cardinals host the first single-admission doubleheader on the Independence Day holiday.
October 12, 1910	Brooklyn hosts a single-admission doubleheader on Columbus Day, in the short-lived experiment to extend the playing season to include a fourth national holiday.
May 30, 1914	The Chicago Cubs and the St. Louis Browns host the first single-admission doubleheaders on the Memorial Day holiday, sparked by competition from the newly created Federal League.
July 4, 1914	All Independence Day matches in the Federal League are played as single-admission doubleheaders, forcing ballclubs in the National and American Leagues to do likewise to stave off the competition on holidays in 1914 and 1915.
October 2, 1920	The Pittsburgh Pirates host the only tripleheader ever played in the major leagues, in which spectators could watch three games for the price of one admission.
July 4, 1923	The New York Yankees host a single-admission doubleheader in the first holiday games ever played in Yankee Stadium, setting the trend for single-admission status by all ballclubs for holiday games.
June 23, 1929	The first time a Sunday doubleheader is stopped prior to completion by a Sunday curfew, due to the Massachusetts law enacted in 1928 that required Sunday games to cease at 6:00 P.M.
September 8, 1929	The first of five consecutive Sunday doubleheaders is hosted by the St. Louis Cardinals, a pattern that escalated in 1930 as the Cardinals popularized the "syn-

	thetic doubleheader" that swamped the Sunday calendar in the major leagues during the Great Depression.
May 28, 1939	The first of numerous scheduled Sunday doubleheaders that appeared on a widespread basis that season on the initial major-league schedule is played.
September 27, 1939	The Chicago White Sox host the first single-admission, day-night doubleheader.
July 24, 1942	The St. Louis Browns and the Cleveland Indians host the first single-admission twilight-night doubleheaders.
June 15, 1943	The Philadelphia Phillies host the first single-admission morning-afternoon doubleheader, known as the "swing-shift" doubleheader.
July 22, 1943	The Washington Senators host the first scheduled twilight-night doubleheader.
August 14, 1946	The Brooklyn Dodgers host the first separate-admission day-night doubleheader.
July 4, 1947	The Brooklyn Dodgers revert to playing separate-admission morning-afternoon two-game sets on the holidays.
April 12, 1950	New York Governor Thomas Dewey vetoes legislation that would have prohibited separate-admission doubleheaders.
April 22, 1952	The Brooklyn Dodgers host the first postwar scheduled twi-night doubleheader.
May 31, 1954	The Philadelphia Phillies decline to schedule a doubleheader on Memorial Day and play just a single game on the holiday (celebrated on Monday since May 30 fell on a Sunday).
June 1, 1955	The Kansas City Athletics host the first scheduled day-night doubleheader.
July 4, 1958	The Los Angeles Dodgers decline to schedule any games on the Independence Day holiday.
July 12, 1959	The last Sunday doubleheader stopped prior to completion by a Sunday curfew is played, as the Pennsylvania law was revoked later that month.
August 26, 1967	The Houston Astros host the last scheduled day-night doubleheader, since the 1968 Basic Agreement prohibited the scheduling of split doubleheaders.
July 4, 1984	The San Francisco Giants host the last scheduled holiday doubleheader.

June 24, 1989	The Boston Red Sox host a day-night doubleheader after obtaining a waiver from the provisions of the Basic Agreement, by vote of the ballplayers, which revives the use of the concept to make up postponed games.
May 26, 2001	The Minnesota Twins host the last scheduled doubleheader in major-league history.

Appendix B: Doubleheader Records*

August 20, 1887	Jim Whitney of the Washington club in the National League is the first pitcher to toss two nine-inning complete games for a victory in both ends of a single-admission doubleheader.
May 30, 1894	Bobby Lowe of the Boston club in the National League hits four home runs in the afternoon game of a Memorial Day two-game set (he had no home runs in the morning game).
August 21, 1894	Boston scores 43 runs in a doubleheader.
August 31, 1903	Joe McGinnity of the New York Giants pitches his third set of double victories in a doubleheader in a span of one month.
September 22, 1903	Mike Donlin of the Cincinnati Reds hits four triples in a doubleheader.
September 26, 1908	Ed Reulbach of the Chicago Cubs pitches two shutout victories in a doubleheader.
August 5, 1909	The Washington Senators play their eighth consecutive doubleheader (streak began on July 27).
July 17–19, 1912	Ty Cobb of the Detroit Tigers is the first to have 14 hits in two consecutive doubleheaders (seven in each).
August 8, 1922	The Pittsburgh Pirates collect 46 hits in a doubleheader.
August 28, 1926	Dutch Levsen of the Cleveland Indians is the last

*Source: Steve Gietschier, ed., Complete Baseball Record Book (St. Louis: Sporting News, 2008).

pitcher to hurl two complete-game victories in a doubleheader.

August 31, 1926   Ray Morehart of the Chicago White Sox is the first modern-era batter to have nine hits in a doubleheader.

September 26, 1926   The New York Yankees and the St. Louis Browns play both games of a doubleheader in two hours and seven minutes, the shortest doubleheader by elapsed time in major-league history.

September 15, 1928   The Boston Braves participate in their ninth consecutive doubleheader (streak began on September 4).

May 21, 1930   Max Bishop of the Philadelphia Athletics collects eight walks in a doubleheader (he tied his own record on July 8, 1934).

September 17, 1930   Earl Averill of the Cleveland Indians is the first American League player to belt four home runs in a doubleheader (he also was the first American Leaguer to have 11 runs batted in).

April 30, 1933   John Stone of the Detroit Tigers is the first player to have six extra-base hits in two nine-inning games of a doubleheader (four doubles and two home runs).

July 25, 1937   Mel Almada of the Washington Senators scores nine runs in a doubleheader.

June 28, 1939   The New York Yankees hit 13 home runs in a doubleheader.

July 4, 1939   The Boston Red Sox and the Philadelphia Athletics score 54 runs in a doubleheader.

June 17, 1943   Joe Cronin of the Boston Red Sox slugs two pinch-hit home runs in a doubleheader.

October 3, 1943   The Chicago White Sox play their 44th doubleheader of the season, the most ever by any ballclub.

July 24, 1948   Pat Seerey of the Chicago White Sox is the first player to strike out seven times in a doubleheader.

August 27, 1948   Hank Majeski of the Philadelphia Athletics hits six doubles in a doubleheader.

August 7, 1952   The Brooklyn Dodgers and the New York Giants take six hours and 46 minutes to play two nine-inning games in a doubleheader at the Polo Grounds.

May 2, 1954   Stan Musial of the St. Louis Cardinals hammers five home runs in a doubleheader.

September 6, 1954	The New York Yankees use 10 pinch-hitters in a doubleheader.
September 12, 1954	Record attendance of 84,578 people watch a doubleheader between the New York Yankees and the Cleveland Indians.
May 3, 1959	Charlie Maxwell of the Detroit Tigers belts four consecutive home runs in a doubleheader.
July 17–18, 1961	Bill White of the St. Louis Cardinals is the first National League player to have 14 hits in two consecutive doubleheaders (eight and six, respectively).
May 31, 1964	The San Francisco Giants and the New York Mets play 32 innings in a nine-hour-52-minute marathon doubleheader.
June 17, 1967	The Kansas City Athletics and the Detroit Tigers take nine hours and five minutes to complete a 28-inning doubleheader.
August 29, 1967	The Boston Red Sox and the New York Yankees play 29 innings in a doubleheader.
June 24, 1970	Bobby Murcer of the New York Yankees slugs four consecutive home runs in a doubleheader.
August 1, 1972	Nate Colbert of the San Diego Padres is the first to have 13 RBIs in a doubleheader, as he hits five home runs to tie Stan Musial's record.
May 30, 1977	The San Diego Padres use 13 different pitchers in both ends of a doubleheader.
May 24, 1995	The Texas Rangers and the Chicago White Sox take seven hours and 39 minutes to play two nine-inning games in a doubleheader.
May 20, 1999	Robin Ventura of the Chicago White Sox hammers a grand slam in both ends of a doubleheader.
September 21, 2000	Boston and Cleveland use 75 players in two nine-inning games of a doubleheader.

Appendix C: Doubleheaders by Year*

In the table below, columns on the left-hand side indicate the number of doubleheaders (DHs), doubleheader games, and total games for each season since the advent of doubleheader play in 1882. The final column expresses the number of doubleheader games as a percentage of all games. To the right of the center rule, the same information is provided for the season as it was originally scheduled.

	Actual Playing Season				Original Season Schedule			
Year	DHs	Games, DHs	Games, Season	Pct.	DHs	Games, DHs	Games, Season	Pct.
1882	7	14	573	2.4%	0	0	588	0.0%
1883	10	20	785	2.5%	10	20	784	2.6%
1884	19	38	1545	2.5%	20	40	1556	2.6%
1885	16	36	891	3.6%	14	28	896	3.1%
1886	30	60	1052	5.7%	14	28	1064	2.6%
1887	34	68	1056	6.4%	17	34	1064	3.2%
1888	51	102	1091	9.3%	16	32	1120	2.9%
1889	76	152	1090	13.9%	10	20	1120	1.8%
1890	118	236	1608	14.7%	38	76	1680	4.5%
1891	59	118	1109	10.6%	25	50	1120	4.5%
1892	97	194	922	21.0%	19	38	924	4.1%
1893	57	114	785	14.5%	17	34	792	4.3%
1894	65	130	799	16.3%	18	36	792	4.5%
1895	64	128	799	16.0%	18	36	792	4.5%
1896	65	130	792	16.4%	18	36	792	4.5%

*Source: Retrosheet database
Two games without regard to admission status

Appendix C: Doubleheaders by Year

	Actual Playing Season				Original Season Schedule			
Year	DHs	Games, DHs	Games, Season	Pct.	DHs	Games, DHs	Games, Season	Pct.
1897	83	166	812	20.4%	18	36	792	4.5%
1898	113	226	921	24.5%	26	52	924	5.6%
1899	107	214	923	23.2%	43	86	924	9.3%
1900	39	78	569	13.7%	12	24	560	4.3%
1901	125	250	1110	22.5%	30	60	1120	5.4%
1902	129	258	1117	23.1%	35	70	1120	6.3%
1903	148	296	1114	26.6%	26	52	1120	4.6%
1904	178	356	1249	28.5%	33	66	1232	5.4%
1905	170	340	1237	27.5%	44	88	1232	7.1%
1906	126	252	1228	20.5%	31	62	1232	5.0%
1907	169	338	1233	27.4%	36	72	1232	5.8%
1908	149	298	1244	24.0%	38	76	1232	6.2%
1909	198	396	1242	31.9%	39	78	1232	6.3%
1910	156	312	1249	25.0%	31	62	1232	5.0%
1911	144	288	1237	23.3%	28	56	1232	4.5%
1912	163	326	1232	26.5%	26	52	1232	4.2%
1913	150	300	1234	24.3%	26	52	1232	4.2%
1914	251	502	1880	26.7%	46	92	1848	5.0%
1915	307	614	1864	32.9%	53	106	1848	5.7%
1916	185	370	1247	29.7%	28	56	1232	4.5%
1917	203	406	1247	32.6%	27	54	1232	4.4%
1918	151	302	1016	29.7%	38	76	1232	6.2%
1919	148	296	1119	26.5%	27	54	1120	4.8%
1920	147	294	1234	23.8%	36	72	1232	5.8%
1921	135	270	1229	22.0%	38	76	1232	6.2%
1922	132	264	1238	21.3%	36	72	1232	5.8%
1923	136	272	1233	22.1%	37	74	1232	6.0%
1924	177	354	1231	28.8%	40	80	1232	6.5%
1925	144	288	1228	23.5%	37	74	1232	6.0%
1926	161	322	1234	26.1%	38	76	1232	6.2%
1927	188	376	1236	30.4%	31	62	1232	5.0%
1928	175	350	1231	28.4%	33	66	1232	5.4%
1929	166	332	1229	27.0%	32	64	1232	5.2%
1930	171	342	1234	27.7%	35	70	1232	5.7%
1931	220	440	1236	35.6%	37	74	1232	6.0%
1932	195	390	1233	31.6%	36	72	1232	5.8%
1933	234	468	1226	38.2%	39	78	1232	6.3%
1934	194	388	1223	31.7%	33	66	1232	5.4%
1935	234	468	1228	38.1%	33	66	1232	5.4%
1936	190	380	1238	30.7%	29	58	1232	4.7%

Appendix C: Doubleheaders by Year

	Actual Playing Season				Original Season Schedule			
Year	DHs	Games, DHs	Games, Season	Pct.	DHs	Games, DHs	Games, Season	Pct.
1937	207	414	1239	33.4%	27	54	1232	4.4%
1938	203	406	1223	33.2%	28	56	1232	4.5%
1939	205	410	1231	33.3%	48	96	1232	7.8%
1940	220	440	1236	35.6%	45	90	1232	7.3%
1941	200	400	1244	32.2%	71	142	1232	11.5%
1942	247	494	1224	40.4%	130	260	1232	21.1%
1943	299	598	1238	48.3%	198	396	1232	32.1%
1944	269	538	1242	43.3%	194	388	1232	31.5%
1945	304	608	1230	49.4%	198	396	1232	32.1%
1946	225	450	1242	36.2%	149	298	1232	24.2%
1947	215	430	1243	34.6%	123	246	1232	20.0%
1948	192	384	1237	31.0%	118	236	1232	19.2%
1949	163	326	1240	26.3%	111	222	1232	18.0%
1950	200	400	1238	32.3%	111	222	1232	18.0%
1951	189	378	1239	30.5%	121	242	1232	19.6%
1952	198	396	1239	32.0%	119	238	1232	19.3%
1953	200	400	1240	32.3%	129	258	1232	20.9%
1954	177	354	1237	28.6%	121	242	1232	19.6%
1955	188	276	1234	30.5%	128	256	1232	20.8%
1956	185	370	1239	29.9%	125	250	1232	20.3%
1957	152	304	1235	24.6%	116	232	1232	18.8%
1958	152	304	1235	24.6%	99	198	1232	16.1%
1959	129	258	1238	20.8%	88	176	1232	14.3%
1960	134	268	1236	21.7%	85	170	1232	13.8%
1961	180	360	1430	25.2%	109	218	1426	15.3%
1962	201	402	1621	24.8%	146	292	1620	18.0%
1963	183	366	1619	22.6%	142	284	1620	17.5%
1964	198	396	1626	24.4%	152	304	1620	18.8%
1965	191	382	1623	23.5%	135	270	1620	16.7%
1966	177	354	1615	21.9%	119	238	1620	14.7%
1967	193	386	1620	23.8%	122	244	1620	15.1%
1968	158	316	1625	19.4%	94	188	1620	11.6%
1969	176	352	1946	18.1%	111	222	1944	11.4%
1970	156	312	1944	16.0%	101	202	1944	10.4%
1971	158	316	1938	16.3%	103	206	1944	10.6%
1972	163	326	1859	17.5%	100	200	1944	10.3%
1973	151	302	1943	15.5%	98	196	1944	10.1%
1974	140	280	1945	14.4%	80	160	1944	8.2%
1975	145	290	1934	15.0%	88	176	1944	9.1%
1976	141	282	1939	14.5%	85	170	1944	8.7%

Appendix C: Doubleheaders by Year

	Actual Playing Season				Original Season Schedule			
Year	DHs	Games, DHs	Games, Season	Pct.	DHs	Games, DHs	Games, Season	Pct.
1977	142	284	2103	13.5%	102	204	2106	9.7%
1978	143	286	2102	13.6%	91	182	2106	8.6%
1979	116	232	2099	11.1%	63	126	2106	6.0%
1980	99	198	2105	9.4%	61	122	2106	5.8%
1981	47	94	1394	6.7%	48	96	2106	4.6%
1982	79	158	2107	7.5%	30	60	2106	2.8%
1983	94	188	2109	8.9%	27	54	2106	2.6%
1984	76	152	2105	7.2%	20	40	2106	1.9%
1985	53	106	2103	5.0%	14	28	2106	1.3%
1986	47	94	2103	4.5%	9	18	2106	0.9%
1987	33	66	2105	3.1%	8	16	2106	0.8%
1988	41	82	2100	3.9%	4	8	2106	0.4%
1989	47	94	2106	4.5%	3	6	2106	0.3%
1990	46	92	2105	4.4%	4	8	2106	0.4%
1991	29	58	2104	2.8%	0	0	2106	0.0%
1992	36	72	2106	3.4%	2	4	2106	0.2%
1993	27	54	2269	2.4%	2	4	2268	0.2%
1994	20	40	1600	2.5%	1	2	2268	0.1%
1995	20	40	2017	2.0%	2	4	2268	0.2%
1996	36	72	2267	3.2%	1	2	2268	0.1%
1997	45	90	2266	4.0%	0	0	2268	0.0%
1998	36	72	2432	3.0%	0	0	2430	0.0%
1999	31	62	2428	2.6%	0	0	2430	0.0%
2000	26	52	2429	2.1%	0	0	2430	0.0%
2001	23	46	2429	1.9%	1	2	2430	0.1%
2002	24	48	2426	2.0%	0	0	2430	0.0%
2003	27	54	2430	2.2%	0	0	2430	0.0%
2004	38	76	2428	3.1%	0	0	2430	0.0%
2005	18	36	2431	1.5%	0	0	2430	0.0%
2006	23	46	2429	1.9%	0	0	2430	0.0%
2007	22	44	2431	1.8%	0	0	2430	0.0%
2008	27	54	2428	2.2%	0	0	2430	0.0%

Chapter Notes

Chapter 1

1. Steve Gietschier, ed., *Complete Baseball Record Book* (St. Louis: The Sporting News, 2008), p. 87.
2. *Worcester Spy*, September 23 and 25, 1882.
3. *Providence Journal*, September 23, 1882.
4. *Worcester Gazette*, September 26, 1882.
5. Peter Morris, *Catcher: How the Man Behind the Plate Became an American Folk Hero* (Chicago: Ivan R. Dee, 2009), p. 144.
6. Alan E. Foulds, *Boston's Ballparks & Arenas* (Lebanon, NH: University Press of New England, 2005), p. 147.
7. Becker College web site, <www.becker.edu/pages/398.asp>.
8. *Boston Globe*, September 29–30, 1882.
9. *Worcester Spy*, September 23 and 29, 1882.
10. Charlie Bevis, *The New England League: A Baseball History, 1885–1949* (Jefferson, NC: McFarland, 2008), p. 57.
11. Constitution of the National League, February 2, 1876; *New York Times*, December 6, 1879.
12. Paul Dickson, *The New Dickson Baseball Dictionary* (New York: Harcourt Brace, 1999), p. 163.
13. *Boston Globe*, September 22, 1892; *Cincinnati Enquirer*, July 24, 1898, as referenced in Peter Morris, *A Game of Inches: The Stories Behind the Innovations That Shaped Baseball, the Game Behind the Scenes* (Chicago: Ivan R. Dee, 2006), p. 128.
14. *New York Times*, January 14, 1885.
15. Ibid.
16. *New York Times*, June 5, 1870, and August 13, 1892.
17. *Grand Forks* (North Dakota) *Herald*, August 4, 1895.
18. Louis Koenig, *Bryan: A Political Biography of William Jennings Bryan* (New York: G.P. Putnam's Sons, 1971), p. 186.
19. *Brooklyn Eagle*, July 10, 1896; *Washington Post*, July 11, 1896.
20. *Boston Globe*, July 24–26, 1896.
21. Charlie Bevis, "Base Ball to Base-Ball to Baseball," *Baseball Research Journal*, 2007.
22. Ibid.
23. Charlie Bevis, "Evolution of the Sunday Doubleheader and Its Role in Elevating the Popularity of Baseball, in *The Cooperstown Symposium on Baseball and American Culture, 2003–2004*, ed. William M. Simons, series ed. Alvin L. Hall (Jefferson, NC: McFarland, 2005), p. 221.

Chapter 2

1. *Pennsylvania Evening Post*, July 5, 1777.
2. Helene Henderson, *Patriotic Holidays of the United States: An Introduction to the History, Symbols, and Traditions Behind the Major Holidays and Days of Observance* (Detroit: Omnigraphics, 2006), p. 127.
3. Robert Myers, *Celebrations: The Complete Book of American Holidays* (New York: Doubleday, 1972), p. 162.
4. *Chicago Inter Ocean*, July 5, 1881.
5. Steven A. Riess, *Touching Base: Professional Baseball and American Culture in the Progressive Era* (Westport, CT: Greenwood Press, 1980), p. 31.
6. *Philadelphia Inquirer*, May 31, 1876.
7. *Buffalo Express*, July 5, 1881.
8. *Worcester Spy*, May 31, 1881; *Worcester Gazette*, July 5, 1881.
9. *Worcester Spy*, May 29–31, 1882.
10. *Troy Daily Times*, May 30–31, 1882; *Albany Morning Express*, May 29, 1882; *The Sporting News*, June 8, 1960.

11. *Boston Globe*, May 31, 1882.
12. *Chicago Inter Ocean*, July 5, 1882.
13. *Boston Globe*, July 5, 1882.
14. *Boston Globe*, May 31, 1883.
15. Stew Thornley, *Land of the Giants: New York's Polo Grounds* (Philadelphia: Temple University Press, 2000), p. 8.
16. *New York Times*, May 31, 1883.
17. *Philadelphia Inquirer*, July 5, 1883.
18. *Brooklyn Eagle*, June 1, 1886.
19. *Brooklyn Eagle*, June 1, 1886; *Boston Globe*, June 1, 1886; *New York Times*, June 1, 1886.
20. *New York Times*, April 4, 1888.
21. Charlie Bevis, "Holiday Doubleheaders," *Baseball Research Journal*, 2004.

Chapter 3

1. *New York Times*, August 12, 1884.
2. *Boston Globe*, August 26, 1884.
3. *Sporting Life*, October 15, 1884; *Baltimore Sun*, October 6, 1884.
4. *Baltimore Sun*, July 16, 1900; Jack Kavanaugh, "William Harrison Barnie," in *Baseball's First Stars*, eds. Frederick Ivor-Campbell, Robert L. Tiemann, and Mark Rucker (Cleveland: Society for American Baseball Research, 1996), p. 6; *Baltimore Sun*, March 5, 1884.
5. *New York Times*, August 25 and 27, 1885.
6. *New York Times*, August 29, 1885.
7. *Buffalo Express*, September 12, 1885.
8. *Buffalo Express*, October 8, 1885.
9. *Boston Globe*, August 27, 1885.
10. *Boston Globe*, October 10, 1885.
11. *Chicago Inter Ocean*, October 10, 1886; *Philadelphia Inquirer*, October 11, 1886.
12. Dan Daniel, "Major League Doubleheader Now Celebrating Sixty-first Anniversary," *Baseball Magazine*, July 1947.
13. *Philadelphia Inquirer*, August 25–26, 1886; *Baltimore Sun*, August 26, 1886.
14. *Philadelphia Inquirer*, September 9, 1886.
15. *Philadelphia Inquirer*, February 3, 1902.
16. Charlie Bevis, *Sunday Baseball: The Major Leagues' Struggle to Play Baseball on the Lord's Day, 1876–1934* (Jefferson, NC: McFarland, 2003), p. 69.
17. *Chicago Inter Ocean*, September 9, 1886.
18. *Boston Globe*, June 7, 1885.
19. *Boston Globe*, September 17, 1924; Peter J. Nash, *Boston's Royal Rooters* (Charleston: Arcadia, 2005), p. 19; *Boston Globe*, June 7, 1885.
20. *Boston Globe*, August 19–20, 1887; Gietschier, p. 87.
21. *Chicago Inter Ocean*, September 10–11, 1887.

Chapter 4

1. *Chicago Inter Ocean*, June 5–6, 1889.
2. *Boston Globe*, September 23–25, 1891.
3. *Boston Globe*, September 15–18, 1891.
4. *Boston Globe*, April 16, 1892.
5. *Boston Globe*, October 1, 1891.
6. *Chicago Inter Ocean*, October 4, 1891.
7. *Boston Globe*, November 12, 1891.
8. *Philadelphia Inquirer*, October 19, 1891.
9. *Brooklyn Eagle*, May 3, 1892.
10. *Chicago Inter Ocean*, April 14 and 19, 1892.
11. *Brooklyn Eagle*, May 3–4, 1892; *Sporting Life*, May 14, 1892.
12. *Philadelphia Inquirer*, July 1, 1892.
13. *Boston Globe*, September 13, 1889.
14. Gietschier, p. 144.
15. Morris, pp. 143–147.
16. *Spalding Guide* 1889, p. 110.
17. Frank B. Latham, *The Panic of 1893: A Time of Strikes, Riots, Hobo Camps, Coxey's "Army," Starvation, Withering Droughts, and Fears of "Revolution"* (New York: Franklin Watts, 1971), p. 3; Charles Hoffman, *The Depression of the Nineties: An Economic History* (Westport, CT: Greenwood Press, 1970), p. 63.
18. Edward Sagendorph Mason, *The Street Railway in Massachusetts: The Rise and Decline of an Industry* (Cambridge: Harvard University Press, 1932), p. 6.
19. Kenneth T. Jackson, *Crabgrass Frontier: The Suburbanization of the United States* (New York: Oxford University Press, 1985), p. 136; Robert M. Fogelson, *Downtown: Its Rise and Fall, 1880–1950* (New Haven: Yale University Press, 2001), pp. 28–29.
20. Sam Bass Warner, Jr., *Streetcar Suburbs: The Process of Growth in Boston (1870–1900)*, 2d ed. (Cambridge: Harvard University Press, 1978), p. 53.
21. Charles R. Morris, *The Tycoons: How Andrew Carnegie, John D. Rockefeller, Jay Gould, and J.P. Morgan Invented the American Supereconomy* (New York: Times Books, 2005), p. 168.
22. Jack Beatty, ed., *Colossus: How the Corporation Changed America* (New York: Broadway, 2001), pp. 46–47.
23. Ibid., pp. 127–128.
24. G. Edward White, *Creating the National Pastime: Baseball Transforms Itself 1903–1953* (Princeton: Princeton University Press, 1996), pp. 64–65.
25. *Boston Globe*, April 20, 1897.
26. *Boston Globe*, April 9, 1899; December 27, 1899; March 15, 1900.
27. *Boston Globe*, September 24, 1897.
28. Nash, pp. 33–34; Roger I. Abrams, *The First World Series and the Baseball Fanatics of 1903* (Boston: Northeastern University Press, 2003), p. 94; *Boston Globe*, February 3, 1943.
29. *Philadelphia Inquirer*, September 1, 1896; *Boston Globe*, September 29, 1897.

30. *Boston Globe*, October 5, 1892.
31. *New York Times*, January 15, 1895, and September 10, 1897.
32. *Cleveland Plain Dealer*, May 17, 1897.
33. Bevis, *Sunday Baseball*, pp. 121–125.
34. *The Sporting News*, March 5, 1898; *Sporting Life*, March 12, 1898.
35. *Boston Globe*, April 29, 1898.

Chapter 5

1. *New York Times*, September 6, 1882; Myers, pp. 210–211.
2. *Boston Globe*, September 6, 1887.
3. *Boston Globe*, September 4, 1888.
4. *Brooklyn Eagle*, September 3, 1888.
5. *Brooklyn Eagle*, September 4, 1888.
6. Foster Rhea Dulles, *A History of Recreation: America Learns to Play* (New York: Appleton-Century-Crofts, 1965), pp. 212–224.
7. *Boston Globe*, March 6, 1889.
8. *Philadelphia Inquirer*, September 2–3, 1889.
9. *Boston Globe*, September 4, 1894.
10. Bevis, *Sunday Baseball*, pp. 131 and 148.
11. Bevis, *The New England League*, p. 90.
12. *New York Times*, February 28 and March 6, 1894.
13. *New York Times*, May 31, 1894; *Philadelphia Inquirer*, May 31, 1894.
14. *Baltimore Sun*, September 3–4, 1894.
15. *Philadelphia Inquirer*, May 31, 1895.
16. *Boston Globe*, July 5, 1895.
17. *Boston Globe*, February 3, 1896.
18. *Philadelphia Inquirer*, May 30, 1897.
19. *Brooklyn Eagle*, September 5, 1899.
20. *Boston Globe*, September 4, 1900.

Chapter 6

1. *Brooklyn Eagle*, September 10, 1888.
2. *Sporting Life*, August 10, 1887.
3. Charlie Bevis, "Rocky Point: A Lone Outpost of Sunday Baseball Within Sabbatarian New England," *NINE: A Journal of Baseball History & Culture*, Fall 2005.
4. *Philadelphia Inquirer*, April 19, 1886.
5. *Rochester Herald*, July 21, 1890; *Sporting Life*, July 26, 1890.
6. Dulles, pp. 4–5, 9.
7. Bruce C. Daniels, *Puritans at Play: Leisure and Recreation in Colonial New England* (New York: St. Martin's, 1995), pp. 166–167.
8. Alexis McCrossen, *Holy Day, Holiday: The American Sunday* (Ithaca: Cornell University Press, 2000), p. 10.
9. Ibid., p. 8.
10. *Philadelphia Inquirer*, September 28, 1890.
11. *Milwaukee Sentinel*, October 5, 1891.
12. Bevis, *Sunday Baseball*, p. 104.
13. *Sporting Life*, October 8, 1892.
14. *Boston Globe*, September 16 and 18, 1893.
15. *Chicago Tribune*, May 1, 1899.
16. *Sporting Life*, September 9, 1899.
17. *Boston Globe*, September 11, 1899.
18. *Chicago Tribune*, October 2, 9, and 16, 1899.

Chapter 7

1. *Boston Globe*, March 22, 1901.
2. *Boston Globe*, April 5, 1902.
3. *Chicago Tribune*, August 25, 1902.
4. *St. Louis Post-Dispatch*, September 22, 1902.
5. Gietschier, p. 144.
6. *Boston Globe*, August 2, 1903.
7. Michael Wells, "Joseph Jerome McGinnity," in *Deadball Stars of the National League*, ed. Tom Simon (Washington, D.C.: Brassey's, 2004), p. 42.
8. *New York Times*, August 9, 1903.
9. *New York Times*, September 1, 1903.
10. Tom Meany, "The Real Man of Iron," *Baseball Digest*, August 1955; Gietschier, p. 56.
11. *New York Times*, October 27, 2004.
12. *The Sporting News*, August 12, 1926.
13. *New York Evening Journal*, August 4, 1898.
14. *New York Evening Journal*, August 4, 1898; *Washington Post*, October 4, 1904.
15. *Sporting Life*, July 16, 1904.
16. *New York Times*, July 16, 1904.
17. Ed Linn, *The Great Rivalry: The Yankees and the Red Sox, 1901–1990* (New York: Ticknor & Fields, 1991), p. 29.
18. Mike Vaccaro, *Emperors and Idiots: The Hundred-Year Rivalry Between the Yankees and Red Sox* (New York: Doubleday, 2005), p. 79.
19. Wayne McElreavy, "John D. Chesbro," in *Deadball Stars of the American League*, ed. David Jones (Dulles, VA: Potomac Books, 2006), p. 700; *New York Times*, October 11, 1904.
20. Linn, *The Great Rivalry*, p. ix.
21. *Boston Globe*, September 11, 1904; *New York Times*, October 9, 1904.
22. *Washington Post*, October 6, 1904; *Detroit News*, October 6, 1904.
23. *Sporting Life*, October 8, 1904.
24. Christopher Finch, *Highways to Heaven: The AUTO Biography of America* (New York: HarperCollins, 1992), p. 45.
25. Ibid., pp. 50 and 64; Frank Coffey and Joseph Layden, *America on Wheels: The First 100 Years, 1896–1996* (Los Angeles: General Publishing, 1996), pp. 38–39.
26. Coffey and Layden, p. 44.
27. *New York Times*, September 21, 1906.
28. Gietschier, p. 143.
29. *St. Louis Post-Dispatch*, August 12, 1907; *Philadelphia Inquirer*, August 12, 1907.

30. *New York Times*, May 1, 1922, and October 9, 1956.
31. *New York Times*, September 5, 1991.
32. Gietschier, p. 141; James Buckley, Jr., *Perfect: The Inside Story of Baseball's Sixteen Perfect Games* (Chicago: Triumph Books, 2002), p. 256; Michael Coffey, *27 Men Out: Baseball's Perfect Games* (New York: Atria Books, 2004), pp. 279–280.
33. *Kansas City Star*, August 11, 2005.
34. *Philadelphia Inquirer*, October 24 and 28, 1907.
35. Gietschier, p. 144; *Chicago Tribune*, September 27, 1908.
36. Emil Rothe, "The Day Ed Reulbach Pitched a Double Header Shutout," *Baseball Digest*, January 1973.
37. *Chicago Tribune*, September 22, 1908; *New York Times*, October 9, 1910.

Chapter 8

1. *Boston Globe*, February 24, 1903.
2. *Boston Globe*, July 5, 1908.
3. *Boston Globe*, October 28, 1906.
4. *Sporting Life*, January 8, 1910.
5. *Boston Globe*, October 13, 1910.
6. *New York Times*, October 13, 1911.
7. *New York Tribune*, September 8, 1903.
8. *Sporting Life*, November 30, 1907.
9. *St. Louis Post-Dispatch*, September 1, 1902.
10. *St. Louis Post-Dispatch*, July 4–5, 1908.
11. *Chicago Tribune*, July 4, 1913.
12. *Chicago Tribune*, May 30, 1914.
13. *New York Times*, April 2.
14. *Boston Globe*, September 8, 1914.
15. *Boston Globe*, October 28, 1906.
16. White, pp. 22–23.
17. Mitchell Nathanson, "Gatekeepers of Americana: Ownership's Never-Ending Quest for Control of the Baseball Creed," *NINE: A Journal of Baseball History & Culture*, Fall 2006, p. 73.
18. Bruce Kuklick, *To Everything a Season: Shibe Park and Urban Philadelphia* (Princeton: Princeton University Press, 1991), p. 26.
19. L. H. Constans, "Forbes Field," *Baseball Magazine*, May 1913.
20. Robin Faith Bachin, *Building the South Side: Urban Space and Civic Culture in Chicago, 1890–1919* (Chicago: University of Chicago Press, 2004), p. 230.
21. Robert Tiemann, "Major League Attendance," in *Total Baseball*, 7th ed., eds. John Thorn, Pete Palmer, and Michael Gershman (Kingston, NY: Total Sports Publishing, 2001), p. 75; Bachin, p. 225.
22. David Nasaw, *Going Out: The Rise and Fall of Public Amusements* (New York: Basic Books, 1993), pp. 97–99.

Chapter 9

1. *Boston Globe*, May 1, 1909; Gietschier, p. 35.
2. Tiemann.
3. *Sporting Life*, January 8, 1910.
4. *New York Times*, February 14 and 17, 1910.
5. *Sporting Life*, January 15, 1910.
6. Michael O'Malley, *Keeping Watch: A History of American Time* (New York: Viking, 1990), p. 291.
7. Bevis, *Sunday Baseball*, p. 172; *New York Times*, September 28, 1914.
8. Marc Okkonen, *The Federal League of 1914–1915: Baseball's Third Major League* (Garrett Park, MD: Society for American Baseball Research, 1989), p. 18.
9. Bevis, *Sunday Baseball*, pp. 184–185.
10. Ben M. Hall, *The Best Remaining Seats: The Story of The Golden Age of the Movie Palace* (New York: Clarkson Potter, 1961), p. 12.
11. *New York Times*, February 1, 1917.
12. Bevis, *Sunday Baseball*, p. 193; *Washington Post*, May 15, 1918.
13. Bevis, *Sunday Baseball*, pp. 187–189; *New York Times*, August 22, 1917.
14. *New York Times*, April 20, 1919.
15. Bevis, *Sunday Baseball*, p. 194.
16. *New York Times*, May 5, 1919.
17. *Boston Globe*, September 1, 1919.
18. *Boston Globe*, June 17–18, 1921.
19. *Boston Globe*, April 18, 1924.
20. A. D. Suehsdorf, "The Last Tripleheader," *Baseball Research Journal*, 1980; Gietschier, p. 35.
21. *Boston Globe*, October 2, 1920.
22. Neil J. Sullivan, *The Diamond in the Bronx: Yankee Stadium and the Politics of New York* (New York: Oxford University Press, 2001), p. 2; *New York Times*, May 17, 1923.
23. *New York Times*, July 5, 1923.
24. *New York Times*, May 31 and September 4, 1923.
25. Kenneth Winter and Michael Haupert, "Yankees Profit and Promise: The Purchase of Babe Ruth and the Building of Yankee Stadium," in *The Cooperstown Symposium on Baseball and American Culture, 2003–2004*, ed. William M. Simons, series ed. Alvin L. Hall (Jefferson, NC: McFarland, 2005), p. 201.
26. *New York Times*, July 5, 1927; Sullivan, p. 36.
27. *New York Times*, September 10, 1928; Sullivan, p. 10.
28. Kathleen Drowne and Patrick Huber, *The 1920s* (Westport, CT: Greenwood Press, 2004), p. 143.
29. Hall, pp. 93 and 248.
30. Jules Tygiel, *Past Time: Baseball as History* (New York: Oxford University Press, 2000), p. 79.

31. Gietschier, pp. 35 and 91.
32. Richard W. Juline, "Doubleheaders Spell Disaster," *Baseball Research Journal*, 1997; *Boston Globe*, September 4, 1928.
33. *Boston Globe*, September 10, 1928.
34. *Boston Globe*, September 6, 1908.
35. Pat Harmon, "Last 'Iron Man' Recalls Feat," *Baseball Digest*, August 1955; Gietschier, p. 144.
36. *Boston Globe*, August 29, 1926.
37. Paul D. Adomites, "Baseball on the Air," in *Total Baseball*, 1se ed., eds. John Thorn and Pete Palmer (New York: Warner, 1989), p. 671.
38. Tygiel, pp. 71–72.

Chapter 10

1. *The Sporting News*, January 25, 1940, and July 1, 1943.
2. Dan Daniel, "Sam Breadon Left Indelible Imprint on Baseball Operation," *Baseball Magazine*, July 1949.
3. Daniel, "Major League Doubleheader Now Celebrating Sixty-first Anniversary."
4. Daniel, "Sam Breadon."
5. *New York Times*, May 18, 1929, and July 1, 1930.
6. *The Sporting News*, July 17, 1930; *New York Times*, May 8, 1931.
7. David N. Laband and Deborah Hendry Heinbuch, *Blue Laws: The History, Economics, and Politics of Sunday-Closing Laws* (Lexington, MA: Lexington Books, 1987), p. 31; John Lucas, "The Unholy Experiment: Professional Baseball's Struggle Against Pennsylvania Blue Laws 1926–1934," *Pennsylvania History*, 1971.
8. Bevis, *Sunday Baseball*, pp. 206–212.
9. Ibid., pp. 220–222.
10. Ibid., pp. 224–227.
11. Ibid., pp. 227–238.
12. *Boston Globe*, May 20, 1932.
13. Charles C. Alexander, *Breaking the Slump: Baseball in the Depression Era* (New York: Columbia University Press, 2002), pp. 4 and 40; Tiemann.
14. Richard Jensen, "The Causes and Cures of Unemployment in the Great Depression," *Journal of Interdisciplinary History*, Spring 1989, p. 557; Bevis, "Evolution of the Sunday Doubleheader and Its Role in Elevating the Popularity of Baseball," p. 219.
15. *Los Angeles Times*, January 29 and February 2, 1933.
16. *New York Times*, August 28, 1933, and September 17, 1934.
17. Jensen, pp. 556 and 561.
18. "Baseball's Synthetic Double-Headers," *Literary Digest*, June 29, 1935.
19. David Surdam, "The New York Yankees Cope with the Great Depression," *Enterprise & Society*, December 2008.
20. James Palmer, "Economic and Social Aspects of Chain Stores," *Journal of Business of the University of Chicago*, July 1929, pp. 272–278.
21. Susan Currell, *The March of Spare Time: The Problem and Promise of Leisure in the Great Depression* (Philadelphia: University of Pennsylvania Press, 2005), p. 2.
22. *New York Times*, December 11, 1931; *The Sporting News*, December 17, 1931.
23. Robert S. McElvaine, *The Great Depression: America, 1929–1941* (New York: Times Books, 1984), p. 90.
24. *The Sporting News*, May 25, 1933, and January 30, 1941.
25. *The Sporting News*, May 25, 1933.
26. *New York Times*, August 24, 1933.
27. "Hard Times Are Baseball's Golden Opportunity," *Baseball Magazine*, September 1933.
28. *New York Times*, December 15, 1933.
29. Bevis, *Sunday Baseball*, pp. 253–259.
30. *New York Times*, September 10, 1934.
31. *Boston Globe*, July 14, 1930; "The Fans Speak Out," *Baseball Digest*, September 2004.
32. *Chicago Tribune*, July 14, 1930.
33. *Chicago Tribune*, July 14 and 18, 1930.
34. *New York Times*, June 7, 1937.
35. *New York Times*, September 4, 1939.
36. *New York Times*, December 13, 1934.
37. David Pietrusza, *Lights On! The Wild Century-Long Saga of Night Baseball* (Lanham, MD: Scarecrow, 1997), p. 71.
38. F.C. Lane, "The Romance of Night Baseball," *Baseball Magazine*, October 1930.
39. Tygiel, pp. 99–106.
40. *New York Times*, July 12, 1935.
41. *New York Times*, August 20, 1936; *Dallas Morning News*, September 29, 1913; *Chicago Tribune*, August 8, 1934.
42. *New York Times*, December 9, 1936, February 3, 1938, and June 8, 1938.
43. *The Sporting News*, February 9, 1939.
44. *Chicago Tribune*, September 27, 1939.
45. *New York Times*, November 11, 1939.
46. *New York Times*, September 7, 1940.
47. *The Sporting News*, January 30 and February 6, 1941.
48. Jonathan Eig, *Luckiest Man: The Life and Death of Lou Gehrig* (New York: Simon & Schuster, 2005), pp. 314–316.
49. *Greensboro News and Record*, July 4, 1989.
50. Eig, p. 361.
51. *Boston Globe*, September 27, 1941.
52. Ted Williams, *My Turn at Bat: The Story of My Life* (New York: Simon & Schuster, 1969), p. 83.
53. Ibid., pp. 85–86.
54. *Boston Globe*, September 29, 1941.

Chapter 11

1. *New York Times*, January 17, 1942.
2. William B. Mead, *Even the Browns* (Chicago: Contemporary Books, 1978), p. 82.
3. *New York Times*, August 4–5, 1942.
4. *St. Louis Post-Dispatch*, July 24, 1942.
5. *St. Louis Post-Dispatch*, July 25, 1942.
6. *New York Times*, July 27, 1942.
7. *St. Louis Post-Dispatch*, September 4–5, 1942.
8. *New York Times*, August 24, 1942.
9. *New York Times*, September 25, 1942.
10. Thomas L. Karnes, "The Sunday Saga of Ted Lyons," *Baseball Research Journal*, 1981; Lyle Spatz, "Ted Lyons's Complete Season of 1942," *The National Pastime*, 1995; *Chicago Tribune*, October 14, 1942.
11. *New York Times*, January 7, 1943.
12. Richard Lingeman, *Don't You Know There's a War On? The American Home Front 1941–1945* (New York: Nation Books, 2003), p. 235.
13. *New York Times*, December 30, 1942, and January 6, 1943.
14. Gietschier, p. 35.
15. George Gmelch, "Bill Kirwin: Pioneering a Community of Baseball Scholars," *NINE: A Journal of Baseball History & Culture*, Spring 2008, p. 155.
16. "1943 Chicago White Sox," Retrosheet database.
17. Mead, p. 77; *The Sporting News*, August 19, 1943.
18. *New York Times*, May 13, 1943.
19. *Chicago Tribune*, June 12, 1943.
20. *Boston Globe*, June 16, 1943; *Boston Post*, June 18, 1943.
21. *Boston Globe*, May 27, 1943; *Boston Globe* (evening edition), May 28, 1943.
22. *New York Times*, August 19, 1943.
23. *New York Times*, August 11, 1944.
24. *Boston Globe*, July 19, 1943.
25. Mead, p. 148.
26. Ibid.
27. Ibid.
28. "Suspended Games," http://www.retrosheet.org; *Boston Globe*, August 2, 1944.
29. *New York Times*, July 12, 1944.
30. Gietschier, p. 90; *Chicago Tribune*, September 17, 1945.
31. F.C. Lane, "The Real Dope on Double Headers," *Baseball Magazine*, October 1928; Michael Goodman, "On the Incidence of Swept Double-Headers," *American Statistician*, December 1969.
32. *The Sporting News*, June 10, 1943.
33. Clifford Bloodgood, "Editorial Comment," *Baseball Magazine*, August 1944.
34. *New York Times*, January 17, 1943.

Chapter 12

1. John Drebinger, "Baseball Crowds," *Baseball Magazine*, July 1946.
2. Ibid.
3. *New York Times*, June 2, 1946.
4. *The Sporting News*, August 21, 1946; *New York Times*, December 13, 1945.
5. *New York Times*, August 14–15, 1946.
6. *New York Times*, August 15–16, 1946.
7. *New York Times*, August 13, 1946.
8. Gietschier, p. 88.
9. *Brooklyn Eagle*, September 7, 1950; Steve Springer, "Let's Play Two! Doubleheaders Have Become Rare and Unpopular Among Players, But Old-Timers Loved Them," *Los Angeles Times*, July 5, 1992.
10. Willis Russell, "Among the New Words," *American Speech*, October 1950, p. 229; George Plimpton, *A Sports Bestiary* (New York: McGraw-Hill, 1982), p. 52.
11. Tiemann.
12. *New York Times*, June 4, 1950, and September 14, 1951.
13. *New York Times*, January 18, 1955.
14. *New York Times*, August 12, 1958.
15. *New York Times*, July 5, 1947.
16. *Brooklyn Eagle*, March 16 and 23, 1950.
17. *Brooklyn Eagle*, April 2, 1950; *New York Times*, April 12, 1950.
18. *New York Times*, April 13, 1950.
19. *Boston Globe*, June 18, 1949; June 18, 1952; and June 18, 1955.
20. *Boston Globe*, April 20, 1966, and April 20, 1968.
21. *New York Times*, March 4, 1946.
22. *New York Times*, May 18, 1946.
23. Stanley Kligfeld, "Big League Magnates Sadly Note Continuing Decline in Attendance," *Wall Street Journal*, August 1, 1952.
24. "Programs on the Air," *New York Times*, June 30, 1949.
25. Andrew Zimbalist, *Baseball and Billions: A Probing Look Inside the Big Business of Our National Pastime* (New York: Basic Books, 1992), p. 48; Henry D. Fetter, *Taking on the Yankees: Winning and Losing in the Business of Baseball, 1903–2003* (New York: W.W. Norton, 2003), p. 397.
26. Murray Schumach, "Big League Baseball Facing Shutout by TV," *New York Times*, September 18, 1955; James R. Walker and Robert V. Bellamy, Jr., *Center Field Shot: A History of Baseball on Television* (Lincoln: University of Nebraska Press, 2008), pp. 324–325.
27. Jim Murray, "The Case for the Suffering Fan," *Sports Illustrated*, August 20, 1956.
28. Michael N. Danielson, *Home Team: Professional Sports and the American Metropolis* (Princeton: Princeton University Press, 1997), p. 32; Fetter, p. 198.

29. Schumach, "Big League Baseball Facing Shutout by TV"; *New York Times*, September 18, 1955; John Drebinger, "24 Games at Night Listed by Dodgers," *New York Times*, January 6, 1952.
30. McCrossen, pp. 105–106.
31. Bill Veeck with Ed Linn, *Veeck—As in Wreck: The Autobiography of Bill Veeck* (New York: G.P. Putnam's Sons, 1962), pp. 11–23; Jim O'Toole, "Bill Veeck and James Thurber: The Literary Origins of the Midget Pinch Hitter," *NINE: A Journal of Baseball History & Culture*, Spring 2002.
32. Veeck, p. 341.
33. *Boston Globe*, June 8, 1959; Veeck, pp. 341–342.
34. Gietschier, p. 26; *St. Louis Post-Dispatch*, May 3, 1954; Stan Musial as told to Bob Broeg, *Stan Musial: "The Man's" Own Story* (Garden City, NY: Doubleday, 1964), pp. 163–164.
35. *New York Times*, December 13, 1949.
36. *Philadelphia Inquirer*, April 29 and August 17, 1957.
37. *Philadelphia Evening Bulletin*, July 24 and 31, 1959; "Suspended Games," http://www.retrosheet.org.
38. *Baltimore Sun*, July 2–5, 1957.
39. Lee Lowenfish and Tony Lupien, *The Imperfect Diamond: The Story of Baseball's Reserve System and the Men Who Fought to Change It* (New York: Stein & Day, 1980), p. 148.
40. Dick Young, "Oh, Those Broken Pledges!" *Baseball Digest*, October 1950; Robert F. Burk, *Much More Than a Game: Players, Owners, & American Baseball Since 1921* (Chapel Hill: University of North Carolina Press, 2001), p. 121.
41. Charles P. Knorr, *The End of Baseball As We Knew It: The Players Union, 1960–81* (Urbana: University of Illinois Press, 2002), p. 271.
42. *New York Times*, June 29 and July 1, 1960.
43. *New York Times*, August 25, 1962.
44. Red Smith, "Greed and Godliness in the Majors," *The Best of Red Smith* (New York: Franklin Watts, 1963), pp. 169–170.
45. *New York Times*, August 24, 1962.
46. "The Fans Speak Out," *Baseball Digest*, June 2004; "Bill White Gets 14 Hits, Ties Ty Cobb Record," *Jet*, August 3, 1961; Gietschier, p. 20.
47. *New York Times*, January 5 and February 10, 1961.
48. *The Sporting News*, February 16, 1963.
49. *New York Times*, November 4, 1965.
50. Gietschier, p. 89.
51. Gietschier, p. 89; *The Sporting News*, July 1, 1967.
52. *Boston Globe*, August 30, 1967.
53. *New York Times*, June 21, 1965.

Chapter 13

1. *New York Times*, February 12, 1967.
2. *The Sporting News*, August 12, 1967.
3. *The Sporting News*, February 10, 1968.
4. *The Sporting News*, March 9, 1968; 2007–2011 Basic Agreement, Section V, Paragraph C, on the web site of the Major League Baseball Players Association, <mlbplayers.mlb.com/pa/pdf/cba_english.pdf>.
5. Marvin Miller, *A Whole Different Ball Game: The Sport and Business of Baseball* (New York: Birch Lane Press, 1991), p. 97.
6. *The Sporting News*, January 13, 1968.
7. *Washington Post*, June 29, 1968.
8. Frank Rinella, "The Fans Speak Out," *Baseball Digest*, January 2005.
9. Clifford Bloodgood, "Holiday Hoopla," *Baseball Magazine*, July 1946.
10. *Chicago Tribune*, May 29 and July 21, 1973.
11. Bevis, "Holiday Doubleheaders."
12. Miller, p. 206.
13. Miller, p. 220; *New York Times*, April 12, 1972.
14. Miller, p. 221; *New York Times*, April 14, 1972.
15. Gietschier, pp. 26, 28, 30; Bob Wolf, "Aug. 1, 1972, Was Nate's Great Day," *Los Angeles Times*, June 21, 1989.
16. Wolf, "Nate's Great Day; *Los Angeles Times*, June 21, 1989; "Colbert Ahead of Aaron's Pace in Homers," *Jet*, August 17, 1972.
17. *The Sporting News*, June 6, 1970; *New York Times*, May 11, 1972.
18. *The Sporting News*, June 10, 1972, and July 25, 1970.
19. *The Sporting News*, August 12, 1972.
20. *The Sporting News*, March 13, 1973; *Chicago Tribune*, June 12, 1975.
21. Robert Burnes, "Are Fans Souring on Twin Bills?" *Baseball Digest*, August 1967; Bevis, "Evolution of the Sunday Doubleheader."
22. James B. Dworkin, *Owners versus Players: Baseball and Collective Bargaining* (Boston: Auburn House, 1981), p. 211, *The Sporting News*, December 25, 1976, and June 7, 1980; Barry Shapiro, "Death of the Doubleheader," *Sport*, July 1983.
23. *New York Times*, June 30, 1978.
24. Leonard Koppett, "Twin Bills No Longer Lure Baseball Fans," *The Sporting News*, February 6, 1982.
25. Meyers, "Baseball Has a Dearth of Doubleheaders"; *Washington Post*, July 4, 1989; Christopher J. Young, "When Fans Wanted to Rock, the Baseball Stopped," *Baseball Research Journal*, 2009.
26. "Tears for Two," *Sports Illustrated*, March 5, 1979; Shapiro.
27. Shapiro.

28. James Quirk and Rodney D. Fort, *Pay Dirt: The Business of Professional Team Sports* (Princeton: Princeton University Press, 1992), p. 138.
29. Zimbalist, pp. 48–51; Burk, p. 242.
30. Burk, p. 249.
31. *Washington Post*, January 6, 1989; Walker and Bellamy, p.168.

Chapter 14

1. Dickson, p. 34.
2. *Chicago Tribune*, April 2, 2008.
3. *New York Times*, January 20, 1977.
4. *Time*, January 31, 1977.
5. *Chicago Tribune*, August 9, 1977.
6. Alan Schwarz, *Once Upon a Game: Baseball's Greatest Memories* (Boston: Houghton Mifflin, 2007), p. 14.
7. Ernie Banks, "Foreword," in *The Golden Age of Baseball*, ed. Paul Adomites (Lincolnwood, IL: Publications International, 2003), p. 5.
8. Glenn Stout, "Play It Again, Ernie," in *The Cubs: The Complete Story of Chicago Cubs Baseball*, eds. Glenn Stout and Richard A. Johnson (Boston: Houghton Mifflin, 2007), pp. 282–283.
9. David Llorens, "New Life for an Old Man," *Ebony*, October 1967.
10. Peter Golenbock, *Wrigleyville: A Magical History Tour of the Chicago Cubs* (New York: St. Martin's Press, 1996), pp. 399, 409, 353; Mark Kram, "A Tale of Two Men and a City," *Sports Illustrated*, September 29, 1969.
11. *Kansas City Star*, October 7, 2006; *Chicago Sun-Times*, October 16, 2006.
12. Stout, p. 283.
13. Kram.
14. *New York Times*, February 2 and July 9, 1969.
15. Golenbock, p. 399.
16. Steve Jacobson, *Carrying Jackie's Torch: The Players Who Integrated Baseball—and America* (Chicago: Lawrence Hill Books, 2007), pp. 69–70.
17. Leo Durocher and Ed Linn, *Nice Guys Finish Last* (New York: Simon & Schuster, 1975), pp. 366–368.
18. Ibid., p. 368.
19. Ibid., pp. 369–370.
20. Jacobsen, p. 70.
21. Schwarz, p. 17.
22. *Cleveland Plain Dealer*, August 13, 1991.

Chapter 15

1. Meyers, "Baseball Has a Dearth of Doubleheaders," *Washington Post*, July 4, 1980.
2. Ibid.
3. Art Turgeon, "Sox Doubleheader is Twin Bill for Fans," *Providence Journal*, June 24, 1989.
4. Ibid.
5. 1990–1993 Basic Agreement, Attachment 2.
6. *Cleveland Plain Dealer*, August 13, 1991.
7. *Boston Globe*, April 13, 1992; Gietschier, p. 39.
8. *Boston Globe*, April 13, 1992; Mike DiGiovanna, "Hitless Victory by Dodgers Puts a Spotlight on Young, *Los Angeles Times*, June 30, 2008.
9. *Rocky Mountain News*, June 26, 1994; Larry Stone, "Doubleheaders Are Passé," *Baseball Digest*, November 2000; Tom Verducci, "Let's Play Two! True Doubleheaders Made Baseball Twice as Nice," *Sports Illustrated*, <http://sportsillustrated.cnn.com/specials/remember-when/baseball/essay.html>.
10. Rick Van Blair, "Dom DiMaggio: An Underrated Star of the 1940s," *Baseball Digest*, August 2006; Meyers, "Baseball Has a Dearth of Doubleheaders," *Washington Post*, July 4, 1980; Paul Sullivan, "Doubleheaders Are Headed for Extinction," *Chicago Tribune*, July 5, 1994.
11. *Chicago Tribune*, July 5, 1994.
12. Burk, pp. 288–298.
13. *Minneapolis Star Tribune*, June 8–9, 1996.
14. 1997–2001 Basic Agreement, Article V, Section (C)(1).
15. 1997–2001 Basic Agreement, Article V, Section (C), Paragraphs (1) and (17).
16. *Denver Post*, April 11, 1997.
17. *New York Times*, June 14, 2000.
18. *New York Times*, July 7, 2000; *New York Post*, July 7, 2000.
19. *Cleveland Plain Dealer*, September 15, 2000; *Minneapolis Star Tribune*, September 26, 2000.
20. *Minneapolis Star Tribune*, May 25, 2001.
21. Ibid.
22. *Minneapolis Star Tribune*, May 27, 2001.
23. Kevin Ausmus, "The Baseball Experience: The Good Old Days, Rainbow Man, and Why There Aren't More Players Named Dick," *Mungebeing Magazine*, Issue 11; Danielson, p. 64.
24. Mark McDonald and Daniel Rascher, "Does Bat Day Make Cents? The Effect of Promotions on the Demand for Major League Baseball," *Journal of Sport Management*, 2000; Daniel Rascher et al, "Variable Ticket Pricing in Major League Baseball," *Journal of Sports Management*, 2007.
25. Verducci.

Bibliography

Adomites, Paul D. "Baseball on the Air." In *Total Baseball*. 1st ed. Eds. John Thorn and Pete Palmer. New York: Warner, 1989.

Alexander, Charles C. *Breaking the Slump: Baseball in the Depression Era*. New York: Columbia University Press, 2002.

"Baseball's Synthetic Double-Headers." *Literary Digest*, June 29, 1935.

Beatty, Jack. *Colossus: How the Corporation Changed America*. New York: Broadway, 2001.

Bevis, Charlie. "Evolution of the Sunday Doubleheader and Its Role in Elevating the Popularity of Baseball." In *Cooperstown Symposium on Baseball and American Culture, 2003–2004*. Ed. William M. Simons. Series ed. Alvin L. Hall. Jefferson, NC: McFarland, 2005.

_____. "Holiday Doubleheaders." *Baseball Research Journal*, 2004.

_____. *Sunday Baseball: The Major Leagues' Struggle to Play Baseball on the Lord's Day, 1876–1934*. Jefferson, NC: McFarland, 2003.

Burk, Robert F. *Much More Than a Game: Players, Owners, & American Baseball Since 1921*. Chapel Hill: University of North Carolina Press, 2001.

Burnes, Robert. "Are Fans Souring on Twin Bills?" *Baseball Digest*, August 1967.

Daniel, Dan. "Major League Doubleheader Now Celebrating Sixty-first Anniversary." *Baseball Magazine*, July 1947.

Danielson, Michael N. *Home Team: Professional Sports and the American Metropolis*. Princeton: Princeton University Press, 1997.

Dickson, Paul. *The New Dickson Baseball Dictionary*. New York: Harcourt Brace, 1999.

Dulles, Foster Rhea. *A History of Recreation: America Learns to Play*. New York: Appleton-Century-Crofts, 1965.

Dworkin, James B. *Owners versus Players: Baseball and Collective Bargaining*. Boston: Auburn House, 1981.

Finch, Christopher. *Highways to Heaven: The AUTO Biography of America*. New York: HarperCollins, 1992.

Fogelson, Robert M. *Downtown: Its Rise and Fall, 1880–1950*. New Haven: Yale University Press, 2001.

Gershman, Michael. *Diamonds: The Evolution of the Ballpark*. Boston: Houghton Mifflin, 1993.

Gietschier, Steve, ed. *Complete Baseball Record Book*. St. Louis: The Sporting News, 2008.

Goodman, Michael. "On the Incidence of Swept Double-Headers." *American Statistician*, December 1969.

Henderson, Helene. *Patriotic Holidays of the United States: An Introduction to the History, Symbols, and Traditions Behind the Major Holidays and Days of Observance*. Detroit: Omnigraphics, 2006.

Jackson, Kenneth T. *Crabgrass Frontier:*

The Suburbanization of the United States. New York: Oxford University Press, 1985.

Kligfeld, Stanley. "Big League Magnates Sadly Note Continuing Decline in Attendance." *Wall Street Journal*, August 1, 1952.

Koppett, Leonard. "Twin Bills No Longer Lure Baseball Fans." *The Sporting News*, February 6, 1982.

Lane, F.C. "The Real Dope on Double Headers." *Baseball Magazine*, October 1928.

Lieb, Fred. "What's Wrong with Baseball?" *Los Angeles Times*, January 29–February 4, February 6–10, 1933.

Lingeman, Richard. *Don't You Know There's a War On? The American Home Front, 1941–1945.* 2d ed. New York: Nation Books, 2003.

Linn, Ed. *The Great Rivalry: The Yankees and the Red Sox, 1901–1990.* New York: Ticknor & Fields, 1991.

Lowenfish, Lee, and Tony Lupien. *Imperfect Diamond: The Story of Baseball's Reserve System and the Men Who Fought to Change It.* New York: Stein & Day, 1980.

McCrossen, Alexis. *Holy Day, Holiday: The American Sunday.* Ithaca: Cornell University Press, 2000.

McDonald, Mark, and Daniel Rascher. "Does Bat Day Make Cents? The Effect of Promotions on the Demand for Major League Baseball." *Journal of Sport Management*, 2000.

Mead, William B. *Even the Browns.* Chicago: Contemporary Books, 1978.

Meyers, Jeff. "Baseball Has a Dearth of Doubleheaders: Two for the Price of One Just Doesn't Make Economic Sense to Big-League Teams." *Washington Post*, July 4, 1989.

Miller, Marvin. *A Whole Different Ball Game: The Sport and Business of Baseball.* New York: Birch Lane Press, 1991.

Murray, Jim. "The Case for the Suffering Fan." *Sports Illustrated*, August 20, 1956.

Nasaw, David. *Going Out: The Rise and Fall of Public Amusements.* New York: Basic Books, 1993.

Nathanson, Mitchell. "Gatekeepers of Americana: Ownership's Never-Ending Quest for Control of the Baseball Creed." *NINE: A Journal of Baseball History & Culture*, Fall 2006.

O'Malley, Michael. *Keeping Watch: A History of American Time.* New York: Viking, 1990.

Quirk, James, and Rodney D. Fort. *Pay Dirt: The Business of Professional Team Sports.* Princeton: Princeton University Press, 1992.

Riess, Steven A. *City Games: The Evolution of American Urban Society and the Rise of Sports.* Champaign: University of Illinois Press, 1991.

Rothe, Emil. "The Day Ed Reulbach Pitched a Double Header Shutout." *Baseball Digest*, January 1973.

Schumach, Murray. "Big League Baseball Facing Shutout by TV." *New York Times*, September 18, 1955.

Shapiro, Barry. "Death of the Doubleheader." *Sport*, July 1983.

Spoelstra, Warren. "Eckert Stays to Bitter End of Tigers' 9-Hour Double Bill." *The Sporting News*, July 1, 1967.

Springer, Steve. "Let's Play Two! Doubleheaders Have Become Rare and Unpopular Among Players, But Old-Timers Loved Them." *Los Angeles Times*, July 5, 1992.

Stone, Larry. "Doubleheaders Are Passé." *Baseball Digest*, November 2000.

Stout, Glenn. "Play It Again, Ernie." In *The Cubs: The Complete Story of Chicago Cubs Baseball.* Eds. Glenn Stout and Richard A. Johnson. Boston: Houghton Mifflin, 2007.

Suehsdorf, A. D. "The Last Tripleheader." *Baseball Research Journal*, 1980.

Sullivan, Paul. "Doubleheaders Are Headed for Extinction—With Few Regrets." *Chicago Tribune*, July 5, 1994.

Tiemann, Robert L. "Major League Attendance." In *Total Baseball*. 7th ed. Eds. John Thorn, Pete Palmer, and Michael Gershman. Kingston, NY: Total Sports Publishing, 2001.

Tygiel, Jules. *Past Time: Baseball as History.* New York: Oxford University Press, 2000.

Walker, James R., and Robert V. Bellamy, Jr. *Center Field Shot: A History of Baseball on Television.* Lincoln: University of Nebraska Press, 2008.

Wells, Michael. "Joseph Jerome McGinnity." In *Deadball Stars of the National League*. Ed. Tom Simon. Washington, D.C.: Brassey's, 2004.

White, G. Edward. *Creating the National Pastime: Baseball Transforms Itself, 1903–1953*. Princeton: Princeton University Press, 1996.

Winter, Kenneth, and Michael Haupert. "Yankees Profit and Promise: The Purchase of Babe Ruth and the Building of Yankee Stadium." In *The Cooperstown Symposium on Baseball and American Culture, 2003–2004*. Ed. William M. Simons. Series ed. Alvin L. Hall. Jefferson, NC: McFarland, 2005.

Zimbalist, Andrew. *Baseball and Billions: A Probing Look Inside the Big Business of Our National Pastime*. New York: Basic Books, 1992.

Baseball Periodicals

Baseball Digest
Baseball Magazine
Sporting Life
The Sporting News

General Newspapers

Baltimore Sun
Boston Globe
Brooklyn Eagle
Buffalo Express
Chicago Inter Ocean
Chicago Tribune
Cincinnati Enquirer
Cleveland Plain Dealer
Detroit News
Kansas City Star
Los Angeles Times
Louisville Courier-Journal
Minneapolis Star Tribune
New York Times
Philadelphia Inquirer
St. Louis Post-Dispatch
San Diego Tribune
Washington Post
Worcester Spy

Index

Numbers in **bold italics** indicate pages with photographs.

Aaron, Henry 188
Almada, Mel 210
Athletic (AA) *see* Philadelphia (AA)
Atlanta (NL) 171, 176, 179, 180, 191
Averill, Earl 210

Baltimore (AA) 19, 24, 27, 28, 33–34, 41, 69
Baltimore (AL) 162, 167, 170, ***171***, 194
Baltimore (NL) 51, 52, 57, 60
Bancroft, Frank 10
Banks, Ernie 186–192, 201
bargain bill 89
Barnie, Billy 27–28, 29, 33–34, 68–69
Basic Agreement *see* Players Association
Bishop, Max 210
Boston (AL): day-night doubleheader 156, 160, 194–195, 198, 208; holiday doubleheader 91, 93, 97–98, 108–109, 160; makeup-game doubleheader 79–82, 104; records set 210, 211; scheduled doubleheader 74; Sunday doubleheader 122, 132, 161, 180; swing-shift doubleheader 147–148; as visiting team 115, 137, 141, 165, 172, 195
Boston (NL): holiday doubleheader 20, 21, 22–24, 55, 56, 58, 59, 62, 63, 91, 93, 97, 108, 160, 205; makeup-game doubleheader 28, 36, 37, 38, 40, 41, 44, 52, 83; records set 114, 209, 210; scheduled doubleheader 101; Sunday doubleheader 120, 122, 130–132, 145, 148–149; twi-night doubleheader 160; as visiting team 12, 41, 42, 76, 86, 147, 148, 157
Breadon, Sam 116–117, 118–120, ***120***, 123, 135, 154, 174
Brooklyn (AA) 24, 55, 62; Sunday doubleheader 64, 205
Brooklyn (NL): day-night doubleheader 154–155, 207; holiday doubleheader 56–57, 58, ***60***, 63, 91, 93–94, 111, 157–158, 205, 206, 207; makeup-game doubleheader 88; records set 210; Sunday doubleheader 135, 161; twi-night doubleheader 164, 168, 207; as visiting team 41, 43, 75, 76, 148, 155
Buffalo (NL) 19, 22, 26–27, 29–31, 205
Bunker Hill Day holiday 24, 59, 93, 109, 157, 160

Canada Day holiday 178, 180
Chesbro, Jack 80–83
Chicago (AL): day-night doubleheader 135, 207; holiday doubleheader 91, 94, 146, 176; records set 145–146, 210, 211; Sunday doubleheader 75, 102, 143, 146, 165; twi-night doubleheader 142, 146, 182; as visiting team 155, 200
Chicago (NL): day-night doubleheader 194–195, 198; holiday doubleheader 17, 20, 22, 23, 24, 61, 62, 91, 96, 189, 196–197, 206; makeup-game doubleheader 26–27, 32–33, 36, 37, 40, 53, 72, 88, 189, ***190***, 196–197; records set 150; scheduled doubleheader 75, 206; Sunday doubleheader 71, 102, 116, 146, 189; as visiting team 20, 25, 43, 130–132, 180
Cincinnati (AA) 19, 23, 24
Cincinnati (NL): holiday doubleheader 62, 91, 94, 107, 167; makeup-game doubleheader 12, 43, 52, 53, 70, 72; night games 133–134; Sunday doubleheader 75, 102, 120, 132, 135, 206; as visiting team 15, 86, 109–110, 198
Clemens, Roger 194, 195, 199
Cleveland (AL): day-night doubleheader 199–200; holiday doubleheader 91, 97; records set 211; scheduled doubleheader 195; Sunday doubleheader 104, 115, 181;

229

swing-shift doubleheader 148; twi-night doubleheader 141–142, 207; as visiting team 102, 135, 142
Cleveland (NL): holiday doubleheader 22, 23, 61; makeup-game doubleheader 26, 53, 72; as visiting team 15, 20, 40, 41, 44
Cobb, Ty 209
Colbert, Nate 179, 211
Colorado (NL) 197, 198
Columbus (AA) 23
Columbus Day holiday 93–94, 103, 206
Cronin, Joe 132, 137, 210

Day, John 23–25, 28–31, 56
day-night doubleheader: ballplayer inconvenience 155, 169–170, 199; home-and-home strategy 199; limits on use 180, 198; scheduled 157, 170–172, 175, 207; separate-admission 154–155, 156–157, 169, 194, 198, 207, 208; single-admission 135, 142, 207
Decoration Day holiday *see* Memorial Day holiday
Detroit (AL): holiday doubleheader 91, 97; makeup-game doubleheader 83; records set 211; scheduled doubleheader 193; twi-night doubleheader 172; as visiting team 142, 155, 165
Detroit (NL): holiday doubleheader 19, 21, 22, 25, 205; makeup-game doubleheader 26, 39; as visiting team 23, 30, 32–33
DiMaggio, Dom 196
Donlin, Mike 209
double bill 28, 50, 89
doubleheader, as term: caricature *13*; definition 9–10, 63; differentiated from two-game set 15; etymology 10–15, 50; first use 9–10; newspaper headline *159*; nicknames for 50, 89, 115; popularized 12
Dreyfuss, Barney 53, 71–72, 79, 92, *92*, 99, 103, 110
Durocher, Leo 189–192

Easter holiday 161
Ebbets, Charlie 93–94, 102–103, 107

factors impacting use of doubleheader: attendance 37, 41, 93, 97–99, 104, 124, 157; ballclub economic models 18, 46, 53, 73, 79, 97, 99–100, 104, 112, 126–128, 162, 184, 201–202; ballpark modernization 98–99, 111, 183, 195; catcher's equipment 7, 44–45, 78; darkness stopping 7, 27, 40, 78, 83, 84, 104, 107, 142; daylight saving time 84, 103–104, 106–107; economic standard for two games 37, 41, 102, 123, 154–155, 157; entertainment alternatives 100, 106, 113–114, 126, 163, 167; franchise relocation 162, 167; free second game 31, 79, 128, 151–152, 154, 161, 164, 167; Great Depression 123–128; league startups 56–57, 74–75, 96–97; marketing 201–202; negatives 78–79; New York legislation 158, 159, 207; night games 139–140, 154; player salaries 175, 181–182, 184–185; Players Association 174–175, 178, 193, 197; promotions 128, 147, 161–162, 164–165, 173, 182, 183; radio 115–116; roster size 7, 38, 44, 45; season, expansion of 32, 39, 43, 50, 71, 79, 103, 170–171, 177; seven-inning games 83–88; spectator complacency 152–154, 172; spectator type 36, 50, 55, 84, 95, 110, 126, 163; spectator value 27, 28, 37–38, 83, 87, 103, 106; television 162–163, 184–185, 195, 201; time length 182, 192, 195, 201; transportation 46, 60, 84–85, 140, 143–144, 149–150, 163–164; weather 39, 102, 195; World War II 139–144, 150–151
Federal League 96–97, 104–106
Fehr, Donald 194
Friend, Bob 169

Gaedel, Eddie 164–165
Galehouse, Denny 149
Gehrig, Lou 112, 136–137, 166
Girardi, Joe 196
Griffith, Clark 81–82, 128

Hargrove, Mike 192
Hart, Jim 42
Hartford (NL) 15
holiday, two games on: advertisements *21*, *30*, *34*, 62; attendance 17, 19–20, 59–60; ballclub finances 17–18, 20, 57–58, 95, 97–98; decline 167, 176–177, *182*, 207; different-opponent strategy 22–24; doubleheaders 94–97, 100, 104, 107–109, 110–112, 153, 160, 167–168, 176–177, 205, 206; first doubleheaders 56, 62, 96, 205, 206; home-and-home two-game sets 63, 94, 97; last doubleheaders 24–25, morning game 24–25, 56, 92, 107; New York legislation 158–159, 207; scheduling 18, 21–22, 25, 57, 59, 90–93; separate-venue strategy 20; two-game sets 14–15, 16–25, 55–58, 90–93, 100, 102, 107, 109, *111*, 157–158, 205, 207; *see also* Bunker Hill Day; Columbus Day; Easter; Independence Day; Labor Day; Memorial Day; Patriots Day
Houston (NL) 171–172, 176, 207

Independence Day holiday 16, 18–19, 93, 176; doubleheaders 96–97, 107, 110, 112, 167; first doubleheader 96, 206; first two-game set 19, 205; last doubleheader 177; scheduled two games 21–22; two-game sets 22–25, 61, 90–93, 157
Indianapolis (AA) 27
Indianapolis (NL) 15, 37
interleague doubleheaders 28–30, 199

Jenkins, Fergie 188, 190
Johnson, Walter 142

Index

Kansas City (AA) 69
Kansas City (AL) 157, 162, 172, 207, 211
Karger, Ed 86–87, *87*

Labor Day holiday 25, 54, 93, 176; doubleheaders 56, 94–95, 107, 108, 168, 176; first doubleheader 56, 205; first two-game set 55, 205; last doubleheader 177; scheduled two games 56; two-game sets 55–58, 62–63, 90–93
levels of doubleheader 14; (Level 1) 36, 39, 79, 101–102, 113, 154, 193, 205; (Level 2) 41, 51, 69–70, 95, 102, 116, 119, 134, 206; (Level 3) 65, 70, 74–75, 117, 120, 127
Levsen, Dutch 115, 209
Los Angeles (AL) 170
Los Angeles (NL) 167–168, 180, 183, 196, 207
Louisville (AA) 19, 24, 30
Louisville (NL) 53, 62, 64, 69, 71–72
Lowe, Bobby 209
Lyons, Ted 143, *144*

Majeski, Hank 210
makeup of postponed game: as doubleheader 5–9, 31–38, 39–40, 42, 43–44, 51, 79, 153–154; as two-game set 15, 26, 32, 147–148, 154–155
Maranville, Rabbit 130–131, *131*
Maxwell, Charlie 211
McGinnity, Joe 44, 75–78, 177, 209
Memorial Day holiday 16–19, 93, 176; doubleheaders 96, 107, 157, 167, 176; first doubleheader 62, 206; first two-game set 20, 205; last doubleheader 177; scheduled two games 22; two-game sets 22–25, 59–62, 90–93
memories of doubleheader, by fans and players 145, 176, 192, 196, 200–201
Metropolitan (AA) *see* New York (AA)
Miller, Marvin 174, 178, 180, 181
Milwaukee (AA) 41, 69
Milwaukee (AL) 181
Milwaukee (NL) 162
Minnesota (AL): holiday doubleheader 170; scheduled doubleheader 197, 200, 208; as visiting team 173, 194, 200
Molitor, Paul 200–201
Montreal (NL) 177, 180
Morehart, Ray 210
Morgan, Joe 196
Murcer, Bobby 211
Musial, Stan 165–166, 179, 210
Mutrie, Jim 23, 29

New York (AA) 22–24, 28–30
New York (AL): holiday doubleheader 91, 94, 110–112, 206; makeup-game doubleheader 79–82, 113; records set 210, 211; Sunday doubleheader 136, 142, 173; twi-night doubleheader 172, 196, 199; as visiting team 132, 141–142, 157, 170, 181

New York Giants (NL): holiday doubleheader 22–25, 56, 58, 59, 62, 63, 91, 94, 102, 111; makeup-game doubleheader 28, 29–30, 40, 42, 75–77, 85, 114, 162; records set 210; Sunday doubleheader 143; as visiting team 36, 94, 154, 157, 166
New York Mets (NL) 172, 180, 196, 199, 211
Newcombe, Don 156
night games 132–135, 139–140, 150, 153–155, 180
nightcap 115
number of doubleheaders 40, 52, *52*, 79, 101, 105, 123, *124*, 127, 140, 144–145, 150, *151*, 168, 176, 184, 212–215

Oakland (AL) 181, 185, 197, 200
O'Malley, Walter 158, 160
O'Neil, Buck 189

Patriots Day holiday 59, 93, 98, 109, 160–161, 175
Philadelphia (AA): holiday doubleheader 19, 23, 24, 56, 205; makeup-game doubleheader 28, 33–34; Sunday doubleheader 69; as visiting team 41
Philadelphia (AL): holiday doubleheader 91; scheduled doubleheader 74; Sunday doubleheader 137–138; swing-shift doubleheader 147; twi-night doubleheader 142; as visiting team 113, 122, 161
Philadelphia (NL): holiday doubleheader 22–25, 56, 58, 60, 61, 63, 91, 94, 167, 205, 207; makeup-game doubleheader 26, 32–33, 41, 44, 83, 114, 205; records set 145; Sunday doubleheader 130, 132, 135, 166, 169; swing-shift doubleheader 147, 207; twi-night doubleheader 155; as visiting team 52, 77
pitchers: shortened no-hitter 85–87; Sunday-only 143, 149; two complete games pitched on one day 7, 19, 37, 44, 75–76, 88, 115, 155, 177
Pittsburgh (AA) 19, 34
Pittsburgh (NL): holiday doubleheader 56, 57, 58, 59, 61, 92, 176, 177; makeup-game doubleheader 39, 43, 86; records set 209; Sunday doubleheader 148, 150, 166, 167, 181; tripleheader 109–110, 206; as visiting team 25, 38, 75, 102, 169
Players Association 168, 174, 194, 198; expansion of doubleheaders 194–195, 198; limits on doubleheaders 169, 172, 174–175, 179–181, 193, 203; player strikes 178, 184, 197; votes by ballplayers 180, 194, 198
Providence (NL): first-ever doubleheader 5–8, 202, 205; holiday doubleheaders 20, 22–24; makeup-game doubleheader 28, 29, 30, 31
Pulliam, Harry 88

Index

records set in doubleheaders 102, 114, 145, 150, 165, 170, 172, 179, 195, 209–211
Reulbach, Ed 88, 209
Rickey, Branch 154, 160, 174
Robison, Frank 53, 95, 96
Rusie, Amos 44
Ruth, Babe 82, 102, 112, 114, 115, 137, 142, 166

St. Louis (AA) 19, 34, 41, 55; Sunday doubleheader 65, 69
St. Louis (AL): holiday doubleheader 91, 94, 96, 107, 206; records set 210; Sunday doubleheader 75, 149, 164–165; twi-night doubleheader 141–142, 155, 156, 207
St. Louis (NL): day-night doubleheader 154, 157; holiday doubleheader 59, 62, 91, 95–96, 107, 206; makeup-game doubleheader 43, 52, 53, 70, 72, 83; scheduled doubleheader 51; Sunday doubleheader 75, 86, 95, 96, 101, 116, 118–120, 161, 165, 176, 206–207; as visiting team 132
San Diego (NL) 179, 193, 211
San Francisco (NL): holiday doubleheader 177, 207; records set 211; scheduled doubleheader 193; Sunday doubleheader 167, 181, 185; as visiting team 172
scheduled doubleheaders 51, 53, 71, 74–75, 101, 128, 206; decline of 185, 193, 197, 202–203; last 200
Seattle (AL) 177
Seerey, Pat 210
separate-admission doubleheader *see* day-night doubleheader; holiday, two games on, two-game sets
Sharsig, Billy 33–35, *35*, 38, 69
spectators 17, 36–37, 46–50, 55–56, 61, 68, 84–85, 95, 98–99, 110–111, 113, 125, 133, 163–164
split doubleheader *see* day-night doubleheader
Stone, John 210
Sunday baseball 17–18, 40, 44, 49, 58; District of Columbia 107; holiday scheduling impact 61, 91–92; Massachusetts 121–123; New York 64, 102, 107–108; Ohio 50–51, 104; Pennsylvania 35, 92, 121, 129–130
Sunday curfew 123, 130–132, *131*, 148, 150, 161, 166–167, 206, 207
Sunday doubleheader: 64, 70–73, 101–103, 105, 116, 118–135, 142–143, 153, 157, 161–162, 180–181; decline 161–162, 164, 180; first played 64–65, 205; first scheduled 53, 71, 207; football impact on 162; limits on 129; night game impact on 132–134; part-time ballplayers 149; in St. Louis 95, 96, 118–120; scheduled 53, 75, 101, 119–120, 128, 132, 134–135; term 134; two-game set 65; war relief 142
suspended game 148, 149
swing-shift doubleheader 147–148, 177, 207
synthetic doubleheader 14, 119, 206–207

Texas (AL) 211
Thomas, Lee 170, 190
three-club doubleheader 53, 71–72, 157
Toledo (AA) 69
tripleheader 57, 109–110, 205, 206
Troy (NL) 19, 20 , 205
twi-night doubleheader 141–142, 145, 150, 154–156, 157, 170–171; first 141, 155, 207; limits on 180, 181; scheduled 145, 157, 168, 170, 207
twin bill 89
two-game set 15; *see also* holiday, two games on, two-game sets; makeup of postponed games, as two-game set
types of doubleheader *see* day-night; holiday; interleague; makeup of postponed game; Sunday; swing-shift; three-club; twi-night

Veeck, Bill 161, 164–165, 182, 197
Ventura, Robin 211
Vickers, Rube 86–87
Von der Ahe, Chris 55, 59, 62

Washington (AA) 24
Washington (AL): makeup-game doubleheader 83, 102; twi-night doubleheader 142, 145, 155, 207; as visiting team 136, 142
Washington (NL) 32, 37, 41, 44, 55, 57, 70
White, Bill 170, 211
Whitney, Jim 37, 209
Williams, Ted 137–138, 192
Wood, Wilbur 177
Worcester (NL): first-ever doubleheader 5–8, 202, 205; holiday doubleheader 19, 20
Wright, Harry 5–6, 25, 31, 33, 35–36, 202

Young, Matt 195–196

www.ingramcontent.com/pod-product-compliance
Lightning Source LLC
Chambersburg PA
CBHW030106170426
43198CB00009B/513